THE DOW JONES-IRWIN

Guide to

Calculating

Yields

THE DOW JONES-IRWIN

Guide to

Calculating Yields

Lawrence R. Rosen

DOW JONES-IRWIN
Homewood, Illinois 60430

This publication is designed to provide accurate and
authoritative information in regard to the subject matter
covered. It is sold with the understanding that the
publisher is not engaged in rendering legal, accounting, or
other professional service. If legal advice or other expert
assistance is required, the services of a competent
professional person should be sought.

*From a Declaration of Principles jointly adopted by a Committee
of the American Bar Association and a Committee of Publishers.*

ISBN 0-87094-532-7

Library of Congress Catalog Card No. 84-71298

Printed in the United States of America

1 2 3 4 5 6 7 8 9 0 MP 2 1 0 9 8 7 6 5

Special thanks are due to Henry Mann, L.L.B.
for his helpful advice and assistance in reviewing
the chapters of this book on matters of real estate law.
The author is indebted to Mr. A.J. Warner, vice
president of Prudential Bache Securities, for his helpful
review of various chapters concerning bonds.

P R E F A C E

I have yet to meet anyone who became wealthy or maximized their assets by putting their money in the bank at a fixed rate of interest. To create wealth and maximize your assets, you will normally need to invest. There are all kinds of potential investments that you can make. And there are all kinds of brokers hoping to sell you one. To name several potential investments, there are:

Common stocks	Preferred stocks
Corporate bonds	Municipal bonds
Real estate	Master recordings
Money market accounts	Certificates of deposits

How do you decide where to put your money? The brokers always have an optimistic view of whatever it is that they are selling. They are hardly likely to be a good source of unbiased knowledge and wisdom. The answer is that you should decide for yourself by analyzing the options available to you and making your own decision. With the liberalization that has taken place in banking regulations starting in late 1982, that place may even be the bank.

This book will give you the tools you need to make important decisions concerning your financial well-being. For example, which would be the best investment for you—assuming that in each case you hold the investment for 15 years?

A common stock in a conservative utility company sells at $100 per share and currently pays a dividend of $10 per year. Your analysis (which may include analysts' forecasts) suggests that the dividend rate is likely to increase at a rate of 5 percent per year. It is assumed that the market value of the stock over the long term will also increase at the same rate as the annual dividend increase, i.e., 5 percent per year.

Or would it be better to buy a corporate bond for $800 that matures in 15 years at $1,000 and pays $120 per year in interest.

Or you could invest in an office building. The current distributable cash (e.g. $17.50) is 1.75 percent of the cash investment (e.g. $1,000). The purchase can be made with 75 percent borrowed funds (e.g. $3,000) and 25 percent cash investment (i.e. $1,000). The loan terms on the borrowed funds are: 12 percent interest per year; 25-year amortization. Assume that you eventually sell it at a 12 percent capitalization rate (i.e. the sale price is 8.3 times the then income) and both annual rents and expenses are expected to increase at an annual inflation rate of 6 percent.

The following table summarizes the known facts about the three investment alternatives.

	Common Stock	Corporate Bond	Office Building
Cash investment	$100	$800	$1,000
Distributable cash (dividend, interest, net rent after loan payment)	$ 10	$120	$ 17.50
Rate of increase per year of:			
dividend	5%		
interest		0%	
net rent			6%
Loan terms for office building:			
Total purchase price			$4,000
Loan amount			3,000
Interest rate on loan			12%
Amortization, years to pay off loan			25 yrs.
Initial pre-tax cash return on cash invested	10%	15%	1.75%

The broker for the common stock will probably talk to you in terms of price-earnings ratios, dividend payout, and current yield. The broker for the corporate bond may speak in terms of yield to maturity and current yield. The real estate broker may speak in terms of cash-on-cash return, equity buildup, and tax savings. Confusing? Yes. Does it have to be? No!

Fortunately, there is a **common denominator to which all forms of investment may be reduced.** A single number that acts as a measure of comparison among investment possibilities A, B, C, etc. That measure is the *internal rate of return* or *IRR*. This book will tell you all about it. It is expressed as a percentage.

Refer back to the three potential investments described above; the common stock, the corporate bond, and the real estate deal. Which one do you think is the best investment, assuming the risks are more or less the same?

Let's see what the *internal rate of return* tells us about choosing among the three alternatives.

Common stock IRR	15.00%
Corporate bond IRR	15.50%
Real estate IRR	19.70%

The IRRs described above are all before tax. But what about Uncle Sam's share of the profits? The government's cut does matter, and the after tax result of the investment is what counts for you. If you are in a 50% tax bracket, the after tax IRR for each is:

Common stock IRR	9.4%
Corporate bond IRR	8.2%
Real estate IRR	20.6%

Now with that knowledge and assuming you had a little more confidence in what IRR really means, isn't it much easier to make the most rational and intelligent choice?

The actual calculation of IRR is exceedingly complex and beyond the capability of all but the most mathematically inclined. In fact, some of the calculations are impossible to perform by solving ordinary equations and require the use of trial and error methods.

The beauty of this book is that even the most complex IRR calculations have been reduced to simple graphs that anybody can use to find answers in seconds. This book will make you a better informed investor. I guarantee it!

All of the calculations and the preparation of the manuscript were performed on my Apple IIe computer, as well as the actual drawing of some of the most complex graphs.

By having and using the book, you will be INVESTING LIKE A COMPUTER WHIZ—without having to learn how to use a computer.

Lawrence R. Rosen

Important Information Regarding Stocks

The analyis of IRR and Revised IRR throughout the text presumes, for STOCKS, that the price at which the stock is sold is based on earnings per share (EPS) at the *end* of the holding period. The earnings per share utilized for this purpose would be effective on the first day *following* the date of sale. Example: If the holding period is 10 years, then the EPS used in determining sales proceeds in the 10th year, is that EPS that would have become effective at the beginning of the 11th year. By using this method, the before tax IRR for all stocks, regardless of the holding period, can be displayed on one chart. If the EPS at the *beginning* of the year of sale had been used instead in determining sales proceeds, one chart would be required for each year. (Let's refer to the latter procedure as the "other method.")

The IRR for stocks, as determined by the method employed, will normally be very close to the IRR that would result from the other method. For example, with a 20 year projection, the method used shows an IRR of 12.0 percent, while the other method produces 11.83 percent. The closeness of the result for the two methods is true for time periods of six years or more (less than 1 percent difference). For periods shorter than six years, the other method will result in progressively lower IRRs as the time period shortens, and the difference becomes more significant. For example, with a three year holding period, the method used shows an IRR of 12 percent and the other method produces 10.08 percent; and for one year, the results would be 12 percent versus 6 percent.

Contents

7.   Real Estate Investing and IRR Analysis **167**

Management. Summary.

8.   Real Estate, IRR Models **176**

Match-Up Worksheet. Sample IRR Calculations. Summary.

After Tax IRR Graphs

9.   Yield to Call **208**

Formula. Graphs or Tables. Municipals and Call Provisions: *Extraordinary, Sinking Fund, and Pre-refunding Calls.*

When to Sell the Investment. The Real McCoy. What Reinvestment Percent Rate Is Needed to Achieve IRR?

Income Tax Effects: *Taxable Premium Bonds. Tax-Exempt Bonds. Premium on Convertible Bonds. Taxable Discount Bonds.* Income Tax Considerations: *Premium Bond. Discount Bond. Par Bond. Summary.* Municipals: *Bond Price Volatility. Bond Price Volatility—Short versus Long Maturities. Bond Price Volatility—High versus Low Coupons. Bond Price Volatility—Magnitude of Yield to Maturity at Purchase. Summary.* Is Yield to Maturity the True Yield? Interest Reinvestment and Bond Maturity. Practical Significance. Price Patterns of Bonds Based on Ratings: *Higher Yields, Lower Ratings. Municipal Bond Quality.* The Dangers of Bonds. Bond Yield Compared to Stock Dividend Yields. Long-Term Bond Yields versus Short-Term Interest Rates. Trading Bonds.

Terminal Value and Reinvestment of Cash Flows. Terminal Values Are Not the Solution: Use Revised IRRs. More Misconceptions. Bond Sale Prior to Maturity.

Municipals or Tax-Exempt IRRs: *Par Bond—Revised IRR for Tax-Exempts. Premium Bond—Revised IRR for Tax-Exempts.* Tax-Exempt Investors; e.g., Pensions, Keoghs, IRAs. Zero Coupon Bonds.

Bond Interest Reinvestment at 4, 8, and 12 Percent (Pre-Tax)

50% Tax Bracket

0% Tax Bracket

Reinvestment of Dividends—Before Tax: *Shrinking P-E Multiples.* Reinvestment of Dividends—After Tax.

Reinvestment of Cash Flow at Various Rates

Before Tax

After Tax

C H A P T E R 1

The Big Picture

If you are going to make the most intelligent, savvy, and logical investment decisions, it is essential to look at the big picture. If you were going to buy a video recorder, you wouldn't buy it just because the case was your favorite color, would you? And if you needed a new car, you would want to consider more than just the passenger capacity. Obviously, there are a number of criteria in either case that you would want to check out and analyze in making your decision.

Things are no different with investments. Some of the factors that need to be considered in the case of an investment in a common stock include: expected growth rate, the price at the time of purchase and the expected sale price, and the cash return from dividends while you hold the investment.

In the final analysis, the only thing that matters is what you get back from an investment. When you make the investment, you invest your money. Forever after, it's a question of what you get back in return, and what you get back usually consists of three benefits:

1. Periodic income, i.e., annual or quarterly (in the form of dividends, interest, or rents).

2. Sales proceeds. The amount of money you expect to ultimately receive when the investment is eventually sold.

3. Tax benefits or cost. Both the periodic income and the sales proceeds need to be adjusted for the cost of taxes. In some cases of tax favored investments, there may be tax savings in some years to take into consideration. For example, in a given year, the investment may produce tax deductions that exceed the revenues; in other words, a net tax loss. If such is the case, then the reduced income taxes that you pay in that year are equivalent to cash received just as if you had received it in the form of tax-free interest from a municipal bond.

For example, if you are in a 50 percent tax bracket and your investment in widgets produces a net loss of $10,000 for the year, and if that loss is allowed to be included on your own personal income tax return, then that deductible loss of $10,000 will result in your paying $5,000 less in income taxes for that year. (The deductible loss of $10,000 times the tax bracket rate of .5 equals the tax savings for the year, $5,000.) This $5,000 tax savings is equivalent to $5,000 in tax-free income. You've got $5,000 more after taxes to spend in that year as the result of the investment. But beware of the possibility that the deductions that made this possible don't come back to haunt you in a different year. More about that later.

The elements of investment decision making couldn't be simpler, could they? There are only three basic considerations: the periodic cash flow, the proceeds from sale, and the adjustment for taxes.

Assume that you have $10,000 to invest and the following two alternatives are offered to you:

Alternative 1: A high-quality corporate bond which you can buy for $9,000 that matures in 20 years for $10,000. It pays annual interest of $1,400.

Alternative 2: A high-quality electric utility common stock that you can buy 900 shares of at $10 per share for a total investment of $9,000. The utility pays a present dividend per year of $1,000 ($1.11 per share). You check it out with various sources and conclude that it is likely that the dividend will increase at 5 percent per year. When you sell the stock in 20 years, the value will have increased from the purchase price at the same 5 percent per year rate that the dividend is expected to increase.

How do we compare these two alternatives to decide which is the more intelligent acquisition? Let's make a comparison chart of what we know about the two alternatives:

Criteria	The Bond	The Stock
Amount invested	$9,000	$9,000
Periodic, annual income (initially)	$1,400	$1,000
Current yield (annual income divided by amount invested)	15.56%	11.11%
Income five years hence	$1,400	$1,276
Current yield in five years	15.56%	14.18%
Number of years investment is expected to be held	20 years	20 years
Proceeds of sale at end of 20 years	$10,000	$23,880

Which Is the Better Investment?

Which is the better investment? The bond provides more current income, but the stock, based on 5 percent per year appreciation, should produce higher sales proceeds 20 years from now. The annual income from the bond, though higher than that of the stock, does not change. The annual income from the stock should increase periodically.

Which is the better investment is not an easy question to answer unless you have the right tools at hand to help you. This book is your tool. When you have read the book, you'll be able to determine the answer in seconds—and without using much math. Certainly, you won't need to use math that is any more complicated than that used by a 10th grader.

The determination of the answer is based upon the principle that the value of any investment is the sum of the future cash flows from that investment. However, we all know that a sum of money, say $10,000, due to be given to you at some time in the future is not worth as much as $10,000 handed to you today. Why? Because the $10,000 that you receive today can be invested to produce more money over the years. The $10,000 that you receive in the future can't be invested until you receive it. Therefore, the future cash flows must be reduced in value by a discount factor, like a negative interest rate, to compare them to money that is in hand today.

Magic Number Concept

If there were only some *magic number,* an interest rate, that could be used to make the initial investment, $9,000 in the above example, **equal to** the future cash flows from that investment (the periodic annual income and the sales proceeds). That magic number would be applied to each of the periodic cash flows and future sales proceeds, and after doing so, the sum would equal the initial investment. Then whichever investment alternative had the higher magic number would be the better investment. Or a series of possible investments could be ranked by the magic number. The magic number would tell us what the true rate of return actually would be from each alternative investment.

Happily there is a magic number. Sometimes it is called *yield to maturity* in the case of a bond, or in the case of real estate investments, it may be called *internal rate of return.* We will use both terms. This book will allow you to determine the yield to maturity (YTM) or internal rate of return (IRR) *in mere seconds of your time.* But first we shall look at some fundamentals concerning the specific types of investments available in the marketplace.

Incidentally, the stock is the better investment. Turn to Graph 1–1, **Stocks: Before Tax Internal Rates of Return.** Enter the graph on the vertical axis at 11.11 percent (the initial yield); proceed horizontally until you reach the 5 percent curve (representing the 5 percent annual increase in both the dividend and market value); then descend to the bottom axis where the graph shows the magic number or internal rate of return to be 16+ percent.

Graph 1–1
Stocks: Before Tax Internal Rate of Return *(Holding Periods: 0–100 Years)*

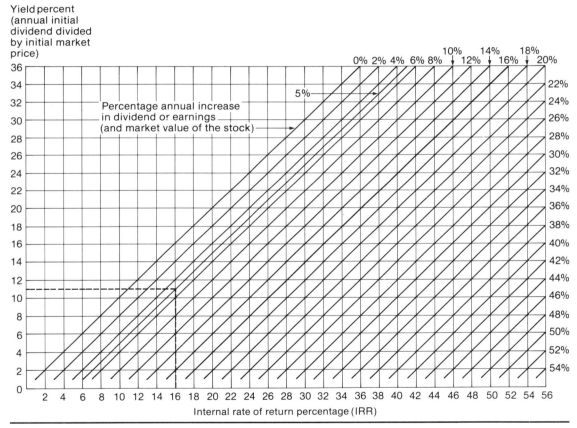

Example:
a. Stock purchase price   = $ 9.00
b. Initial dividend/year   = $ 1.00
c. Percent yield (b ÷ a)   = 11.11%
d. Assumed annual increase
    in dividend (and market value
    of the stock)   =   5.00%

Enter graph at 11.1 percent on vertical axis. Go horizontally to 5 percent curve, then proceed down to the bottom axis. The intersection at the bottom axis is the IRR, i.e., 16 percent.

Graph 1–2
Bond Yield to Maturity: 20 Years

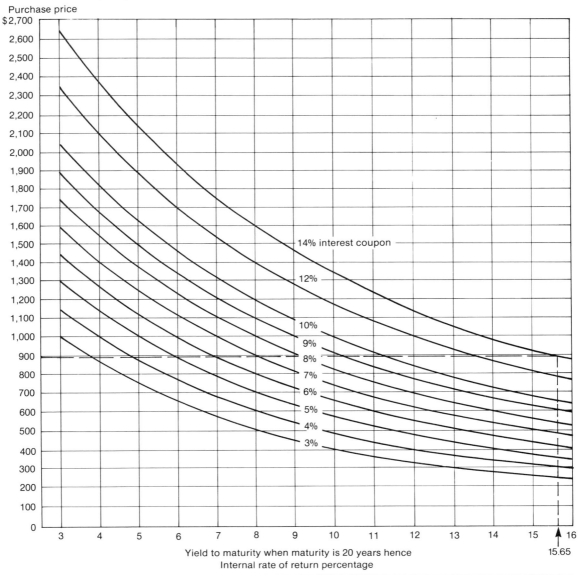

Purchase price

Yield to maturity when maturity is 20 years hence
Internal rate of return percentage

Example: *a.*   Bond purchase price   = $900.00
           b.   Annual bond interest   = $140.00
           c.   Interest coupon ($140 ÷ $1000) =   14.00%

Enter graph at $900 on vertical axis. Go horizontally to 14 percent curve, then proceed down to bottom axis. Intersection at bottom axis is the IRR, i.e., ± 15.65 percent.

For the bond, refer to Graph 1–2, **Bond Yield to Maturity: 20 Years,** which provides the magic number. Enter the chart on the vertical axis at the purchase price of one bond, $900. (Note: 10 bonds were purchased at $900 each, for a total investment of $9,000.) Proceed horizontally until the 14 percent curve is reached (which represents the $140 annual interest revenue divided by the $1,000 maturity value of the bond); then move vertically to the bottom axis where it shows that the yield to maturity (or internal rate of return) is about 15.65 percent.

That's all there is to it.

A Little Interest Makes a Big Difference

The difference between 15.65 percent in the case of the bond and 16 percent in the case of the stock may not sound like much. Consider, however, that if you invest $9,000 today in a lump sum and earn 15.65 percent compound annual interest, at the end of 20 years your account will be worth $164,875. The same investment at 16 percent would be worth $175,147.

The moral of this story is that when it comes to interest rates, and internal rates of return in particular, a mole hill can be like a mountain. Every little bit counts.

Next we shall see how internal rates of return are calculated and how all forms of investment, stocks, bonds and real estate, may be evaluated using IRR as the yardstick for comparison.

CHAPTER 2

Internal Rate of Return, the Magic Number

A businessman's staff proposes to him two alternate courses of action.

Proposal 1: This proposal requires a capital investment of $100,000 and the estimated revenues for the first five years are forecast below:

Year	Estimated Revenues
1	$ 0
2	10,000
3	10,000
4	50,000
5	60,000
Total	$130,000

The revenues forecast are net, after expenses, taxes, and so on, and the businessman has investigated the underlying assumptions which he believes to be accurate.

Proposal 2: The capital investment required is also $100,000, and revenues forecast are given below:

Year	Estimated Revenues
1	$ 40,000
2	20,000
3	20,000
4	20,000
5	20,000
Total	$120,000

The businessman's financial limitations are such that he must choose between the two proposals. He decides that he will select the one that offers him the best return on investment during the ensuing five years. Which proposal does he choose?

In both cases, it is necessary to determine what the future revenues are worth today based on discounting such revenues back from the date they occur to the present at an appropriate interest rate. The interest rate selected should be at least the same as the company could obtain by investing its funds elsewhere. Let's assume that 10 percent per year is selected.

Determination of the Present Value of Future Revenue

Proposal 1: The formula is:

$$P = a(1 + i)^{-n} + b(1 + i)^{-n_1} + \text{etc.}$$

where,

P = present value of the future revenues.

i = 10 percent.

$n, n_1, n_2, \ldots$ = the number of years hence that the revenues of a, b, and so on will be received.

Thus,

$$P = 10,000(1.1)^{-2} + 10,000(1.1)^{-3} + 50,000(1.1)^{-4} + 60,000(1.1)^{-5}$$
$$P = 8,264 + 7,513 + 34,151 + 37,653$$
$$P = \$87,183.$$

Proposal 2:

$$P = 40,000(1.1)^{-1} + 20,000(1.1)^{-2} + 20,000(1.1)^{-3} + 20,000(1.1)^{-4} + 20,000(1.1)^{-5}$$
$$P = 36,364 + 16,529 + 15,026 + 13,660 + 12,418$$
$$P = \$93,997.$$

As Proposal 2 affords the businessman the prospect of about $6,800 more in present value of future income, it (other things being equal) should be chosen even though Proposal 1 would produce $10,000 more total cash over the entire five-year period.

Discounted Cash Flow

The above analysis is commonly known as the discounted cash flow method of investment analysis. It illustrates a key element in decision making with respect to investments—that it is important to note *both* the *amount* of money one expects to earn as well as *when* one will receive it.

The discounted cash flow is also referred to as net present value or NPV. The net present value of Proposal 1 is $87,183 when the discount rate is 10 percent. But how confusing NPV can be. Why use 10 percent as the discount rate? What if a different discount rate were used? The NPV analysis does prove that Proposal 2 is better than Proposal 1. How much better? The difference between $87,183 and $93,997, if money is worth 10 percent.

However, wouldn't it be much better if we could simply analyze the two proposals in terms of some common denominator? The magic number concept, or internal rate of return (IRR), that we discussed earlier is equally applicable here. In this case, the IRR is that compound interest rate which will equate the initial cash outflow of $100,000 and the future cash inflows in years one through five. In other words, it is the true rate of return on the money invested.

The internal rate of return for Proposal 1 is 6.44 percent and for Proposal 2 is 7.3 percent. Besides telling us that Proposal 2 is superior to Proposal 1, the IRR is also telling us the true earnings percentage from each proposal. One should really be asking, if the rate of return on both proposals is so low, should I be making this investment at all?

The magic number, IRR, allows you to compare alternate proposals or to compare the prospective results from such diverse investment possibilities as stocks, bonds, and real estate. Table 2–1 shows the comparison of NPV to IRR for the example proposals.

IRR, to repeat, is the interest rate that equates the expected cash inflows from an investment to the initial (and subsequent, if any) cash outlays. Without a computer and without this book, IRR is found by trial and error. You calculate the present value of the expected cash

Table 2–1
Internal Rate of Return Compared to Discounted Present Value

Year	Revenues: Proposal 1	Revenues: Proposal 2
0	$ – 100,000	$ – 100,000
1	0	40,000
2	10,000	20,000
3	10,000	20,000
4	50,000	20,000
5	60,000	20,000
Total revenues	$ 130,000	$ 120,000
Present value at 10 percent discount rate	$ 87,183	$ 93,997
Internal rate of return or IRR percent	.06437 6.44%	.07295 7.30%

inflows from the investment using an estimated interest rate. The present value obtained from the first trial is compared to the initial cash outlay. *If it is larger than the cash outlay, the next trial interest rate should be a higher number.* On the other hand, *if the present value of the cash inflows is smaller than the initial cash outlay, the next trial should be performed with a lower interest rate.* You continue this process of repeated trials until the present value of the cash inflows is equal to the initial cash outlay. (At this point, when the present value of the cash inflows is equal to the initial cash investment, the net present value is zero.) The interest rate that equates the present value of the cash inflows to the initial investment is the IRR.

In the following chapters, we will determine the IRR for stocks, bonds, and real estate investments. Both before tax and after tax calculations will be performed. By using the simple graphs within each chapter, you will be able to make these calculations yourself in mere seconds for varying investment possibilities.

IRR Calculation with Negative Cash Flows

A tax shelter deal is proposed to you as follows. Invest $100,000 in widgets now and receive tax deductions in the first year of $300,000; second-year deductions of $250,000; third-year deductions of $200,000; and fourth-year deductions of $100,000; in the fifth year, the widgets are sold for $750,000 to end the investment. For an investment of only $100,000, you receive $850,000 in deductions. You can't lose, right?

If the deductions are valid (and there must be economic substance to the deal so that it is not disallowed with penalties by the IRS as a "tax sham"), how good a deal is it? Can we apply IRR analysis? Of course. Set it up as follows (in a 50 percent tax bracket):

Year	Net Deductions	Cash Flow	
0	—	($100,000)	Initial cash investment
1	$300,000	150,000	From tax savings
2	250,000	125,000	From tax savings
3	200,000	100,000	From tax savings
4	100,000	50,000	From tax savings
5	(750,000)	(375,000)	Tax payable on sale
5	—	750,000	Cash from sale
5	—	(750,000)	Repay loan
	100,000	(50,000)	Total

The widgets were bought in year 0 for $100,000 cash and with the proceeds of a $750,000 loan, payable interest only for five years with a balloon payment in the fifth year. When the widgets are sold in year 5 for $750,000, the entire sales proceeds repay the outstanding loan balance. At this point, the widgets have been fully depreciated so the tax "cost basis" is zero and the entire gain of $750,000 is recapturable as ordinary income. The resulting tax must be paid out of pocket by the investor in the amount of $375,000 because there are no investment proceeds left (after repaying the loan) with which to pay the taxes.

So we have negative cash flows of $100,000 at point 0, and $375,000 at the end of year 5. Here's the IRR formula:

$$100,000 = \frac{150,000}{(1 + i)^1} + \frac{125,000}{(1 + i)^2} + \frac{100,000}{(1 + i)^3} + \frac{50,000}{(1 + i)^4} - \frac{375,000}{(1 + i)^5}$$

The equation may be solved by trial and error, substituting trial values for i in the equation and continuing to try new values for i until the right-hand side of the equation is equal to $100,000 (the value of the left-hand side).

If i Is	The Right Side Is	
50%	$145,679	Try higher i
60	138,859	Try higher i
110	103,960	Try higher i
115	101,048	Try higher i
117	99,917	

Thus i is about 1.17 or 117 percent. This is the internal rate of return for this investment. If this mythical investment were real, the return would be terrific.

The critical factor in tax shelter situations is to be sure to provide for the unpleasant tax effects in the year of sale, disposition, or foreclosure. That is the year when all or part of those wonderful distributions in prior years suddenly come back to haunt you as ordinary income, capital gains, or both.

Bear in mind that the above analysis is an economic one. Equally important is the legal or accounting analysis in any proposed deal whose merits reside in the availability of large tax deductions. Read the legal "tax opinion" carefully. Does it state that the proposed accounting and tax treatment is valid, or does it raise the various tax issues and hedge the conclusion with wording like "it is more likely than not that the tax deductions are valid"? In any event, have your own tax expert advise you on the tax and accounting aspects (not the investment merits) before you invest one penny.

C H A P T E R 3

Stocks, Internal Rate of Return Analysis (Before Tax)

Why would anyone be interested in the before tax rate of return from an investment in a stock? There could be several reasons. First of all, the investor might be tax-exempt, such as a pension fund, Keogh plan, or individual retirement account (IRA). Or the investor might be the custodian for a child who is in a zero tax bracket, due to the effect of the child's personal income tax exemption.

In order to determine the internal rate of return from a stock investment, all you have to do is use Graph 3–1, and the IRR can be determined in mere seconds. There are two items that must be determined in order to use the graph and make the determination.

1. Percent yield. This is the annual dividend from the security divided by the initial market price of the stock. For example, if the purchase price of the stock is $100 and the initial dividend per year is $6 per share, then the percent yield is 6% ($6 ÷ $100). Refer to Graph 3–1. The left axis of the graph is percent yield, and whatever amount you determine as the yield will be your starting point on the left axis.

2. Percentage annual increase in dividend (and market value of the stock). There are a number of lines or curves running across the graph which represent percentage annual increases in dividend ranging from 0 to 54 percent per year. You must decide, for the particular stock you are contemplating purchasing, your best estimate for the percentage annual increase in dividend. Stock market analyst reports may help you make this estimate as may brokerage firms, discussions with officers of the company, or your own analysis. For example, let's assume that you decide the best estimate of such future growth is 6 percent. To find the IRR for this stock, enter the graph at the 6 percent point on the left axis, go across until you reach the 6 percent curve; then from that point of intersection, proceed down until you reach the bottom axis. That point of intersection with the bottom axis is the IRR, which in this case is 12 percent. That's all there is to it. If the stock does not pay any dividend, simply enter the graph at the 0 point on the left axis and proceed to the curve that represents your estimate of the annual increase in earnings per share.

There is an implicit assumption in the graph that the market value of the stock will increase over the long term at the same rate as the annual increase in dividends. This is a reasonable assumption but it may not always be the case. Inherent in such an assumption is the fact that the price-earnings ratio will remain constant. In actual practice, a rapid-growth company is likely to see its price-earnings multiple decrease as time passes, and a depressed company that is "turned around" may enjoy an expanded or increased price-earnings ratio. Where the P-E multiple shrinks with the passage of time, the realized IRR, as a result, will be less than that obtained by use of Graph 3–1. In such cases, Graph 3–1 overstates the IRR.

The actual computation of the 12 percent IRR determined above is shown in Table 3–1. The example is based on an initial purchase of $100 and a starting annual cash flow of $6. The $338.87 shown in the 20th year includes both the dividend in that year and the proceeds of sale.

Table 3–1
Complete Calculation of IRR

Number	Cash Value	No. × CV	Iterations
0	− 100.00	0.00	441.45
1	6.00	6.00	9150.36
2	6.36	12.72	0.05
3	6.74	20.22	152.53
4	7.15	28.60	3886.32
5	7.57	37.85	0.09
6	8.03	48.18	43.89
7	8.51	59.57	1982.87
8	9.02	72.16	0.11
9	9.56	86.04	7.61
10	10.14	101.40	1371.62
11	10.75	118.25	0.12
12	11.40	136.80	0.36
13	12.07	156.91	1251.93
14	12.80	179.20	0.12
15	13.57	203.55	0.00
16	14.38	230.08	1246.07
17	15.24	259.08	0.12

Table 3–1 *(concluded)*

Number	Cash Value	No. × CV	Iterations
18	16.16	290.88	0.00
19	17.13	325.47	1246.06
20	338.87	6777.40	0.12

	IRR	12%	

Stocks:	Tax bracket	0%	
	Initial yield	6%	
	Annual increase in yield		
	and market value	6%	
	Holding period	20 yrs.	

The actual formulas in each cell of a spreadsheet computer program that made the calculation are shown in Table 3–2. Readers with some knowledge of spreadsheet computer programs may find it of interest. If you are not in that category, skip the table altogether.

Table 3–2
Formulas for IRR Calculation

Number	Cash Value	No.*CV	Iterations
0	− 100	0	@NPV(0,D4 . . . D63) + D3
+ C3 + 1	6	+ D4*C4	@NPV(0,F4 . . . F63)
+ C4 + 1	6.36	+ D5*C5	+ G3/G4
+ C5 + 1	6.74	+ D6*C6	@NPV(G5,D4 . . . D63) + D3
+ C6 + 1	7.15	+ D7*C7	@NPV(G5,F4 . . . F63)
+ C7 + 1	7.57	+ D8*C8	+ G5 + (G6*(1 + G5)/G7)
+ C8 + 1	8.03	+ D9*C9	@NPV(G8,D4 . . . D63) + D3
+ C9 + 1	8.51	+ D10*C10	@NPV(G8,F4 . . . F63)
+ C10 + 1	8.02	+ D11*C11	+ G8 + (G9*(1 + G8)/G10)
+ C11 + 1	9.56	+ D12*C12	@NPV(G11,D4 . . . D63) + D3
+ C12 + 1	10.14	+ D13*C13	@NPV(G11,F4 . . . F63)
+ C13 + 1	10.75	+ D14*C14	+ G11 + (G12*(1 + G11)/G13)
+ C14 + 1	11.4	+ D15*C15	@NPV(G14,D4 . . . D63) + D3
+ C15 + 1	12.07	+ D16*C16	@NPV(G14,F4 . . . F63)
+ C16 + 1	12.8	+ D17*C17	+ G14 + (G15*(1 + G14)/G16)
+ C17 + 1	13.57	+ D18*C18	@NPV(G17,D4 . . . D63) + D3
+ C18 + 1	14.38	+ D19*C19	@NPV(G17,F4 . . . F63)
+ C19 + 1	15.24	+ D20*C20	+ G17 + (G18*(1 + G17)/G19)
+ C20 + 1	16.16	+ D21*C21	@NPV(G20,D4 . . . D63) + D3
+ C21 + 1	17.13	+ D22*C22	@NPV(G20,F4 . . . F63)
+ C22 + 1	338.87	+ D23*C23	+ G20 + (G21*(1 + G20)/G22)

@ IRR(D3, D4 . . . D23)

Stocks:	Tax bracket	− 0	
	Initial yield	6%	
	Annual increase in yield		
	and market value	6%	
	Holding period	20 yrs.	

Graph 3–1 in this chapter may be used for any holding period; it doesn't matter whether the time period is 5 years or 50 years. The one graph does it all in a zero tax bracket provided the price earnings ratio is the same at purchase and sale.

Interestingly, for a zero bracket, you will note if you study the graph that **the IRR is always the sum of the initial yield percentage and the annual increase in dividend or earnings percentage.** For example, without looking at the graph for the moment, what do you think the IRR is for a 10 percent initial yield with 6 percent annual increases in dividend? If you said 16 percent, congratulations. If you said anything else, reread this paragraph.

Shrinking P-E Multiples

The assumption that the rate of change in both dividends and earnings per share will be the same is reasonable in most cases. In other words, if a company's earnings per share are increasing at 8 percent per year, then its dividend is also going to increase at about that rate.

And it is reasonable that the P-E multiple for an average stock will remain stable provided that the stock is selling at a P-E multiple near that of the stock market averages. In other words, if the market averages are selling at a P-E multiple of 12, and Hagaan Ice Cream Company is selling at a P-E multiple of 11, then 3, 5 or 10 years later, it is reasonable to expect that Hagaan Ice Cream Company's multiple will still be around that of the stock market averages.

However, for a stock which is anticipated to increase dividends and earnings per share at a growth rate substantially greater than the market averages, it is likely that over a period of years the P-E multiple will decrease. For example, the Jerome Hotel Company was started 10 years ago and has enjoyed 50 percent per year growth in earnings per share. Its annual revenues are now $2 million, and its P-E multiple is 40. As the company matures and gets bigger, it is likely that its rapid growth rate will subside and that its P-E multiple will shrink from the lofty level of 40 to a figure near the market averages. To see the effects of a shrinking multiple, please refer to Graph 3–2, **IRR of Stocks: 67 Percent Drop in P-E Multiple.** The assumptions underlying this chart are:

The P-E multiple shrinks from 30 to 1 at purchase to 10 to 1 at sale.

The stock is held for 10 years before sale.

The owner's tax bracket is zero.

(Graph 3–1 is based on the assumption that the P-E multiple remains the same from the date of purchase to the date of sale.)

Graph 3–1
Stocks: Before Tax Internal Rate of Return *(Holding Periods: 0–100 Years/Tax Bracket: Zero)*

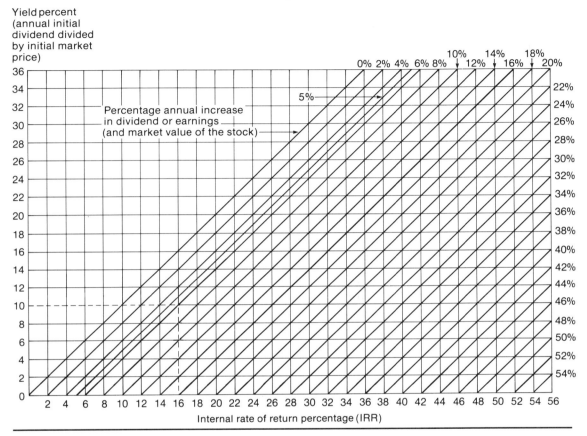

Yield percent
(annual initial
dividend divided
by initial market
price)

Internal rate of return percentage (IRR)

Example: *a.* Stock purchase price = $100
  b. Initial dividend/year = $ 10
  c. Percent yield (b ÷ a) = 10%
  d. Assumed annual increase = 6%
    in dividend (and market
    value of the stock)

Enter graph at 10 percent on vertical axis. Go horizontally to 6 percent curve, then proceed down to the bottom axis. The intersection at the bottom axis is the IRR, i.e., 16 percent.

Referring to Graph 3–2, for a stock with a dividend rate of zero (and thus an initial yield of 0 percent) and an expected growth rate of 40 percent per year in earnings per share, the chart shows that the IRR is 25.4 percent. This is true despite a drop in the P-E multiple from 30:1 at purchase to 10:1 at sale. As shown in Graph 3–1, when the multiple remained unchanged, the IRR would have been 40 percent. Thus it is evident that a large change in the P-E multiple will have a significant effect on the IRR.

Graph 3–2
IRR of Stocks: 67 Percent Drop in P-E Multiple

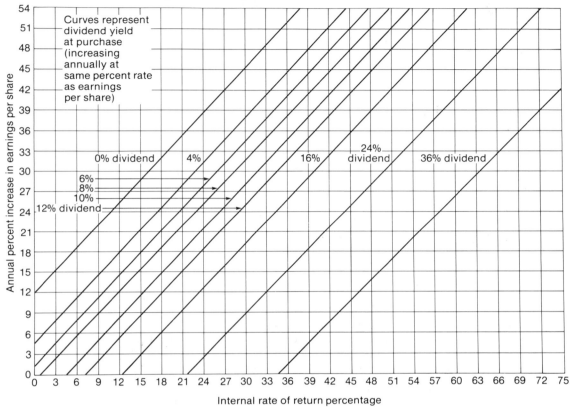

Note: P-E multiple at purchase = 30
P-E multiple at sale   = 10
Tax bracket   = 0%
Holding period   = 10 yrs.

What if the P-E multiple drops by half from let's say a multiple at purchase of 20:1 to a multiple at sale of 10:1? Graph 3–3 has the answer. Please refer to it. The stock described in the preceding paragraph would show an IRR of 30.6 percent with a 50 percent drop in the multiple over the 10-year holding period.

The following table summarizes the illustrations of the effect of a shrinking P-E multiple on a stock paying zero dividend:

P-E Multiple Decrease	Earnings Growth Rate	IRR
0.00%	40%	40.00%
50.00	40	30.63
66.67	40	25.40

Graph 3–3
IRR of Stocks: 50 Percent Drop in P-E Multiple

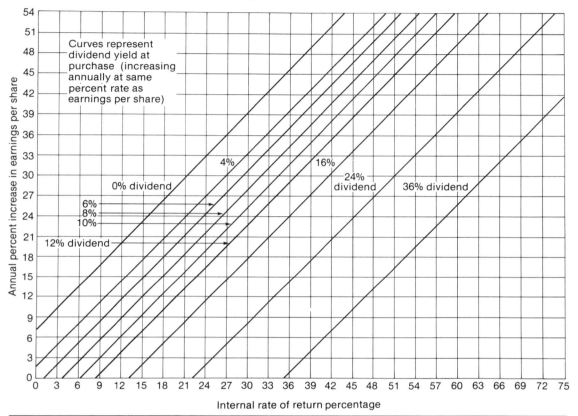

Note: P-E multiple at purchase = 20
        P-E multiple at sale   = 10
        Tax bracket   =   0%
        Holding period   = 10 yrs.

But what happens to the internal rate of return if the holding period, the length of time between purchase and sale, is shortened from 10 years? The effect of a shrinking P-E multiple becomes more significant; that is, drop in IRR is more dramatic. Graph 3–4 shows the results of a *five-year holding period* with a 50 percent drop in the P-E multiple from a 20:1 ratio at purchase to a 10:1 ratio at sale, and Graph 3–5 shows the results of a five-year holding period with a 66.67 percent drop in P-E multiple from a 30:1 ratio at purchase to a 10:1 ratio at sale.

Graph 3–4
IRR of Stocks: 50 Percent Drop in P-E Multiple

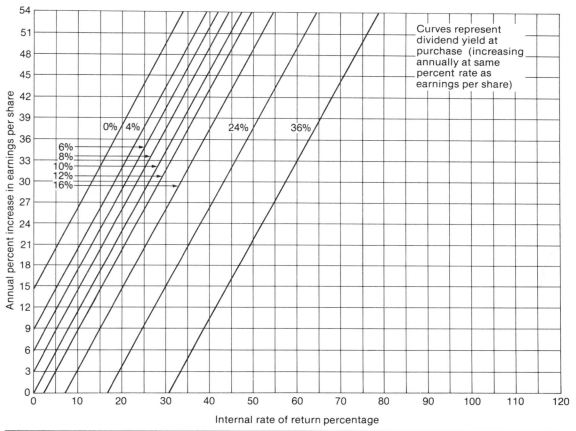

Note: P-E multiple at purchase = 20
       P-E multiple at sale   = 10
       Tax bracket   = 0%
       Holding period   = 5 yrs.

It may help you to visualize the concepts involved to think of the P-E ratio as "How many cents do I have to invest to acquire $1 of company earnings!"

Let's continue the example of a stock paying zero dividend, held for five years, with an expected earnings per share growth rate of 40 percent. Refer to Graph 3–4. Enter the left axis at 40 percent (EPS growth rate) and proceed horizontally across to the 0 percent dividend curve. At that intersection, drop vertically until the intersection with the bottom axis. That point of intersection shows the IRR to be about

22 percent. For a 66.67 percent drop in the P-E multiple, Graph 3–5 shows the IRR to be about 12.5 percent.

So for a five-year holding:

P-E Multiple Decrease	Earnings Growth Rate	IRR
0%	40%	40.0%
50	40	22.0
67	40	12.5

Graph 3–5
IRR of Stocks: 67 Percent Drop in P-E Multiple

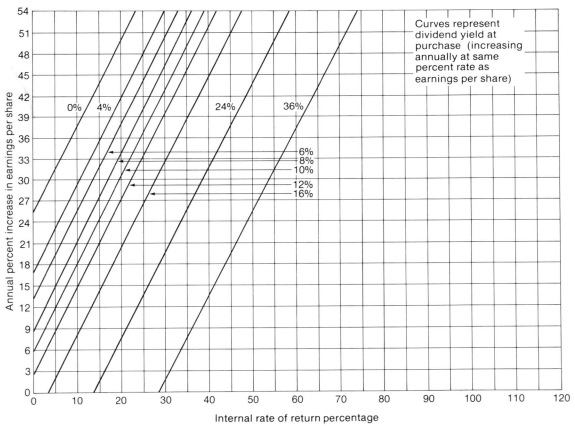

Note: P-E multiple at purchase = 30
        P-E multiple at sale   = 10
        Tax bracket   = 0%
        Holding period   = 5 yrs.

Mounting Multiples

What about the contrary situation where the P-E multiple at purchase is less than the P-E multiple at sale? In other words, we have a mounting multiple! For example, the stock of Abelson R-T Envelopes Company is selling at a P-E multiple of 10 and pays no dividend. In the past, Abelson R-T Envelopes has increased its earnings per share annually at a rate of only 3 percent. However, you have met the management and studied analytical information about the company. The president, Sally Abelson, tells you that the company is going to enter

Graph 3–6
IRR of Stocks: 200 Percent Increase in P-E Multiple

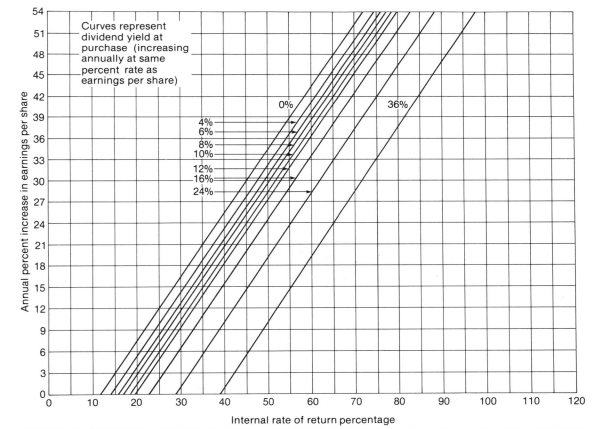

Note: P-E multiple at purchase = 10
P-E multiple at sale   = 30
Holding period   = 10 yrs.
Tax bracket   = 0%

a new field, stationery for home computers—including personalized form-fed checks, envelopes, and stationery. Your best estimate is that earnings per share will increase at a compound rate of 30 percent annually for the next 10 years and that, as a result of such growth, the P-E multiple will mount to 30:1 by the end of 10 years. Under such circumstances, what will be the internal rate of return from buying this stock?

Refer to Graph 3–6 (**IRR of Stocks: 200 Percent Increase in P-E Multiple**). Enter the graph on the left axis at 30 percent; proceed horizontally to the 0 percent dividend curve; at its intersection, de-

Graph 3–7
IRR of Stocks: 100 Percent Increase in P-E Multiple

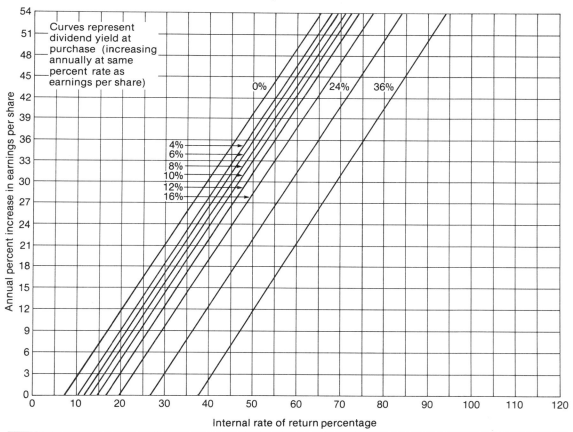

Note: P-E multiple at purchase = 10
        P-E multiple at sale   = 20
        Holding period   = 10 yrs.
        Tax bracket   = 0%

scend to the bottom axis. The point of intersection at the bottom axis is the IRR, 45 percent. Had the P-E multiple remained constant, the IRR would have been only 30 percent (Graph 3–1).

But suppose you are too optimistic in your projections and the P-E multiple for Abelson R-T Envelopes increases, but only by double instead of triple. What would the IRR be then? Refer to Graph 3–7. The IRR in this event would be 39.5 percent.

Perhaps you aren't comfortable projecting earnings and P-E multiples for as long a period as 10 years. You might feel that Abelson R-T Envelopes will boom, but only for the next five years. If its earnings

Graph 3–8
IRR of Stocks: 200 Percent Increase in P-E Multiple

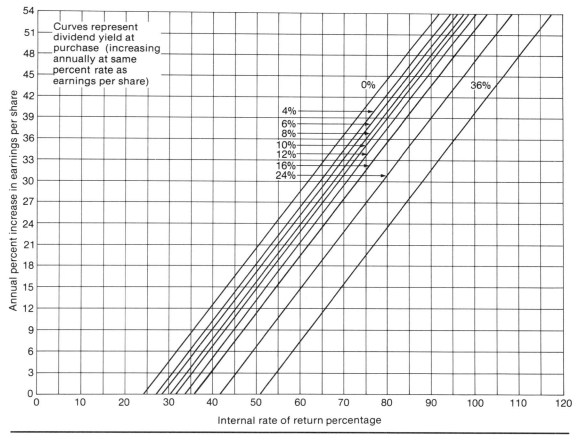

Note: P-E multiple at purchase = 10
       P-E multiple at sale   = 30
       Holding period   = 5 yrs.
       Tax bracket   = 0%

per share increase at 30 percent annually for five years and the P-E multiple mounts, what will the IRR be then? If the P-E multiple triples, then the IRR will be a rousing 62.5 percent. (Graph 3–8 performs the analysis in seconds.) And if the P-E multiple merely mounts by double, then you will still derive a highly respectable IRR of 49.5 percent from your intelligent investing (Graph 3–9).

Graph 3–9
IRR of Stocks: 100 Percent Increase in P-E Multiple

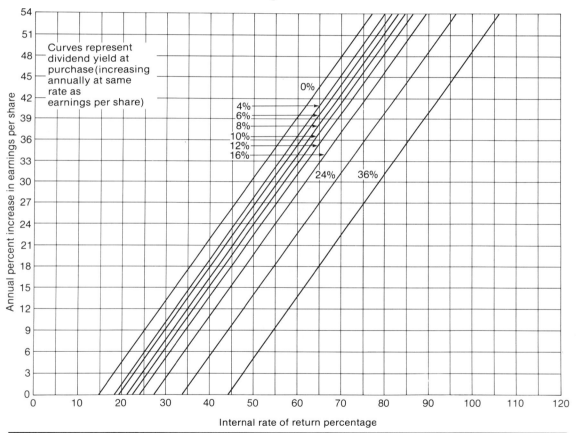

Note: P-E multiple at purchase = 10
        P-E multiple at sale   = 20
        Holding period   =   5 yrs.
        Tax bracket   =   0%

The following table summarizes the results of the Abelson R-T Envelope investment:

P-E Mounts by	Number of Years Held	Annual EPS Increase	IRR
300%	10	30%	45.0%
200	10	30	39.5
0	10	30	30.0
300	5	30	62.5
200	5	30	49.5
0	5	30	30.0

A mounting multiple has a more significant effect on the IRR realized when the holding period is shorter. This is true because the proceeds of sale magnified by the mounting multiple are realized sooner.

Stocks, Internal Rate of Return Analysis (After Tax)

As we saw in the preceding chapter, there are three cash-flow elements to consider in determining the IRR for a stock investment: (*a*) the initial yield and, (*b*) the subsequent years yield or earnings, and (*c*) the proceeds of sale at the end of the holding period. If the investor is in other than a zero tax bracket, things become more complicated.

The three cash flow elements are all reduced to the extent of applicable taxes. The initial yield and subsequent years cash flow are all reduced by the appropriate level of federal and state income taxes. Finally, the proceeds of sale at the end of the holding period are reduced by the relevant capital gains tax.

The calculations assume that the capital gains tax (maximum 20 percent) is 40 percent of the income tax bracket rate; thus, for a 50 percent tax bracket, the tax applied to the annual cash flows is 50 percent, and from the capital gain resulting from sale, 20 percent (.5 × .4) is deducted. For an investor in a 30 percent tax bracket, 30 percent is deducted from the annual cash flows, and 12 percent (.4 × .3) of the gain is deducted from the sales proceeds as capital gains tax.

In order to determine the internal rate of return from a stock investment in other than a zero tax bracket, all you have to do is use the appropriate graph. Two factors govern the selection of the proper graph: *the number of years that the investment is to be held* and *the applicable tax bracket.*

There are three choices for the tax bracket, 50 percent, 30 percent, or 0 percent, as described in the preceding chapter. Select the bracket closest to that of the investor. Within the tax bracket category, select the number of years the investment is to be held, ranging from 1 to 30 years. Let's say, the investors, Joyce and Don, are in the 50 percent tax bracket and they wish to find the IRR for a proposed stock investment to be held for 15 years. Refer to Graph 4–15, which is the graph for a 15-year holding and a 50 percent (or 30 percent) bracket. Joyce and Don must determine two items in order to use the graph and calculate the IRR:

1. Percent yield. This is the annual dividend from the security divided by the initial market price of the stock. For example, if the purchase price of the stock is $100 and the initial dividend per year is $6 per share, then the percent yield is 6 percent ($6 ÷ $100). Refer to the graph. The left axis of the graph is percent yield, and 6 percent, in this case, will be the starting point on the left axis.

2. Percentage annual increase in dividend or earnings per share (and market value of the stock). There are a number of lines or curves running across the graph which represent percentage annual increases in dividends or earnings per share ranging from 0 to 40 percent per year. You must decide your best estimate for the percentage annual increase in dividend or earnings per share for the particular stock you are evaluating. Stock market analyst reports may help you make this estimate as may brokerage firms, discussions with officers of the company, or your own analysis. For example, let's assume that Joyce and Don decide the best estimate of such future growth is 5 percent. (The choices for annual increase are 0, 5, 10, 15, 20, 25, 30, and 40 percent. Values other than these would lie proportionately between the curves for the next smaller and larger values.)

To find the IRR for the proposed investment, enter the graph at the 6 percent point on the left vertical axis, go across until you reach the 5 percent curve (for five percent growth)—for the 50 percent tax bracket (the solid curve); (dashed line curves are for 30 percent tax brackets). From that point of intersection, proceed down until you reach the bottom axis. That point of intersection with the bottom axis is the IRR, which in this case is 7.38 percent. The IRR, after 50 percent income tax and 20 percent capital gains tax, is 7.38 percent.

There is an implicit assumption in the Graph that the market value of the stock will increase over the long term at the same rate as the annual increase in dividends or earnings per share. This is a reasonable assumption, but it may not always be the case. It would not be the case if the present price-earnings ratio changes in the future.

If the stock does not pay any dividend, simply enter the graph at the 0 point on the left axis and proceed to the curve that represents your estimate of the annual increase in earnings per share.

The actual computation of the 7.38 percent IRR determined earlier is shown in Table 4–1. The example is based on an initial purchase of $100 and a starting annual cash flow of $6. The $192.25 cash flow shown in the 15th year includes both the dividend, after tax, in that year and the proceeds of sale after deduction of capital gains tax.

Table 4–1
Computation of IRR

Number	Cash Flow	Year × Cash Flow		
0	($100.00)		Initial dividend rate	6%
1	$3.00	3.000	Annual increase	5%
2	$3.15	6.300	After O.I. tax	50%
3	$3.31	9.923	After capital gains tax	80%
4	$3.47	13.892	Tax bracket	50%
5	$3.65	18.233	Number of years	15
6	$3.83	22.973	IRR percentage	7.38%
7	$4.02	28.142		
8	$4.22	33.770		
9	$4.43	39.891		
10	$4.65	46.540		
11	$4.89	53.754		
12	$5.13	61.572		
13	$5.39	70.038		
14	$5.66	79.197		
15	$192.25	2,883.811		

Table 4–2 shows the actual formulas in each cell of the spreadsheet computer program that made the calculation. Readers with some knowledge of spreadsheet computer programs may find it of interest. If you are not in that category, skip the table.

The graphs in this chapter may be used for any holding period from 1 to 30 years.

A summary of the steps to determine IRR after tax for a stock investment follows:

1. Find the graph based on tax bracket (zero bracket in Chapter 3, 50 percent or 30 percent in this chapter) and number of years the investment is to be held.

2. Enter the graph with the initial yield and proceed to the curve for the appropriate tax bracket which represents the annual growth rate of dividends or earnings. Then, descend to the horizontal axis to find the IRR.

Shrinking and Mounting P-E Multiples

The Graphs 4–1 to 4–30 assume that the market value of a stock will increase over the long term at the same rate as the annual increase in

Table 4–2
Formulas for IRR Computation

	1	2	3	4	5	6
1	"NUMBER"	"CFLOW"	"= = = = = = = = = ="	"YR*CF"	"INIT.DIV.RATE"	0.06
2	0	−100	"IRR%"		"ANN.INCREASE"	0.05
3	1	+R1C6*(−R2C2)*R3C6	"= = = = = = = = = ="	RC[−2]*RC[−3]	"AFTER O.I.TAX"	1 − R5C6
4	2	−R2C2*R1C6*((1+R2C6)^(R4C1 − 1))*R3C6		RC[−2]*RC[−3]	"AFTER CG TAX"	1 − 0.4*R5C6
5	3	R[−1]*(1+R2C6)	ITERCNT() = 9	RC[−2]*RC[−3]	"TAX BRACKET"	0.5
6	4	R[−1]*(1+R2C6)	IF(ISERROR(R[−1]C), 0,N+1)	RC[−2]*RC[−3]	"NO. YRS."	15
7	5	R[−1]*(1+R2C6)	IF(OR(N=0,R2C2=0),0 ,X+(NPV(X,CF)+INV)* (1+X)/NPV(X,CF1))	RC[−2]*RC[−3]		
8	6	R[−1]*(1+R2C6)		RC[−2]*RC[−3]		
9	7	R[−1]*(1+R2C6)		RC[−2]*RC[−3]		
10	8	R[−1]*(1+R2C6)		RC[−2]*RC[−3]		
11	9	R[−1]*(1+R2C6)		RC[−2]*RC[−3]		
12	10	R[−1]*(1+R2C6)		RC[−2]*RC[−3]		
13	11	R[−1]*(1+R2C6)		RC[−2]*RC[−3]		
14	12	R[−1]*(1+R2C6)		RC[−2]*RC[−3]		
15	13	R[−1]*(1+R2C6)		RC[−2]*RC[−3]		
16	14	R[−1]*(1+R2C6)		RC[−2]*RC[−3]		
17	15	R[−1]*(1+R2C6)+((−R2C2*((1+ R2C6)^C[−1]) − 100)*R4C6)+(−R 2C2)		RC[−2]*RC[−3]		

dividends or earnings per share. This is a reasonable assumption, but it may not always be the case. Inherent in such an assumption is the fact that the price-earnings ratio will remain constant. In actual practice, a rapid growth company is likely to see its price-earnings multiple decrease as time passes, and a depressed company that is "turned around" may enjoy an expanded or increased price-earnings ratio. Where the P-E multiple shrinks with the passage of time, the realized IRR, as a result, will be less than that obtained by use of Graphs 4–1 to 4–30. In such cases, those Graphs overstate the IRR.

Shrinking P-E Multiples

The assumption is reasonable, in most cases, that the rate of change in both dividends and earnings per share will be about the same. In other words, if a company's earnings per share are increasing at 8 percent per year, then its dividend is also going to increase at about that rate. And it is reasonable that, for an average stock, the P-E multiple will remain stable, provided the stock is selling at a P-E multiple near that of the stock market averages. In other words, if the market is selling at a P-E multiple of 9, then 3, 5 or 10 years later, it is reasonable to expect that McClain Light and Power's multiple will still be around that of the stock market averages.

But for a stock which is anticipated to increase earnings per share at a growth rate substantially greater than the market averages, it is likely that, over a period of years, the P-E multiple will decrease. For example, Pidgeons Pottery opened its doors 10 years ago and has increased its earnings per share 45 percent each year. Its annual sales are now $75 million, and its P-E multiple is 35. As the company matures, it is likely that its rapid growth rate will subside, and in anticipation of that occurrence, its P-E multiple will *shrink* from the elevated 30–40 range to somewhere between 8 and 12 where the averages reside.

Graphs 4–31, 4–32, 4–35, and 4–36 show the effects of shrinking multiples, as follows:

Graph 4–31	67% drop in multiple	50% investor tax bracket
Graph 4–32	50 drop in multiple	50 investor tax bracket
Graph 4–35	67 drop in multiple	30 investor tax bracket
Graph 4–36	50 drop in multiple	30 investor tax bracket

The graphs are based on a holding period of five years between purchase and sale.

Suppose you are considering an investment in Connie's Quick-Grow Company, which has a projected earnings per share growth rate of 40 percent per year. You are in a 50 percent tax bracket. Connie's Quick-Grow is plowing its earnings back into the business and pays no dividend. The present P-E multiple is 30:1; that is, each $30 of market price buys $1 of present earnings. If the multiple drops to 10:1 over a five-year holding period, what will your IRR be? Refer to Graph 4–31. Enter the left axis at the 40 percent earnings per share growth rate; proceed horizontally to the 0 percent dividend curve. Then go vertically to the bottom axis. The intersection at the bottom axis is the IRR, about 11.5 percent. Compare this result to the following:

0% tax bracket	no change in P-E multiple	IRR = 40%	(Graph 3–1)
50 tax bracket	no change in P-E multiple	IRR = 35	(Graph 4–5)
50 tax bracket	drop in P-E from 30:1 to 10:1	IRR = 11	(Graph 4–31)
50 tax bracket	drop in P-E from 20:1 to 10:1	IRR = 19	(Graph 4–32)
30 tax bracket	no change in P-E multiple	IRR = 37	(Graph 4–5)
30 tax bracket	drop in P-E from 30:1 to 10:1	IRR = 12	(Graph 4–35)
30 tax bracket	drop in P-E from 20:1 to 10:1	IRR = 20	(Graph 4–36)

What conclusions can you draw from the foregoing? First, think carefully about your own situation and the assumptions that underlie your analysis. Apply the same criteria to your alternative investment possibilities, stocks, bonds, tax-exempts, and real estate. Second, if you must buy high growth stocks at lofty P-E multiples, get rid of them before they enter the shrinking multiple phase.

Mounting Multiples

A *turnaround* or *special situation* stock may exhibit characteristics quite the opposite of the shrinking multiple company. Suppose you are considering an investment in McGrewders Muffler Company (MMC). As a muffler company, it has exhibited unspectacular growth, increasing earnings per share at only an average of 8 percent per year over the past 10 years. However, a year ago it formed a research and development arm that has been engaged in research on an electrically powered automobile motor. You have reason to think that a commercially viable product will result that will allow the consumer to drive at a cost of only 2 cents per mile, and with the motor in mass production, the cost of cars will decline by 20 percent. MMC is selling at only seven times its $1 per share earnings. You buy it on the expectation that its earnings will increase 40 percent per year over the next five years and that its P-E multiple will triple from 7:1 to 21:1. MMC pays no dividend, and you are in a 50 percent tax bracket. What will your IRR be if this works out as you anticipate? Refer to Graph 4–33. Enter the graph on the left axis at 40 percent growth of earnings per share; proceed horizontally to the intersection with the 0 percent dividend curve; then, vertically to the bottom axis where it is seen that the IRR for this investment is 66.5 percent. Compare this to several other possibilities at 40 percent EPS growth:

0% tax bracket	P-E multiple remains unchanged	IRR = 40%	(Graph 3–1)
50 tax bracket	P-E multiple triples	IRR = 66	(Graph 4–33)
50 tax bracket	P-E multiple doubles	IRR = 55	(Graph 4–34)
30 tax bracket	P-E multiple doubles	IRR = 57	(Graph 4–38)
30 tax bracket	P-E multiple triples	IRR = 70	(Graph 4–37)

It is so much better to own a stock with a mounting rather than a shrinking multiple! Compare the results of owning McGrewders Mufflers to Connie's Quick-Grow Company. Now compare the results of an investment of $1,000 growing at 12 percent after tax to the results of $1,000 growing at 70 percent.

12% Connie's Quick-Grow Company will be worth $3,105
70% McGrewders Mufflers will be worth $202,000.

In both cases we are talking about a stock with earnings per share growth rate of 40 percent per year, zero dividend, an investor in the 30 percent tax bracket, and a holding period of 10 years. The difference between the two cases is that the first stock (Connie's Quick-Grow) has a multiple *shrink* from 30:1 to 10:1 and the second stock (McGrewders Mufflers) has a multiple *mount* from 10:1 to 30:1.

Graph 4–1
After Tax Internal Rates of Return

Yield percentage
(annual initial
dividend divided
by initial market
price)

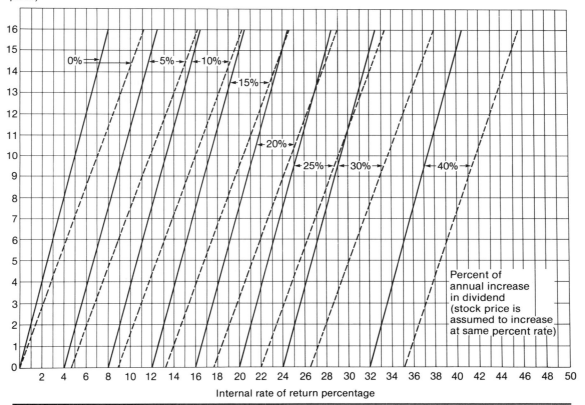

Internal rate of return percentage

Note: —— 50 percent tax bracket.
         ---- 30 percent tax bracket.
         Investment is held 1 year.

Graph 4–2
After Tax Internal Rates of Return

Yield percentage
(annual initial
dividend divided
by initial market
price)

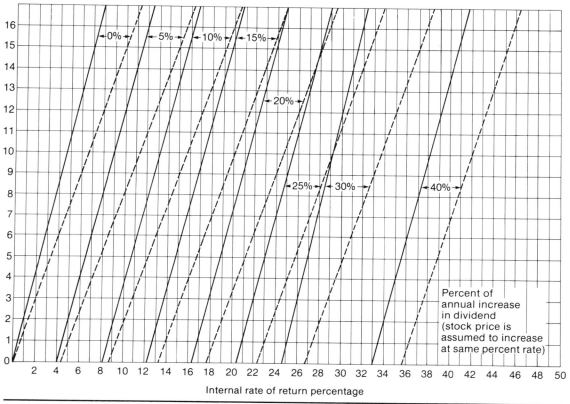

Internal rate of return percentage

Note: —— 50 percent tax bracket.
        ---- 30 percent tax bracket.
        Investment is held 2 years.

Graph 4–3
After Tax Internal Rates of Return

Yield percentage
(annual initial
dividend divided
by initial market
price)

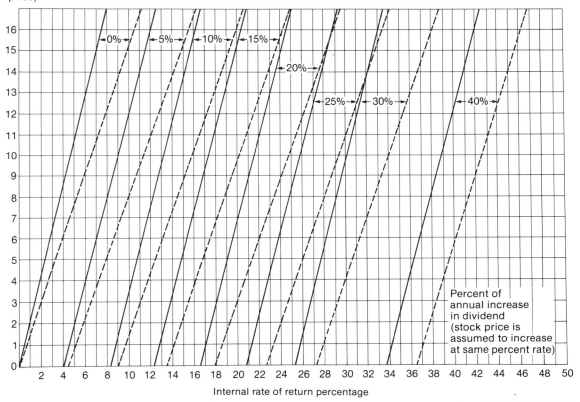

Internal rate of return percentage

Note: —— 50 percent tax bracket.
           ---- 30 percent tax bracket.
           Investment is held 3 years.

Graph 4–4
After Tax Internal Rates of Return

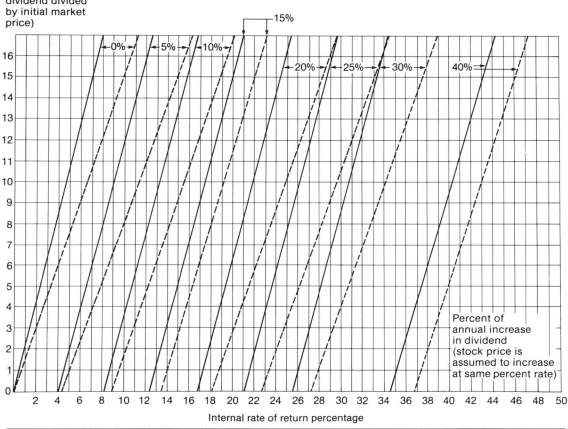

Yield percentage
(annual initial
dividend divided
by initial market
price)

Internal rate of return percentage

Note: —— 50 percent tax bracket.
       ---- 30 percent tax bracket.
       Investment is held 4 years.

Graph 4–5
After Tax Internal Rates of Return

Yield percentage
(annual initial
dividend divided
by initial market
price)

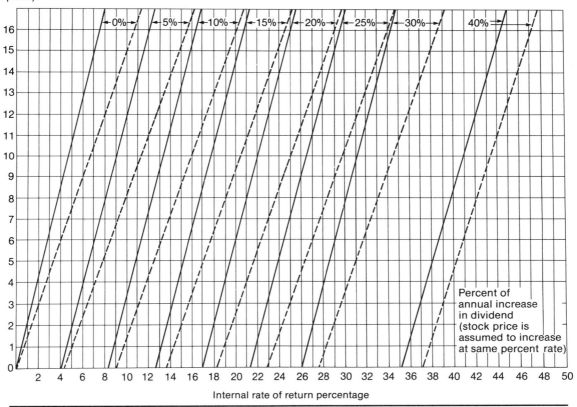

Internal rate of return percentage

Note: —— 50 percent tax bracket.
 ---- 30 percent tax bracket.
 Investment is held 5 years.

Graph 4–6
After Tax Internal Rates of Return

Yield percentage
(annual initial
dividend divided
by initial market
price)

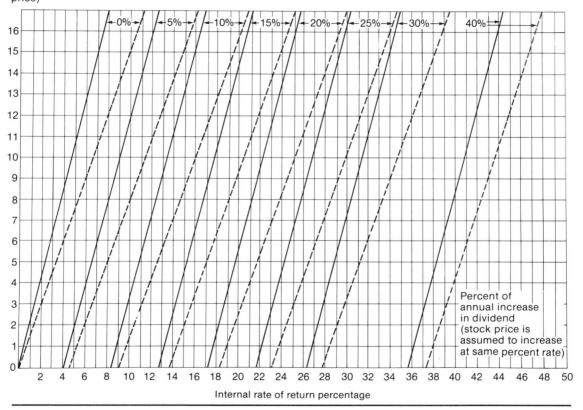

Internal rate of return percentage

Note: —— 50 percent tax bracket.
         ---- 30 percent tax bracket.
         Investment is held 6 years.

Graph 4–7
After Tax Internal Rates of Return

Yield percentage
(annual initial
dividend divided
by initial market
price)

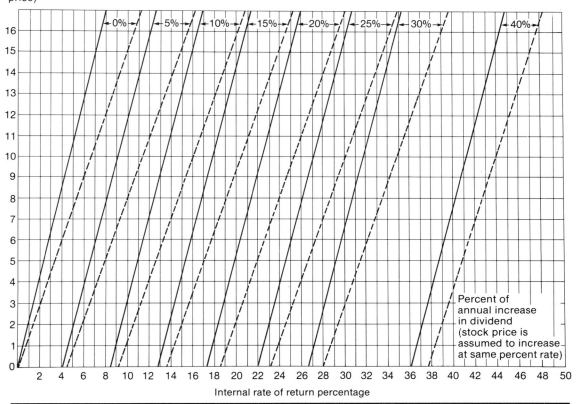

Internal rate of return percentage

Note: —— 50 percent tax bracket.
         ---- 30 percent tax bracket.
         Investment is held 7 years.

Graph 4–8
After Tax Internal Rates of Return

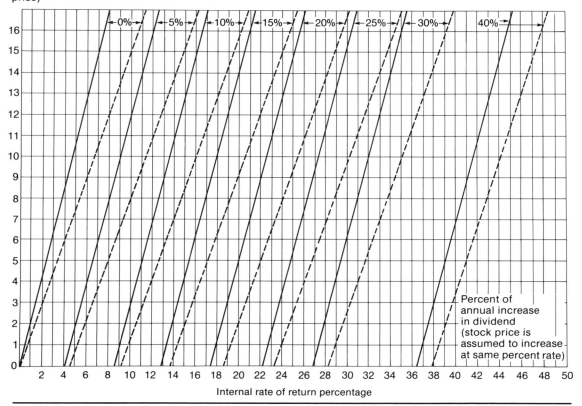

Yield percentage
(annual initial
dividend divided
by initial market
price)

Internal rate of return percentage

Note: —— 50 percent tax bracket.
         ---- 30 percent tax bracket.
         Investment is held 8 years.

Graph 4–9
After Tax Internal Rates of Return

Yield percentage
(annual initial
dividend divided
by initial market
price)

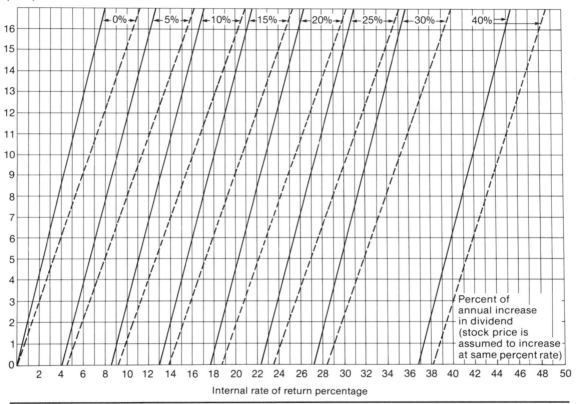

Internal rate of return percentage

Note: —— 50 percent tax bracket.
      ---- 30 percent tax bracket.
      Investment is held 9 years.

Graph 4–10
After Tax Internal Rates of Return

Yield percentage
(annual initial
dividend divided
by initial market
price)

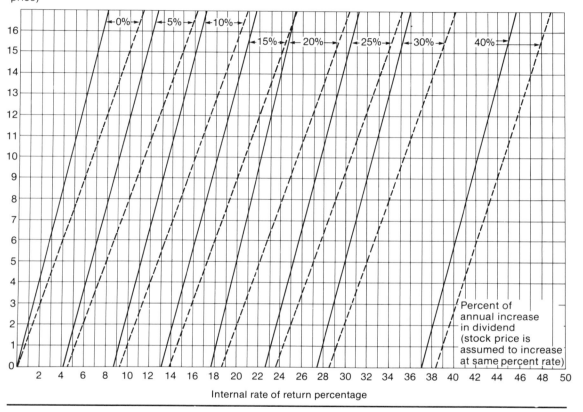

Internal rate of return percentage

Note: —— 50 percent tax bracket.
         ---- 30 percent tax bracket.
         Investment is held 10 years.

Graph 4–11
After Tax Internal Rates of Return

Yield percentage
(annual initial
dividend divided
by initial market
price)

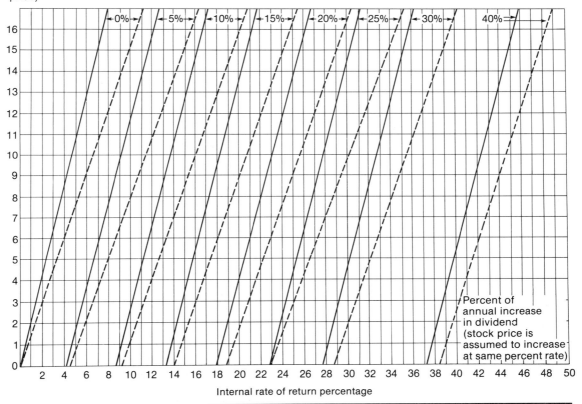

Internal rate of return percentage

Note: —— 50 percent tax bracket.
         ---- 30 percent tax bracket.
         Investment is held 11 years.

Graph 4–12
After Tax Internal Rates of Return

Yield percentage
(annual initial
dividend divided
by initial market
price)

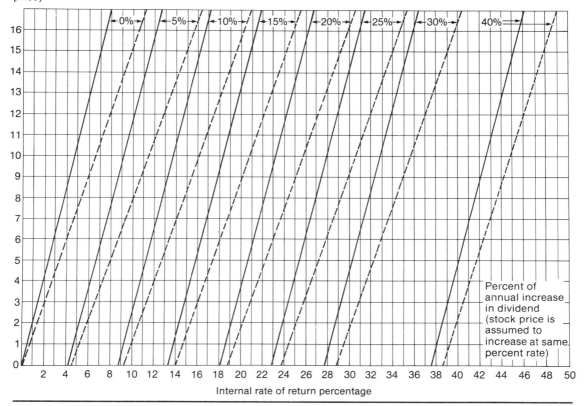

Note: —— 50 percent tax bracket.
‑‑‑‑ 30 percent tax bracket.
Investment is held 12 years.

Graph 4–13
After Tax Internal Rates of Return

Yield percentage
(annual initial
dividend divided
by initial market
price)

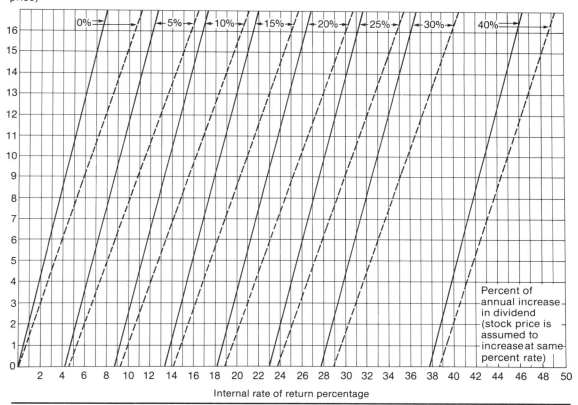

Internal rate of return percentage

Note: —— 50 percent tax bracket.
       ---- 30 percent tax bracket.
       Investment is held 13 years.

Graph 4–14
After Tax Internal Rates of Return

Yield percentage
(annual initial
dividend divided
by initial market
price)

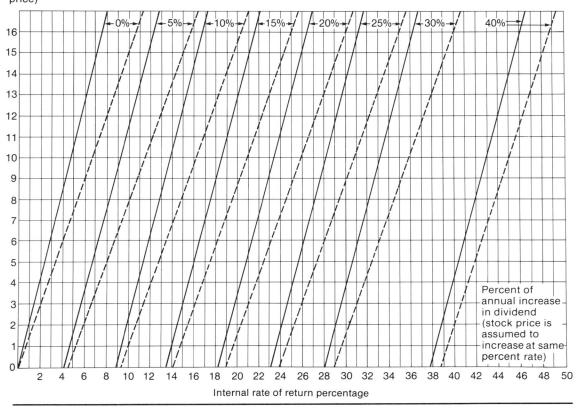

Note: —— 50 percent tax bracket.
         ---- 30 percent tax bracket.
         Investment is held 14 years.

Graph 4–15
After Tax Internal Rates of Return

Yield percentage
(annual initial
dividend divided
by initial market
price)

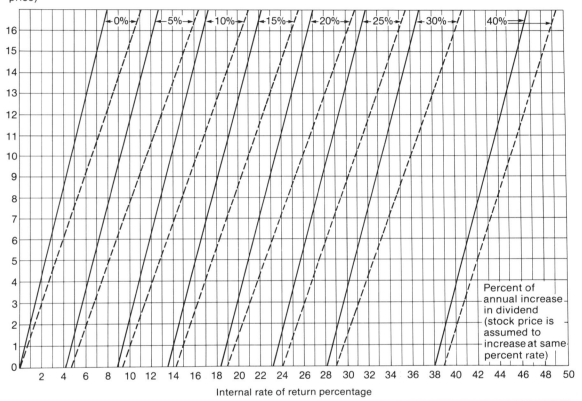

Internal rate of return percentage

Note: —— 50 percent tax bracket.
        ---- 30 percent tax bracket.
        Investment is held 15 years.

Graph 4–16
After Tax Internal Rates of Return

Yield percentage
(annual initial
dividend divided
by initial market
price)

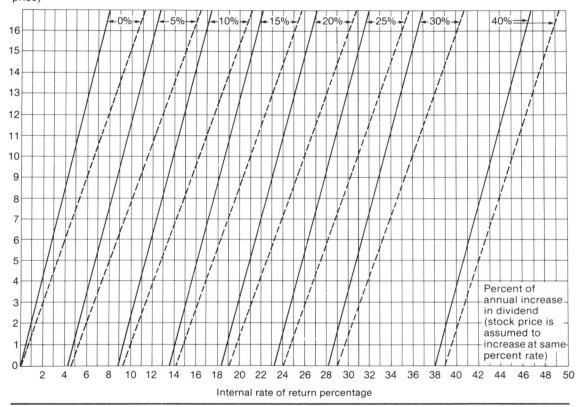

Internal rate of return percentage

Note: —— 50 percent tax bracket.
       ---- 30 percent tax bracket.
       Investment is held 16 years.

Graph 4–17
After Tax Internal Rates of Return

Yield percentage
(annual initial
dividend divided
by initial market
price)

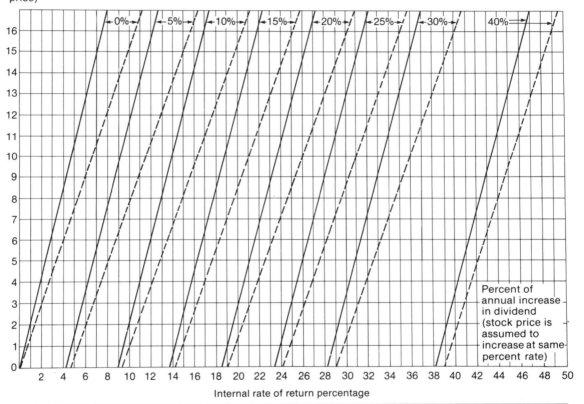

Internal rate of return percentage

Note: —— 50 percent tax bracket.
         ---- 30 percent tax bracket.
         Investment is held 17 years.

Graph 4–18
After Tax Internal Rates of Return

Yield percentage
(annual initial
dividend divided
by initial market
price)

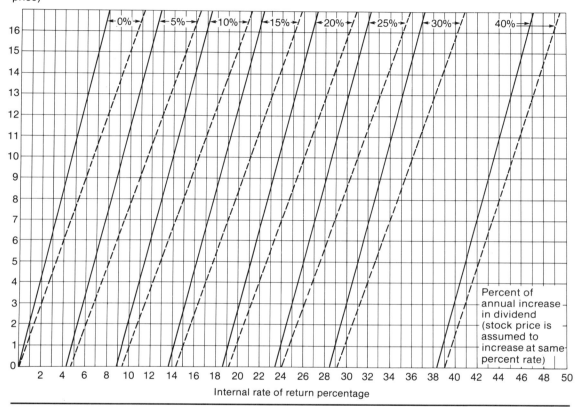

Internal rate of return percentage

Note: —— 50 percent tax bracket.
         ---- 30 percent tax bracket.
         Investment is held 18 years.

Graph 4–19
After Tax Internal Rates of Return

Yield percentage
(annual initial
dividend divided
by initial market
price)

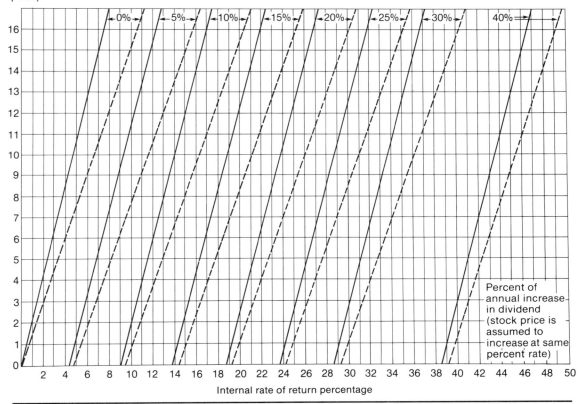

Internal rate of return percentage

Graph 4–20
After Tax Internal Rates of Return

Yield percentage
(annual initial
dividend divided
by initial market
price)

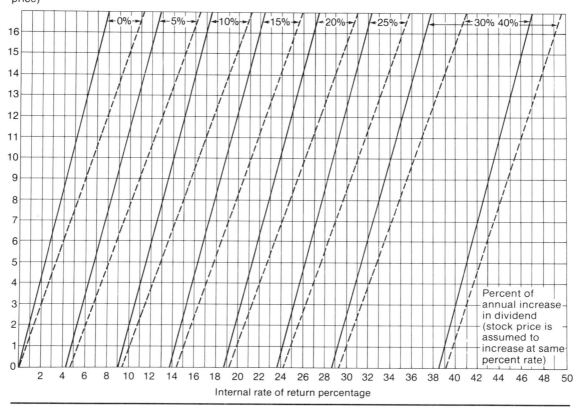

Internal rate of return percentage

Note: —— 50 percent tax bracket.
          ---- 30 percent tax bracket.
          Investment is held 20 years.

Graph 4–21
After Tax Internal Rates of Return

Yield percentage
(annual initial
dividend divided
by initial market
price)

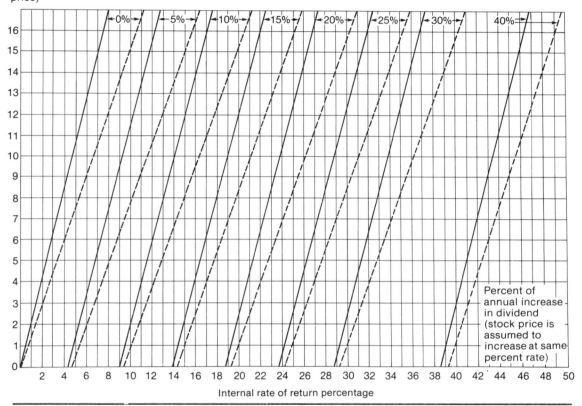

Internal rate of return percentage

Note: —— 50 percent tax bracket.
‑‑‑‑ 30 percent tax bracket.
Investment is held 21 years.

Graph 4–22
After Tax Internal Rates of Return

Yield percentage
(annual initial
dividend divided
by initial market
price)

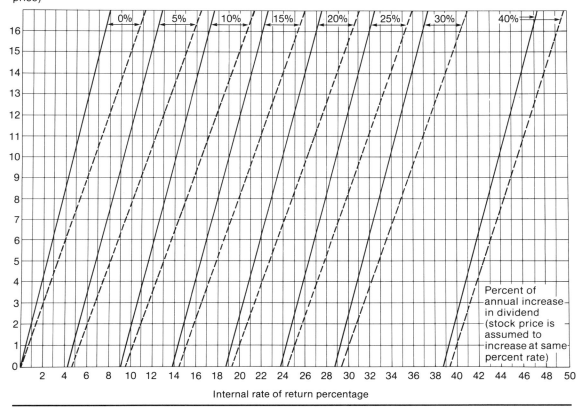

Internal rate of return percentage

Note: ⎯⎯ 50 percent tax bracket.
       ---- 30 percent tax bracket.
       Investment is held 22 years.

Graph 4–23
After Tax Internal Rates of Return

Yield percentage
(annual initial
dividend divided
by initial market
price)

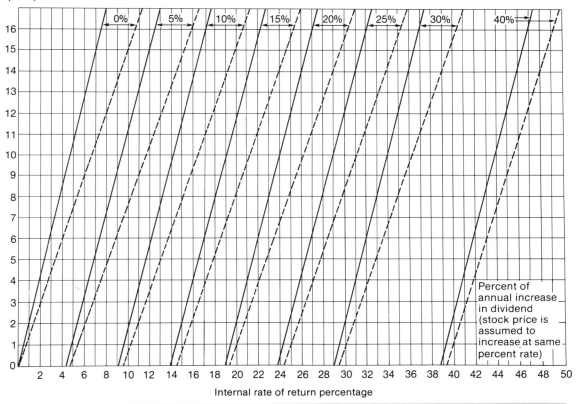

Internal rate of return percentage

Note: —— 50 percent tax bracket.
         ---- 30 percent tax bracket.
         Investment is held 23 years.

Graph 4–24
After Tax Internal Rates of Return

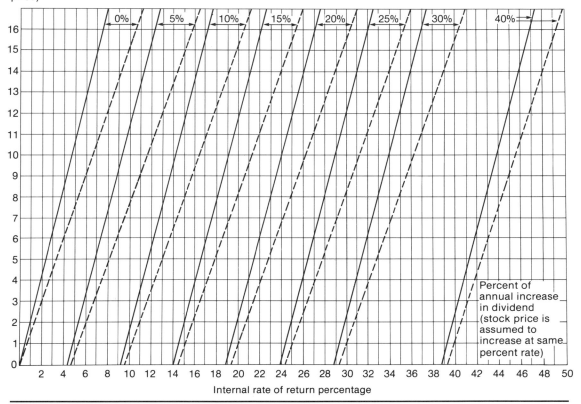

Yield percentage
(annual initial
dividend divided
by initial market
price)

Note: —— 50 percent tax bracket.
        ---- 30 percent tax bracket.
        Investment is held 24 years.

Graph 4–25
After Tax Internal Rates of Return

Yield percentage
(annual initial
dividend divided
by initial market
price)

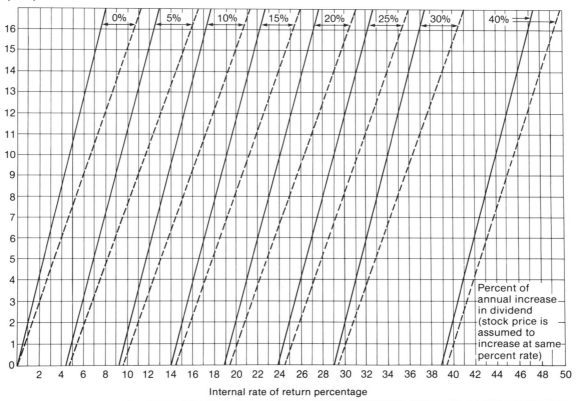

Internal rate of return percentage

Note: —— 50 percent tax bracket.
---- 30 percent tax bracket.
Investment is held 25 years.

Graph 4–26
After Tax Internal Rates of Return

Yield percentage
(annual initial
dividend divided
by initial market
price)

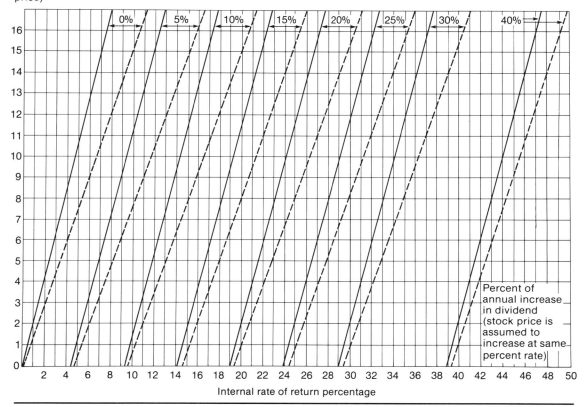

Internal rate of return percentage

Note: —— 50 percent tax bracket.
         ---- 30 percent tax bracket.
         Investment is held 26 years.

Graph 4–27
After Tax Internal Rates of Return

Yield percentage
(annual initial
dividend divided
by initial market
price)

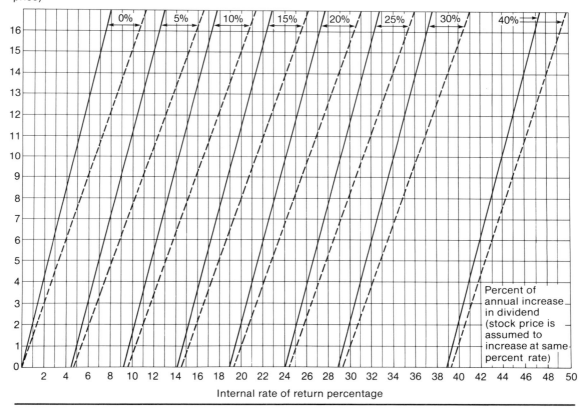

Internal rate of return percentage

Note: —— 50 percent tax bracket.
---- 30 percent tax bracket.
Investment is held 27 years.

Graph 4–28
After Tax Internal Rates of Return

Yield percentage
(annual initial
dividend divided
by initial market
price)

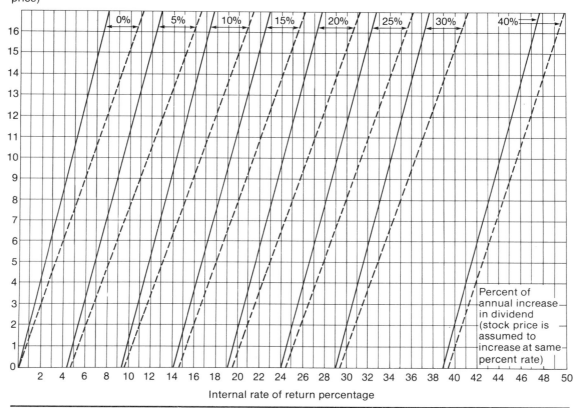

Internal rate of return percentage

Note: ——— 50 percent tax bracket.
       ----- 30 percent tax bracket.
       Investment is held 28 years.

Graph 4–29
After Tax Internal Rates of Return

Yield percentage
(annual initial
dividend divided
by initial market
price)

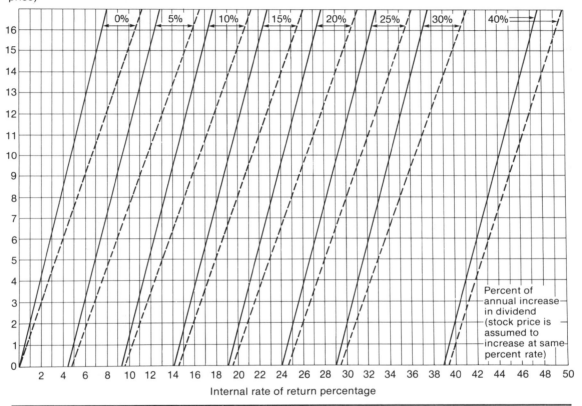

Internal rate of return percentage

Note: —— 50 percent tax bracket.
   ---- 30 percent tax bracket.
   Investment is held 29 years.

Graph 4–30
After Tax Internal Rates of Return

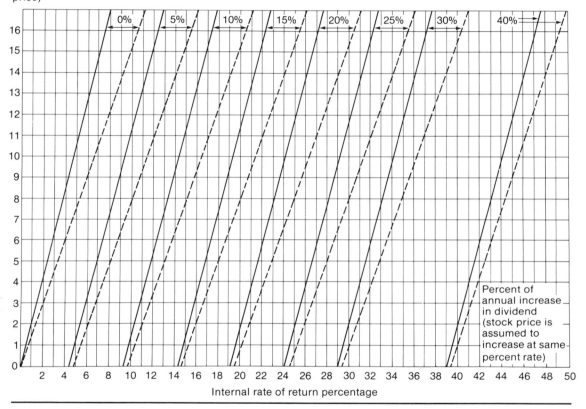

Yield percentage
(annual initial
dividend divided
by initial market
price)

Internal rate of return percentage

Note: ——— 50 percent tax bracket.
         ---- 30 percent tax bracket.
         Investment is held 30 years.

Graph 4–31
IRR of Stocks: 67 Percent Drop in P-E Multiple

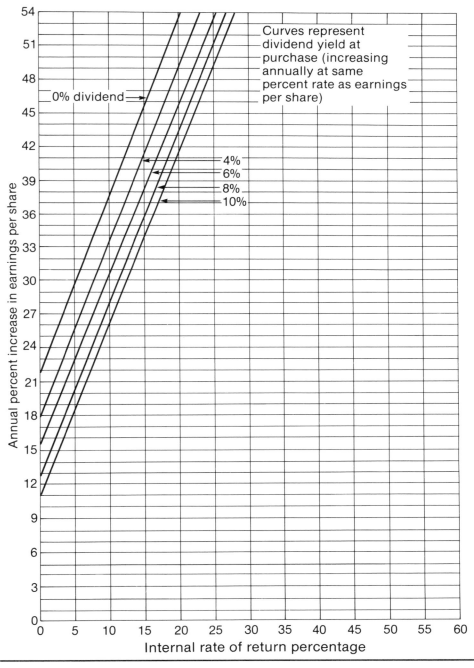

Curves represent dividend yield at purchase (increasing annually at same percent rate as earnings per share)

0% dividend →

4%
6%
8%
10%

Annual percent increase in earnings per share

Internal rate of return percentage

Note: P-E multiple at purchase = 30
P-E multiple at sale   = 10
Tax bracket   = 50
Holding period   = 5 yrs.

Graph 4–32
IRR of Stocks: 50 Percent Drop in P-E Multiple

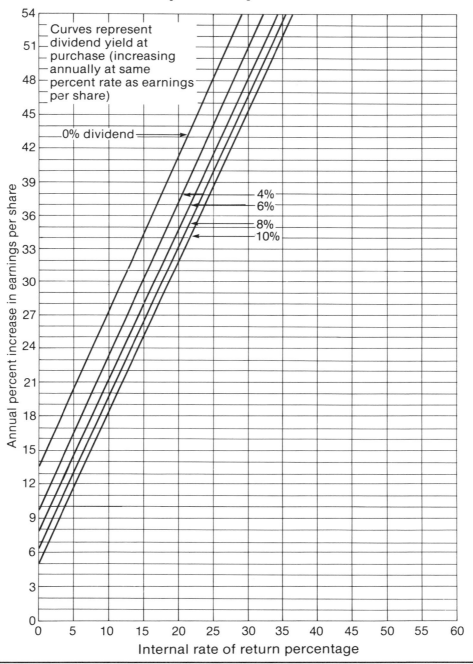

Note: P-E multiple at purchase = 20
      P-E multiple at sale   = 10
      Tax bracket   = 50
      Holding period   = 5 yrs.

Graph 4–33
IRR of Stocks: 200 Percent Increase in P-E Multiple

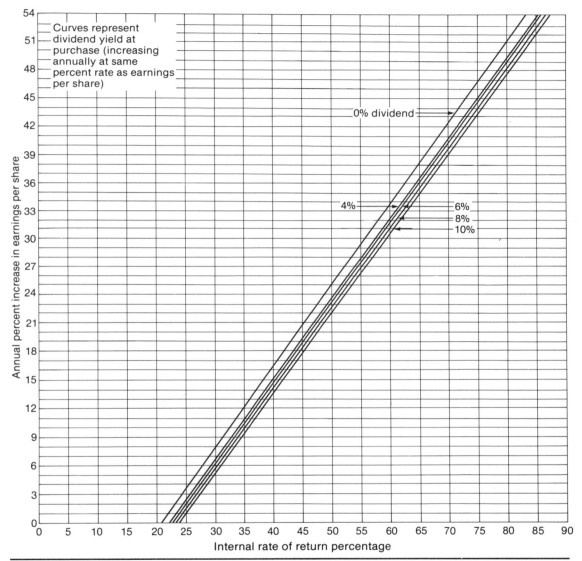

Note: P-E multiple at purchase = 10
P-E multiple at sale = 30
Tax bracket = 50
Holding period = 5 yrs.

Graph 4–34
IRR of Stocks: 100 Percent Increase in P-E Multiple

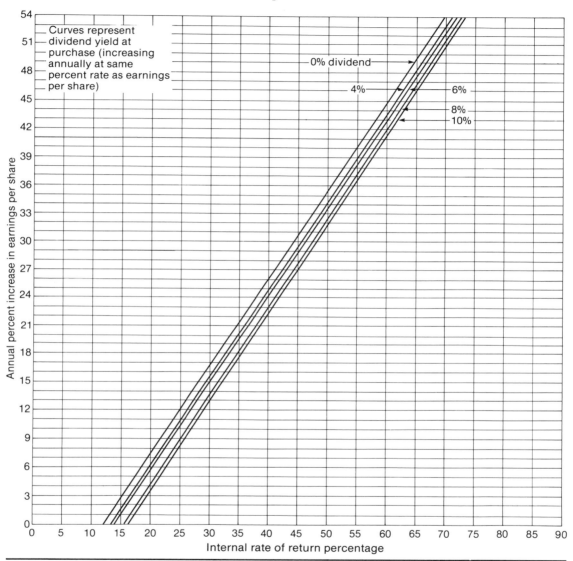

Note: P-E multiple at purchase = 10
P-E multiple at sale   = 20
Tax bracket   = 50
Holding period   = 5 yrs.

Graph 4–35
IRR of Stocks: 67 Percent Drop in P-E Multiple

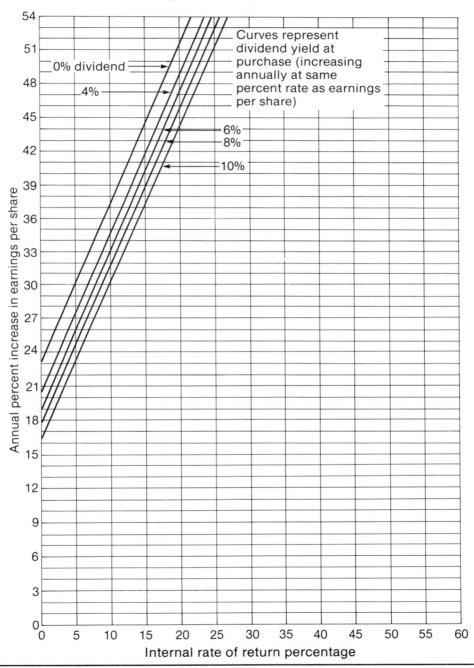

Note: P-E multiple at purchase = 30
P-E multiple at sale   = 10
Tax bracket   = 30
Holding period   = 5 yrs.

Graph 4–36
IRR of Stocks: 50 Percent Drop in P-E Multiple

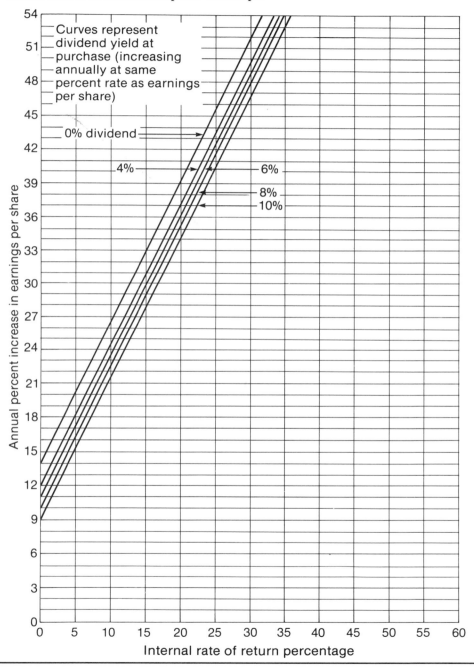

Note: P-E multiple at purchase = 20
P-E multiple at sale = 10
Tax bracket = 30
Holding period = 5 yrs.

Graph 4–37
IRR of Stocks: 200 Percent Increase in P-E Multiple

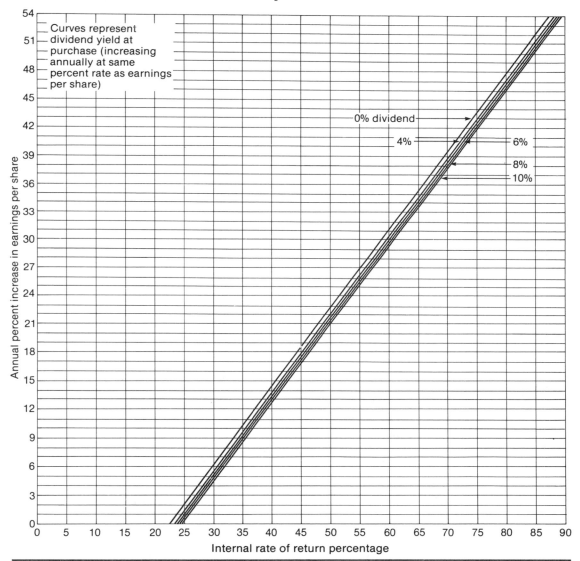

Note: P-E multiple at purchase = 10
P-E multiple at sale   = 30
Tax bracket   = 30
Holding period   = 5 yrs.

Graph 4–38
IRR of Stocks: 100 Percent Increase in P-E Multiple

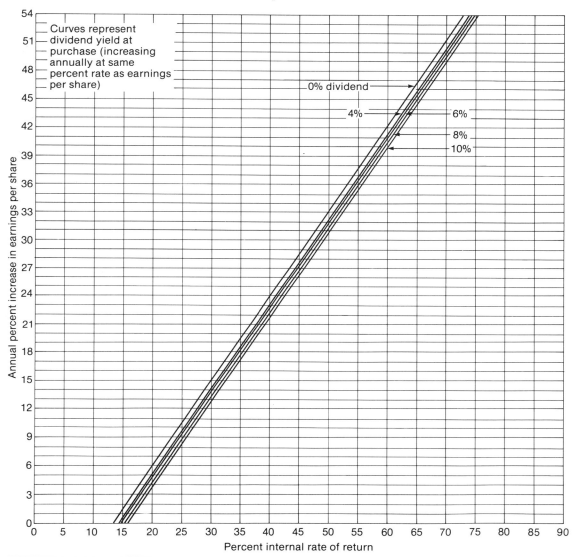

Note: P-E multiple at purchase = 10
        P-E multiple at sale   = 20
        Tax bracket   = 30
        Holding period   = 5 yrs.

CHAPTER 5

Bonds, Internal Rate of Return Analysis (Before Tax)

Why would anyone be interested in the before-tax rate of return from an investment in a bond? There could be several reasons. First of all the investor might be tax-exempt, such as a pension fund, Keogh plan, or individual retirement account (IRA). Or the investor might be the custodian for a child who is in a zero tax bracket, due to the effect of the child's personal income tax exemption. (Note: This chapter is not applicable to tax-exempt bonds unless such bonds are purchased at par value of $1,000. IRR for tax-exempts is covered in Chapter 6.)

In order to determine the internal rate of return from a bond investment, without regard to tax consequences, all you have to do is use Graphs 5–1 to 5–30. The term *yield to maturity* is frequently used with respect to bonds. It means precisely the same thing as internal rate of return. So don't be confused. Yield to maturity and internal rate of return are synonymous.

There are two items that must be determined in order to use the graphs and make the determination:

1. Purchase price. This is just what the name implies—the price you would pay to acquire each bond. If you wish to determine the internal rate of return for an existing bond, use the current market price in lieu of the purchase price.

2. Percent interest coupon. This is an expression of the annual income received from the bond as a percentage of the par value of $1,000. For example, a 10 percent bond is one that pays annual interest totaling $100 per bond (0.10 × $1,000 is $100).

There are 30 graphs in this chapter. Each graph represents the *number of years* from the present *until* the *maturity* date of the bond. The range of years covered is from 1 to 30.

Let's find the yield to maturity for the following bond. It matures 30 years from now; it can be purchased for $1,050, and it pays $120 per year (12 percent in interest).

To find the YTM or IRR for this bond, refer to the 30-year graph, 5–30. Enter the graph at the $1,050 point on the left vertical axis, go across until you reach the 12 percent curve; then from that point of intersection, proceed down until you reach the bottom axis. That point is the YTM or IRR, which in this case is 11.4 percent. (There is an implicit assumption in the graph that the maturity value of the bond is $1,000.)

The actual computation of the 11.4 percent YTM or IRR determined above is shown in Table 5–1. The cash flow in the 30th year is comprised of both the $1,000 maturity value and the interest for that year of $120.

Table 5–1
IRR Calculation

Year	Cash Flow	Year × Cash Flow	Iterations	30-year bond $ 120 coupon
0	− 1050	0	3550.00	Purchase price $1,050 *******
1	120	120	85800.00	
2	120	240	.0413753	Internal rate of return 11.41%
3	120	360	1287.16	
4	120	480	34472.09	
5	120	600	.0802595	
6	120	720	396.30	
7	120	840	16672.98	
8	120	960	.105936	
9	120	1080	76.29	
10	120	1200	11054.75	
11	120	1320	.1135677	
12	120	1440	4.39	
13	120	1560	9882.22	
14	120	1680	.1140625	
15	120	1800	0.02	
16	120	1920	9812.14	
17	120	2040	.1140644	
18	120	2160	0.00	
19	120	2280	9811.87	
20	120	2400	.1140644	
21	120	2520		
22	120	2640		
23	120	2760		
24	120	2880		
25	120	3000		
26	120	3120		
27	120	3240		
28	120	3360		
29	120	3480		
30	1120	33600		

Interestingly, for a zero bracket, you will note if you study the graphs that, at a $1,000 purchase price, the YTM is always equal to the coupon rate. For example, without looking at the graph for the moment, what do you think the IRR is for a 10 percent coupon with a $1,000 purchase price and a 20-year maturity? If you said 10 percent, congratulations. If you said anything, else, reread this paragraph.

In the next chapter, we will look at IRR for bonds, after tax.

Graph 5–1
Bond Yield to Maturity: 1 Year *(curves represent annual interest as a percentage of maturity value)*

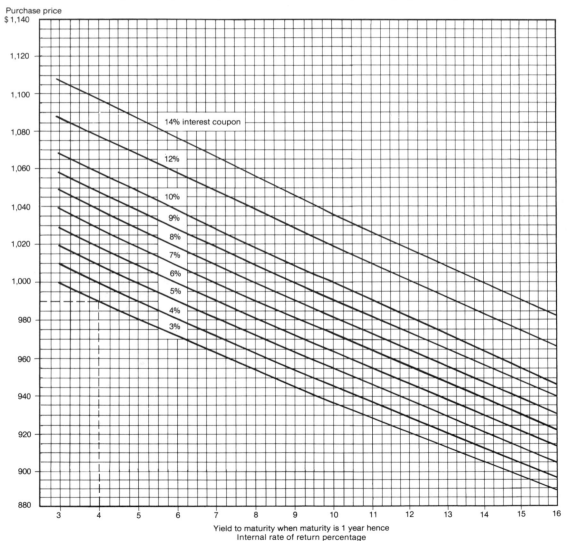

Graph 5–2
Bond Yield to Maturity: 2 Years *(curves represent annual interest as a percentage of maturity value)*

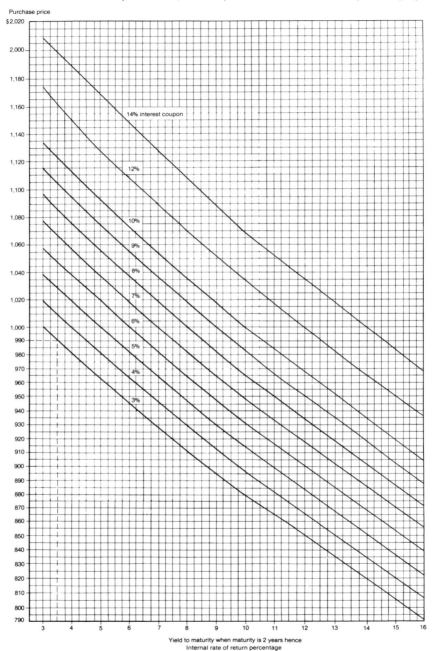

Purchase price

Yield to maturity when maturity is 2 years hence
Internal rate of return percentage

Graph 5–3
Bond Yield to Maturity: 3 Years *(curves represent annual interest as a percentage of maturity value)*

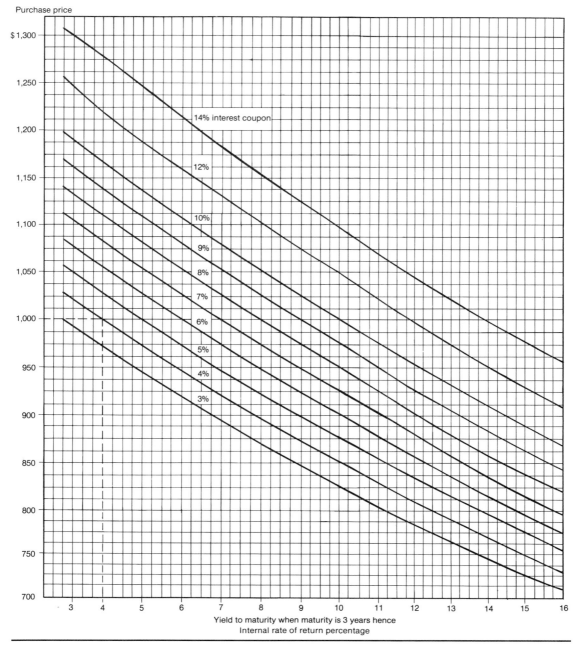

Purchase price

14% interest coupon

12%

10%

9%

8%

7%

6%

5%

4%

3%

Yield to maturity when maturity is 3 years hence
Internal rate of return percentage

Graph 5–4
Bond Yield to Maturity: 4 Years *(curves represent annual interest as a percentage of maturity value)*

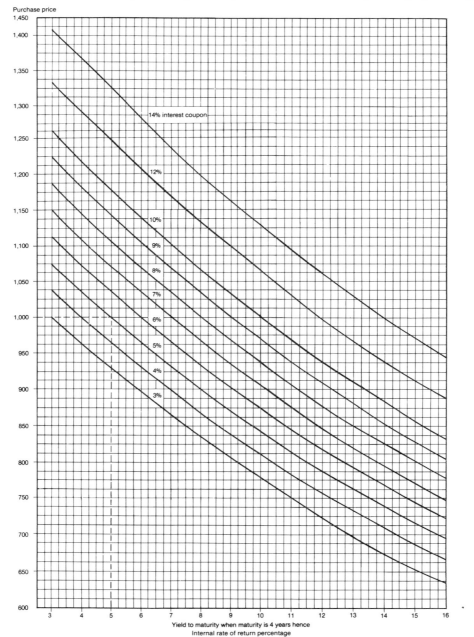

Purchase price

14% interest coupon

12%

10%

9%

8%

7%

6%

5%

4%

3%

Yield to maturity when maturity is 4 years hence
Internal rate of return percentage

Graph 5–5
Bond Yield to Maturity: 5 Years *(curves represent annual interest as a percentage of maturity value)*

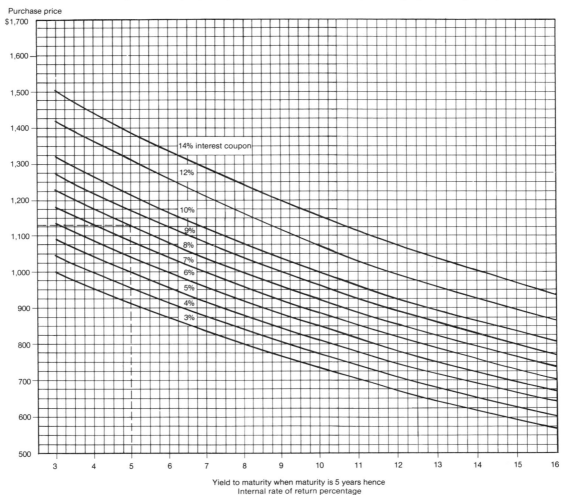

Yield to maturity when maturity is 5 years hence
Internal rate of return percentage

Graph 5–6
Bond Yield to Maturity: 6 Years *(curves represent annual interest as a percentage of maturity value)*

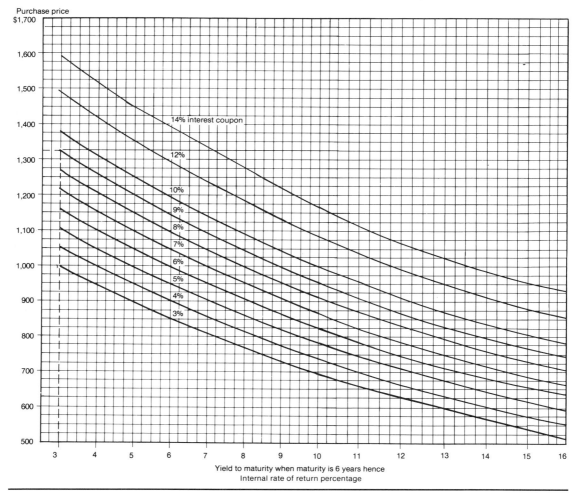

Purchase price

14% interest coupon
12%
10%
9%
8%
7%
6%
5%
4%
3%

Yield to maturity when maturity is 6 years hence
Internal rate of return percentage

Graph 5–7
Bond Yield to Maturity: 7 Years *(curves represent annual interest as a percentage of maturity value)*

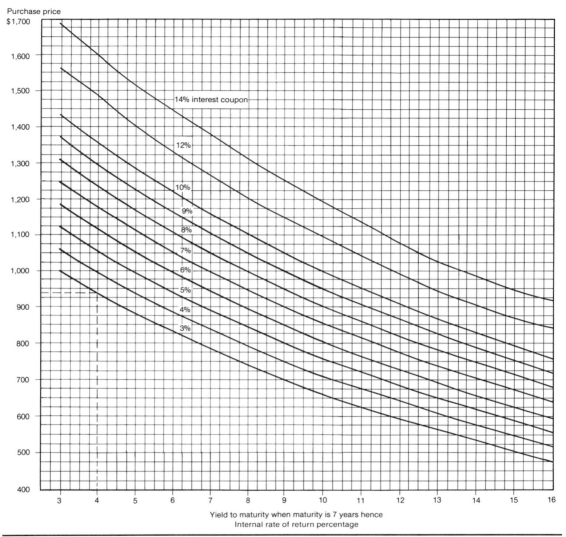

Purchase price

14% interest coupon

12%

10%
9%
8%
7%
6%
5%
4%
3%

Yield to maturity when maturity is 7 years hence
Internal rate of return percentage

Graph 5–8
Bond Yield to Maturity: 8 Years *(curves represent annual interest as a percentage of maturity value)*

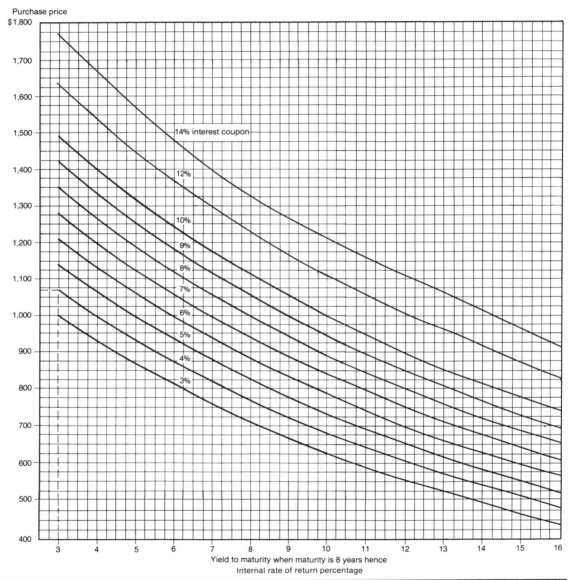

Purchase price

Yield to maturity when maturity is 8 years hence
Internal rate of return percentage

Graph 5–9
Bond Yield to Maturity: 9 Years *(curves represent annual interest as a percentage of maturity value)*

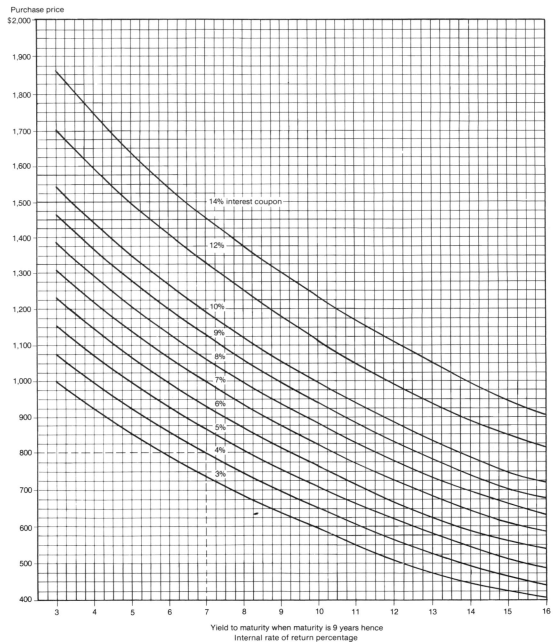

Purchase price

14% interest coupon

12%

10%

9%

8%

7%

6%

5%

4%

3%

Yield to maturity when maturity is 9 years hence
Internal rate of return percentage

Graph 5–10
Bond Yield to Maturity: 10 Years *(curves represent annual interest as a percentage of maturity value)*

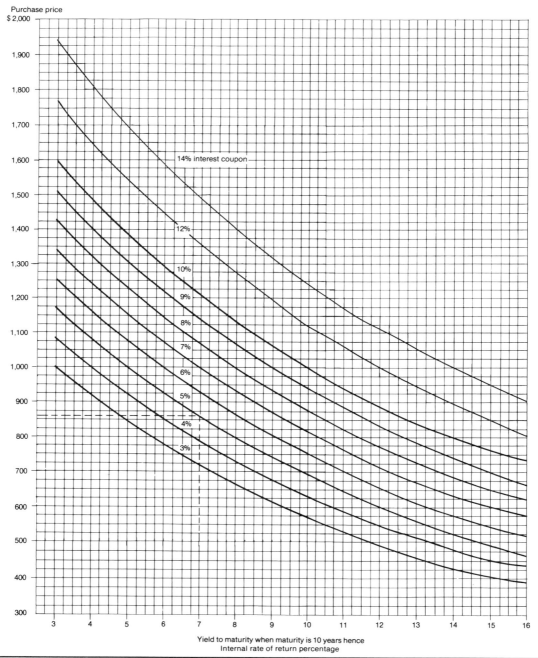

Purchase price

14% interest coupon

12%

10%

9%

8%

7%

6%

5%

4%

3%

Yield to maturity when maturity is 10 years hence
Internal rate of return percentage

Graph 5–11
Bond Yield to Maturity: 11 Years *(curves represent annual interest as a percentage of maturity value)*

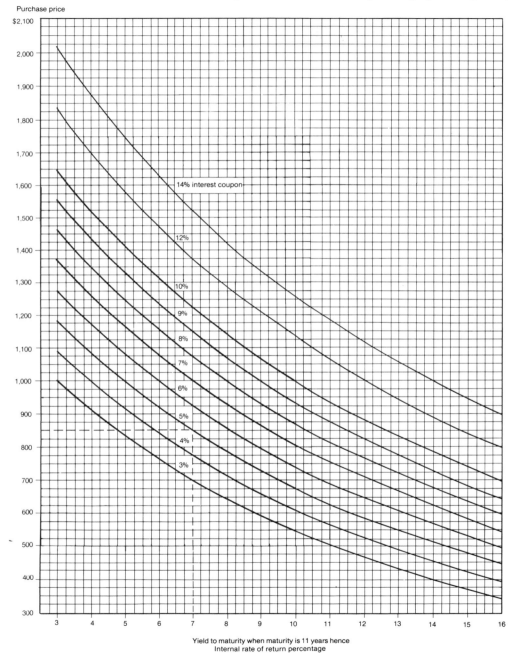

Purchase price

14% interest coupon

12%

10%

9%

8%

7%

6%

5%

4%

3%

Yield to maturity when maturity is 11 years hence
Internal rate of return percentage

Graph 5–12
Bond Yield to Maturity: 12 Years *(curves represent annual interest as a percentage of maturity value)*

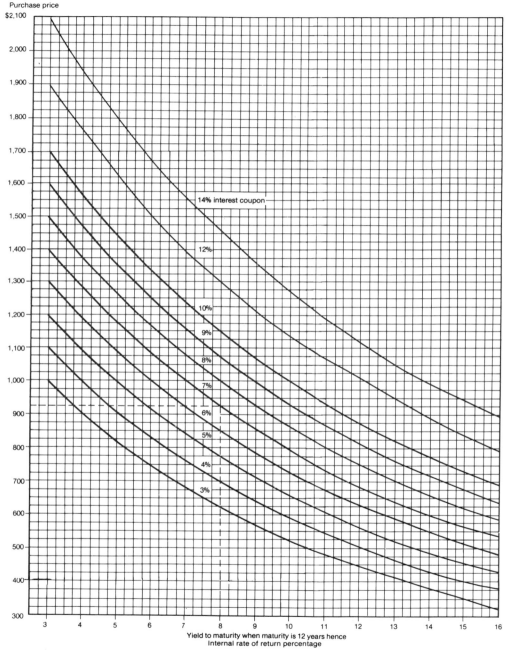

Purchase price

Yield to maturity when maturity is 12 years hence
Internal rate of return percentage

Graph 5–13
Bond Yield to Maturity: 13 Years *(curves represent annual interest as a percentage of maturity value)*

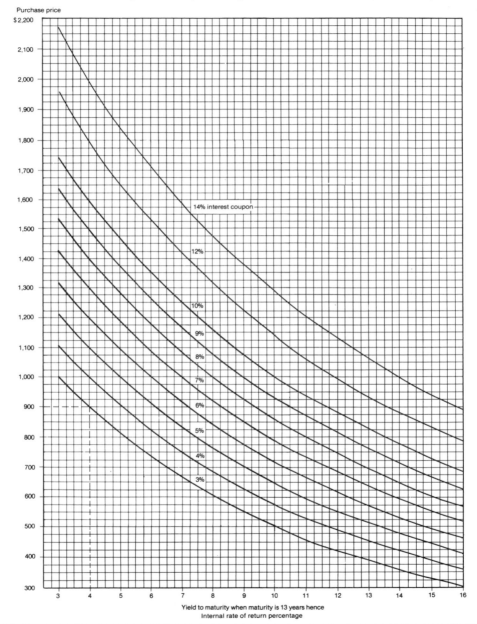

Purchase price

14% interest coupon

12%

10%

9%

8%

7%

6%

5%

4%

3%

Yield to maturity when maturity is 13 years hence
Internal rate of return percentage

Graph 5–14
Bond Yield to Maturity: 14 Years *(curves represent annual interest as a percentage of maturity value)*

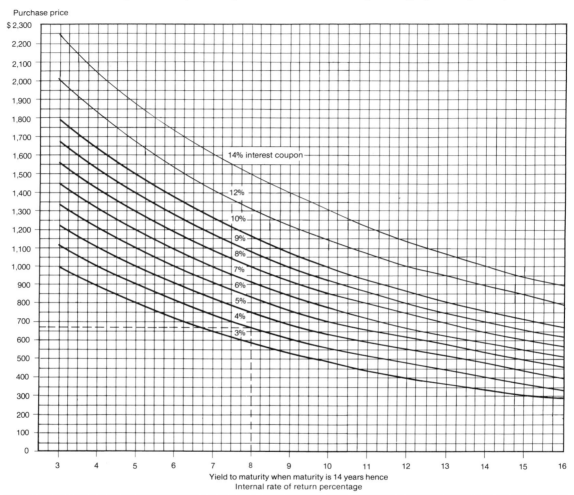

Purchase price

14% interest coupon

12%

10%

9%

8%

7%

6%

5%

4%

3%

Yield to maturity when maturity is 14 years hence
Internal rate of return percentage

Graph 5–15
Bond Yield to Maturity: 15 Years *(curves represent annual interest as a percentage of maturity value)*

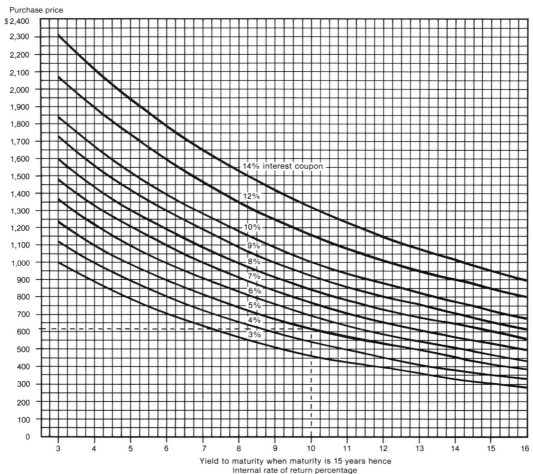

Purchase price

Yield to maturity when maturity is 15 years hence
Internal rate of return percentage

Graph 5–16
Bond Yield to Maturity: 16 Years *(curves represent annual interest as a percentage of maturity value)*

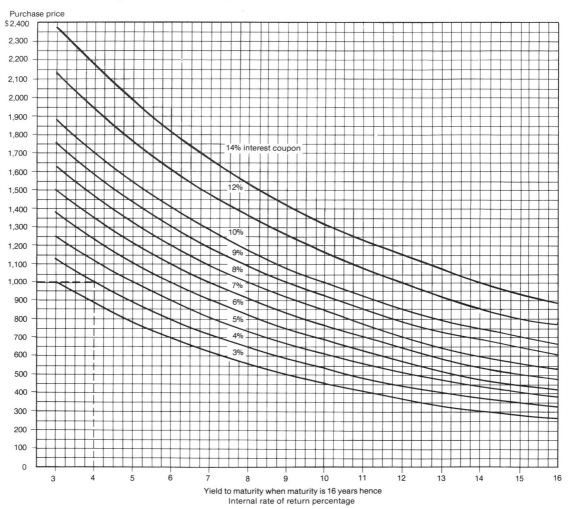

Purchase price

14% interest coupon

12%

10%

9%

8%

7%

6%

5%

4%

3%

Yield to maturity when maturity is 16 years hence
Internal rate of return percentage

Graph 5–17
Bond Yield to Maturity: 17 Years *(curves represent annual interest as a percentage of maturity value)*

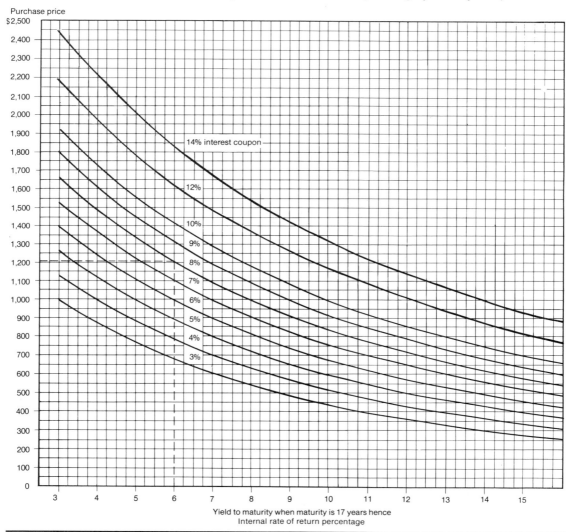

Purchase price

Yield to maturity when maturity is 17 years hence
Internal rate of return percentage

Graph 5–18
Bond Yield to Maturity: 18 Years *(curves represent annual interest as a percentage of maturity value)*

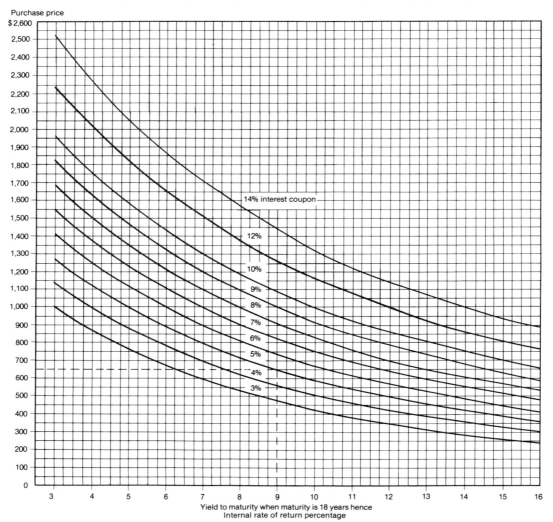

Purchase price

14% interest coupon

12%

10%

9%

8%

7%

6%

5%

4%

3%

Yield to maturity when maturity is 18 years hence
Internal rate of return percentage

Graph 5–19
Bond Yield to Maturity: 19 Years *(curves represent annual interest as a percentage of maturity value)*

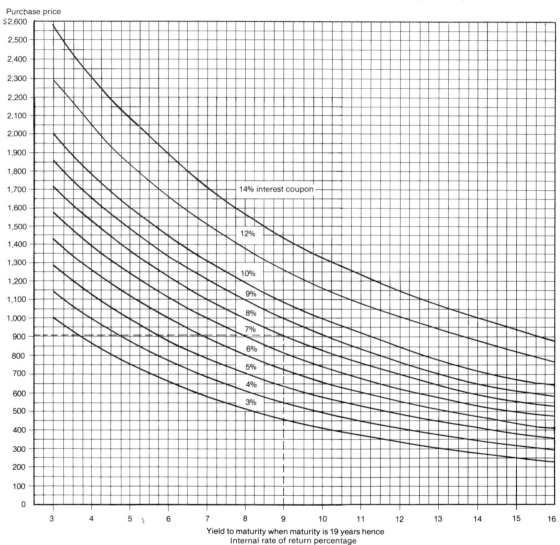

Purchase price

Yield to maturity when maturity is 19 years hence
Internal rate of return percentage

Graph 5–20
Bond Yield to Maturity: 20 Years *(curves represent annual interest as a percentage of maturity value)*

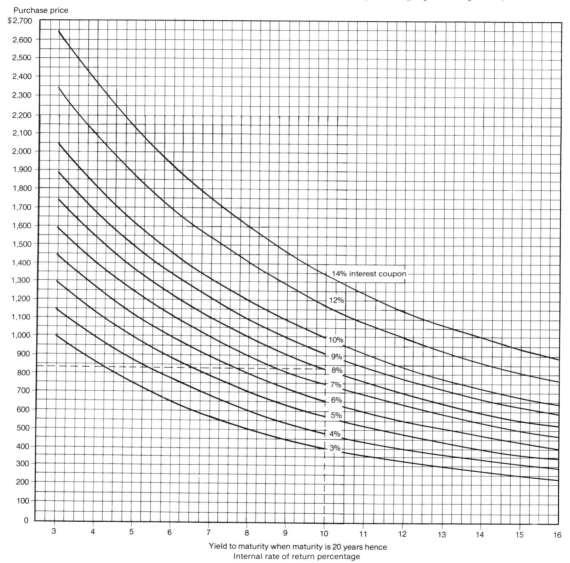

Purchase price

Yield to maturity when maturity is 20 years hence
Internal rate of return percentage

Graph 5–21
Bond Yield to Maturity: 21 Years *(curves represent annual interest as a percentage of maturity value)*

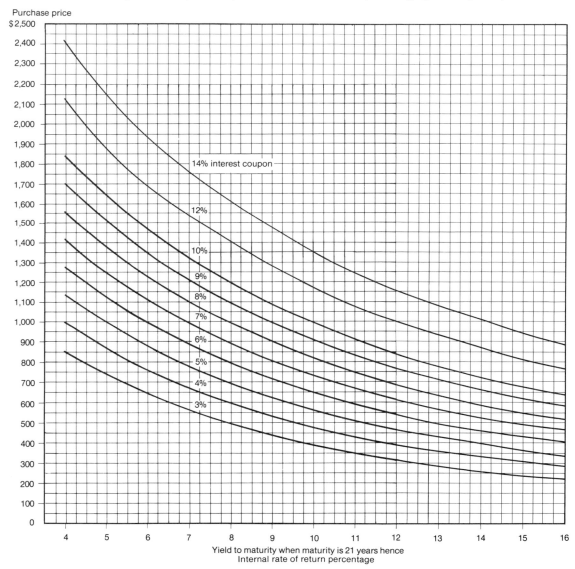

Purchase price

Yield to maturity when maturity is 21 years hence
Internal rate of return percentage

Graph 5–22
Bond Yield to Maturity: 22 Years *(curves represent annual interest as a percentage of maturity value)*

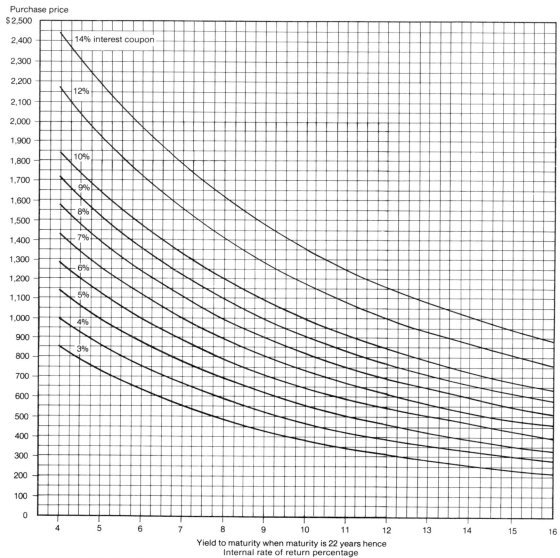

Purchase price

Yield to maturity when maturity is 22 years hence
Internal rate of return percentage

Graph 5–23
Bond Yield to Maturity: 23 Years *(curves represent annual interest as a percentage of maturity value)*

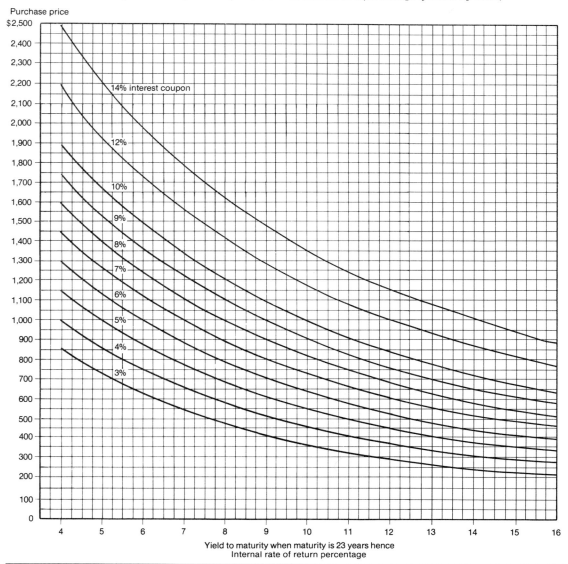

Purchase price

Yield to maturity when maturity is 23 years hence
Internal rate of return percentage

Graph 5–24
Bond Yield to Maturity: 24 Years *(curves represent annual interest as a percentage of maturity value)*

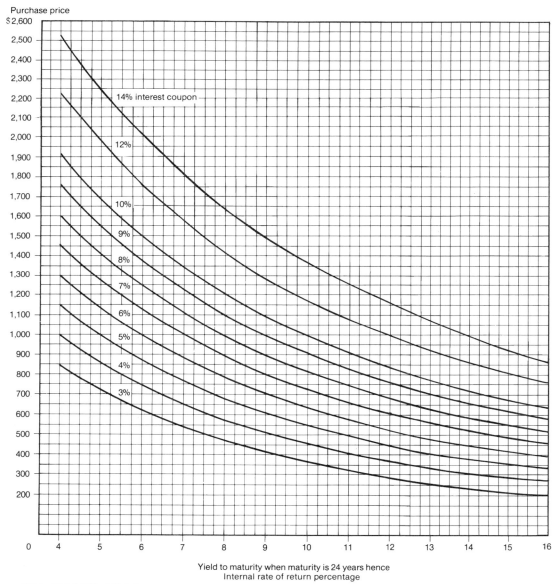

Purchase price

Yield to maturity when maturity is 24 years hence
Internal rate of return percentage

Graph 5–25
Bond Yield to Maturity: 25 Years *(curves represent annual interest as a percentage of maturity value)*

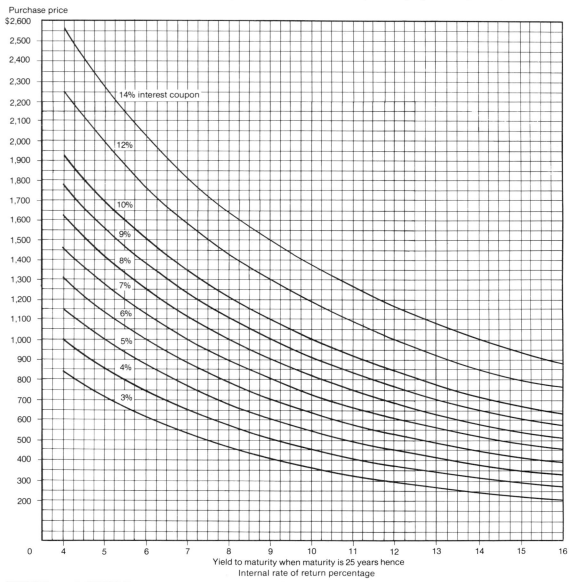

Purchase price

14% interest coupon

12%

10%

9%

8%

7%

6%

5%

4%

3%

Yield to maturity when maturity is 25 years hence
Internal rate of return percentage

Graph 5–26
Bond Yield to Maturity: 26 Years *(curves represent annual interest as a percentage of maturity value)*

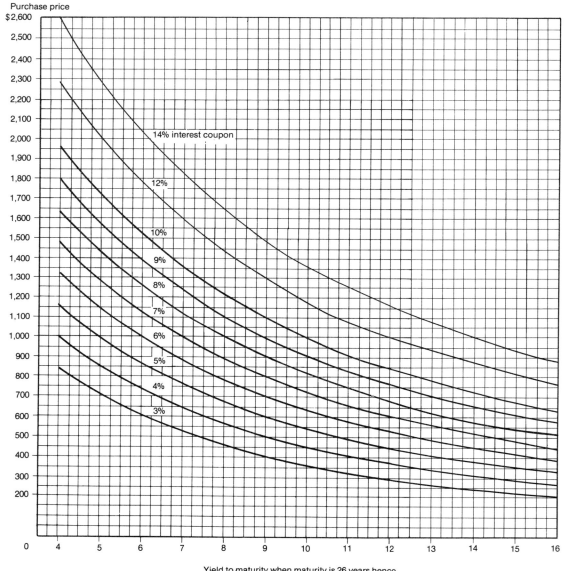

Purchase price

14% interest coupon

12%

10%

9%

8%

7%

6%

5%

4%

3%

Yield to maturity when maturity is 26 years hence
Internal rate of return percentage

Graph 5–27
Bond Yield to Maturity: 27 Years *(curves represent annual interest as a percentage of maturity value)*

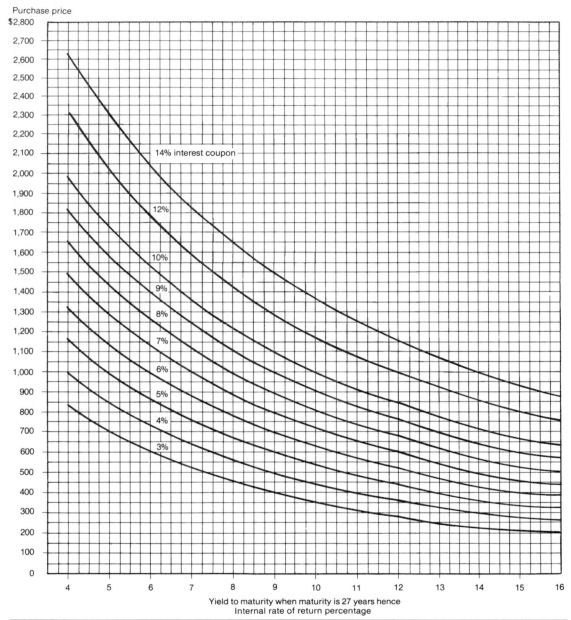

Purchase price

14% interest coupon

12%

10%

9%

8%

7%

6%

5%

4%

3%

Yield to maturity when maturity is 27 years hence
Internal rate of return percentage

Graph 5–28
Bond Yield to Maturity: 28 Years *(curves represent annual interest as a percentage of maturity value)*

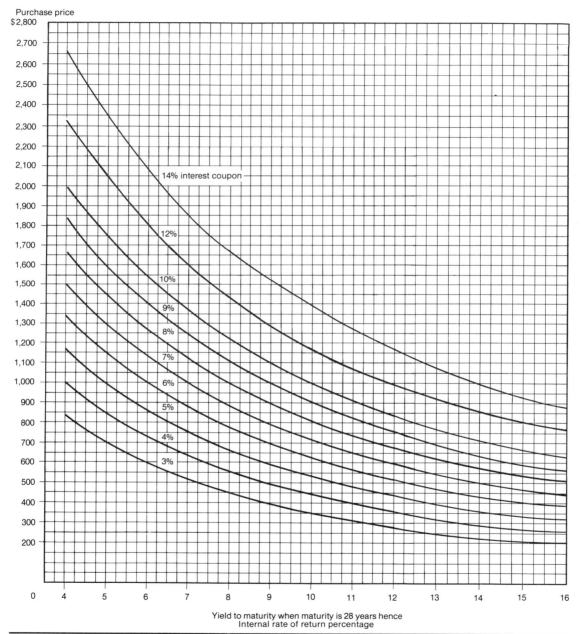

Purchase price

14% interest coupon

12%

10%

9%

8%

7%

6%

5%

4%

3%

Yield to maturity when maturity is 28 years hence
Internal rate of return percentage

Graph 5–29
Bond Yield to Maturity: 29 Years (*curves represent annual interest as a percentage of maturity value*)

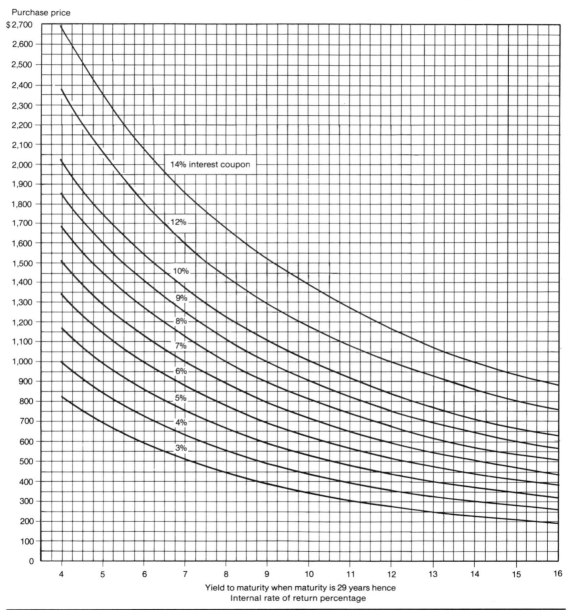

Purchase price

14% interest coupon

12%

10%

9%

8%

7%

6%

5%

4%

3%

Yield to maturity when maturity is 29 years hence
Internal rate of return percentage

Graph 5–30
Bond Yield to Maturity: 30 Years *(curves represent annual interest as a percentage of maturity value)*

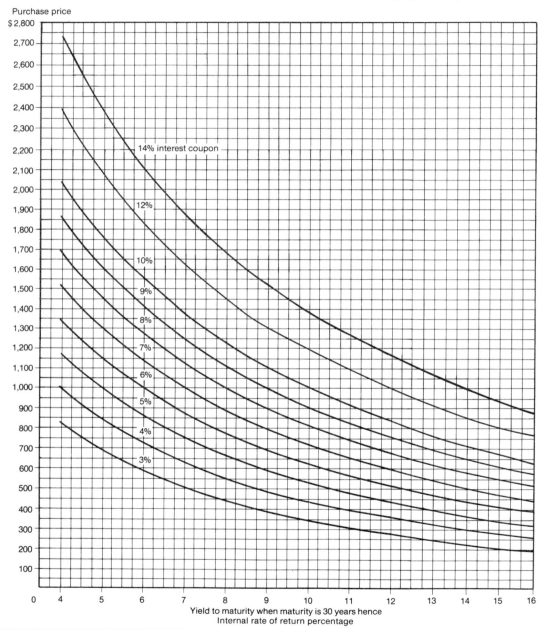

Purchase price

C H A P T E R   6

Bonds, Internal Rate of Return Analysis (After Tax)

As we saw in the preceding chapter, there are two cash flow elements to consider in determining the before tax IRR for a bond investment: the annual interest yield and the proceeds of sale at the end of the holding period. If the investor is in other than a zero tax bracket, things become slightly more complicated. The cash flow elements are all reduced (or increased in the case of a premium bond which gives birth to a capital loss at maturity) to the extent of applicable taxes. The annual cash flow from interest receipts is reduced by the appropriate level of federal and state income taxes. Finally, the proceeds of sale at the end of the holding period are reduced by the relevant capital gains tax (or increased by the tax savings resulting from a capital loss).

The calculations assume that the capital gains tax (maximum 20 percent) is 40 percent of the income tax bracket rate (maximum 50 percent); thus, for a 50 percent tax bracket, the tax applied to the annual cash flows is 50 percent and 20 percent of the gain is deducted from the capital gain resulting from sale. If the investment is a loss, 20 percent of the loss is added to the sales proceeds. For an investor in a 30 percent tax bracket, 30 percent is deducted from the annual cash flows and 12 percent of the gain is deducted from (or added to) the sales proceeds as capital gains tax (or benefit).

Taxable Bonds

In order to determine the internal rate of return for a *taxable* bond investment, you have to use the appropriate graph. (*Tax-exempt* bond calculations are described later in this chapter.) Two factors govern the selection of the proper graph: the *number of years* until the bond's maturity, and the applicable tax *bracket*. There are three choices for the tax bracket, 50 percent, 30 percent, and 0 percent (0 percent bracket and before tax IRR are described in the preceding chapter). Select the bracket closest to that of the investor. Within the applicable tax bracket category, select the number of years until the bond's maturity, ranging from 1 year to 30 years. Let's say, the investors, Samantha and Gene, are in the 50 percent tax bracket, and they wish to find the IRR for a proposed taxable bond investment that matures in 30 years. Refer to Graph 6–30, which is the graph for 30 years until maturity and a 50 percent tax bracket. Samantha and Gene must determine two items in order to use the graph and calculate the IRR:

1. Purchase price of each bond. This is nothing more than what the name implies—the price that Samantha and Gene paid for each bond, or if the bond is not being purchased presently, then the market value of the bond. Refer to the graph. The left (vertical) axis of the graph is "Bond Purchase Price." The bonds Sam and Gene are thinking of buying are priced at $1,050 each.

2. Coupon rate percentage. There are a number of lines or curves running across the graph which represent percentage annual interest or, expressed another way, the coupon rate, which is the annual interest divided by the bond's $1,000 maturity value. Thus if the annual interest is $120, the coupon rate is 12 percent. The bonds that Sam and Gene are thinking of buying have a 12 percent coupon rate.

To find the IRR for this bond, enter the graph at the $1,050 point on the vertical axis and go across until you reach the 12 percent curve. From that point of intersection, proceed down until you reach the bottom axis. That point of intersection with the bottom axis is the IRR, which in this case is 5.66 percent. That's all there is to it. The IRR, after 50 percent income tax and 20 percent capital gains tax, is 5.66 percent. Note, however, that the effect of the capital gains tax is to add $10 to the proceeds of the sale, as the redemption of the bond at maturity creates a $50 long-term capital loss ($1,050 − $1,000). The $10 addition to the maturity value is the tax savings [the product of the $50 loss times 50 percent (the bracket) of 40 percent (portion of loss which is deductible)].

The actual computation of the 5.66 percent IRR determined earlier is shown in Table 6–1. The cash flows are displayed after tax.

The graphs in this chapter may be used for any holding period from 1 to 30 years and for either a 50 percent or 30 percent tax bracket. For a 0 percent tax bracket, use the graphs in Chapter 5.

Table 6–1
Computation of IRR

Year	Cash Flow	Year × Cash Flow	Iterations	30-year bond $ 120 coupon
0	−1050	0	1760.00	Purchase price $1,050 *******
1	60	60	58200.00	Tax bracket 50%
2	60	120	.03024055	
3	60	180	535.58	Internal rate of return 5.66%
4	60	240	27985.46	
5	60	300	.04995708	
6	60	360	106.78	
7	60	420	18066.99	
8	60	480	.05616236	
9	60	540	7.01	
10	60	600	15850.76	
11	60	660	.05662929	
12	60	720	0.04	
13	60	780	15697.56	
14	60	840	.05663168	
15	60	900	0.00	
16	60	960	15696.78	
17	60	1020	.05663168	
18	60	1080	−0.00	
19	60	1140	15696.78	
20	60	1200	.05663168	
21	60	1260		
22	60	1320		
23	60	1380		
24	60	1440		
25	60	1500		
26	60	1560		
27	60	1620		
28	60	1680		
29	60	1740		
30	1070	32100		

A summary of the steps to determine IRR after tax for a taxable bond investment follows:

1. Find the graph based on tax bracket (0 percent, 30 percent, or 50 percent) and number of years (1 to 30) until the bond matures.

2. Enter the graph with the purchase price and proceed to the curve representing the annual coupon rate.

Tax-Exempt IRRs

With slight adaptation, the charts in this and the preceding chapter may also be used to calculate the IRR or YTM after tax from investments in municipals or tax-exempts. Although the interest receipts from a municipal are not normally subject to federal income tax, the capital gain upon sale or redemption at maturity is taxable. The premium paid for a tax-exempt bond *must* be amortized to reduce the bond's tax basis. Thus, by the bond's maturity date, the adjusted basis will equal the maturity value; hence there is no capital loss that may be deducted for a tax-exempt bond purchased at a premium. The procedure to follow for obtaining the after tax yield to maturity (IRR) from an investment in a "tax-exempt" bond is as follows:

1. For tax-exempt bonds purchased at a discount or at par use the set of graphs that is closest to the investor's tax bracket (50 percent, 30 percent, or 0 percent). For tax-exempt bonds purchased at a premium, however, one *must use* the graphs in Chapter 5.

2. Choose the graph which is closest to the bond's number of years until maturity (1 to 30 years).

3. Calculate an *adjusted coupon rate*, as follows:

$$\text{Adjusted coupon rate} = \frac{\text{Tax-exempt bond's coupon rate}}{(1 - \text{Investor's tax bracket})}$$

Example: Sally Abelson, who is in a 30 percent tax bracket, is considering the purchase of a tax-exempt sewer bond for $650 with 30 years until maturity. It pays $70 per year in interest per bond. The adjusted coupon rate (for using the graphs) for Sally's bond is:

$$\begin{aligned} \text{Adjusted coupon rate} &= \frac{\$70 \ (\text{Tax-exempt's coupon rate})}{(1 - 0.3)\ (1 - \text{Sally's tax bracket})} \\ &= \frac{70}{0.7} \\ &= \$100.00 \end{aligned}$$

To find the after-capital-gains-tax yield to maturity, for Sally's bond, refer to Graph 6–60. Enter the graph on the vertical axis at the bond's purchase price, $650. Proceed across to the *adjusted coupon rate*, 10 percent ($100); then descend to the horizontal axis. The intersection at the horizontal axis is the after tax yield to maturity, 11 percent. It takes into consideration both the tax-free nature of the $70 annual interest as well as the ultimate capital gains tax of $42 (capital gains tax rate of 12 percent, for 30 percent ordinary income tax bracket, of $350 gain— $1,000 redemption less $650 cost).

A 50 percent or 30 percent tax bracket investor in a *tax-exempt* bond **must** use the adjusted coupon rate as described and determined earlier. A 0 percent tax bracket investor in a tax-exempt bond can use the graphs in Chapter 5 without adjustment because in a zero bracket the adjusted coupon rate will always equal the unadjusted coupon rate.

Next, we shall explore the application of internal rate of return analysis to real estate investment transactions.

Graph 6–1
Bond Yield to Maturity: 1 Year/50 Percent Tax Bracket *(curves represent annual interest as a percentage of maturity value)*

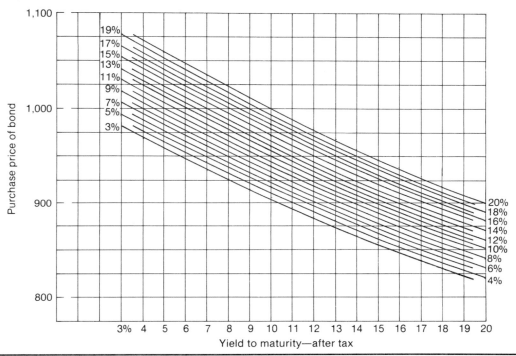

Graph 6–2
Bond Yield to Maturity: 2 Years/50 Percent Tax Bracket *(curves represent annual interest as a percentage of maturity value)*

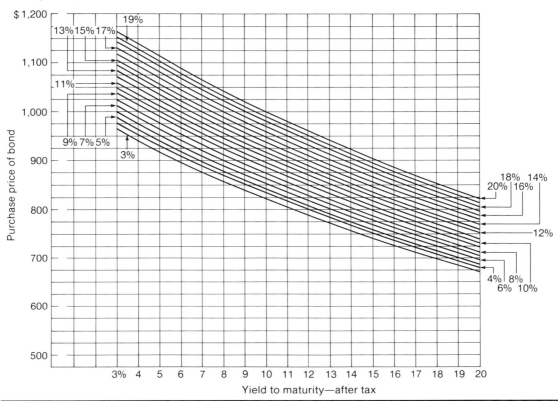

Graph 6–3
Bond Yield to Maturity: 3 Years/50 Percent Tax Bracket *(curves represent annual interest as a percentage of maturity value)*

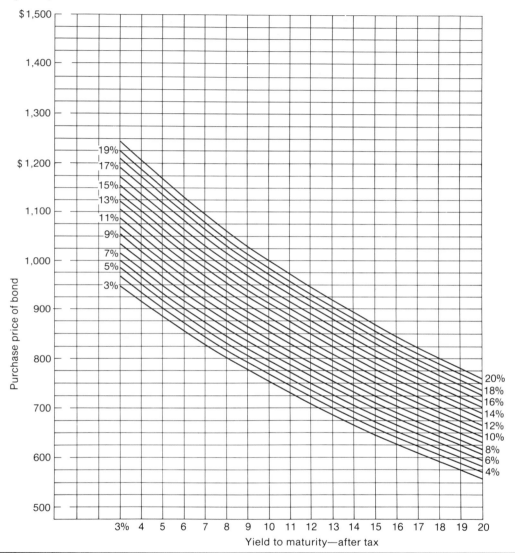

Graph 6–4
Bond Yield to Maturity: 4 Years/50 Percent Tax Bracket *(curves represent annual interest as a percentage of maturity value)*

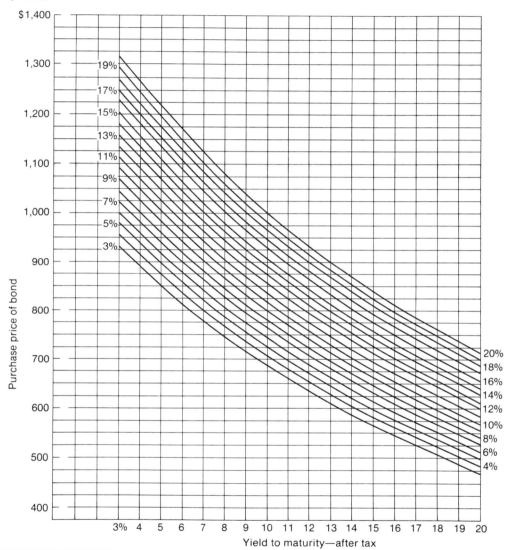

Graph 6–5
Bond Yield to Maturity: 5 Years/50 Percent Tax Bracket *(curves represent annual interest as a percentage of maturity value)*

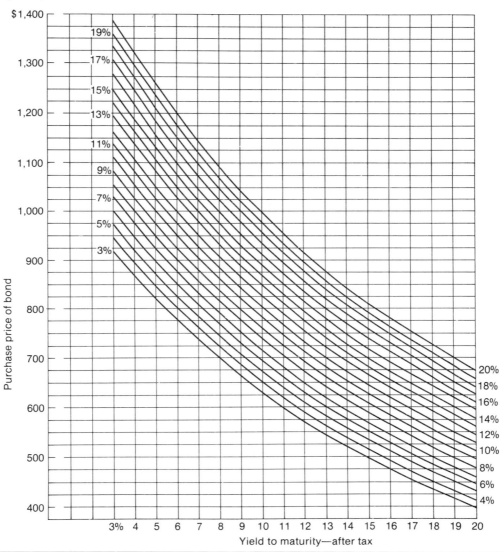

Graph 6–6
Bond Yield to Maturity: 6 Years/50 Percent Tax Bracket *(curves represent annual interest as a percentage of maturity value)*

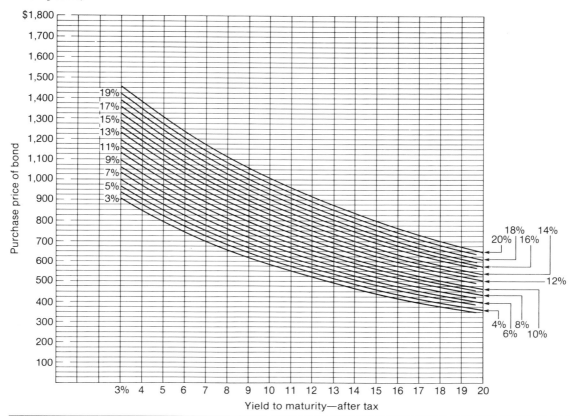

Graph 6–7
Bond Yield to Maturity: 7 Years/50 Percent Tax Bracket *(curves represent annual interest as a percentage of maturity value)*

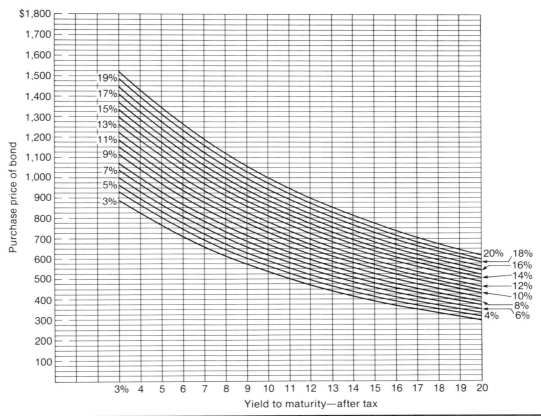

Graph 6–8
Bond Yield to Maturity: 8 Years/50 Percent Tax Bracket *(curves represent annual interest as a percentage of maturity value)*

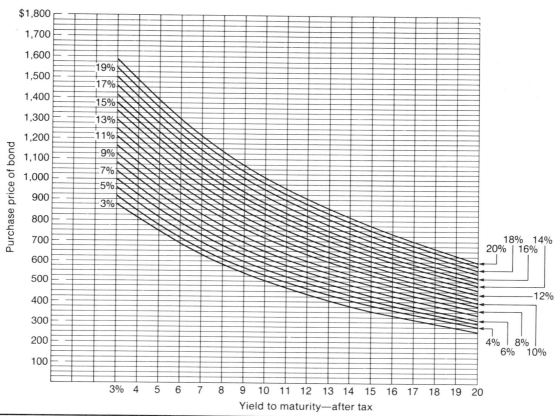

Graph 6–9
Bond Yield to Maturity: 9 Years/50 Percent Tax Bracket *(curves represent annual interest as a percentage of maturity value)*

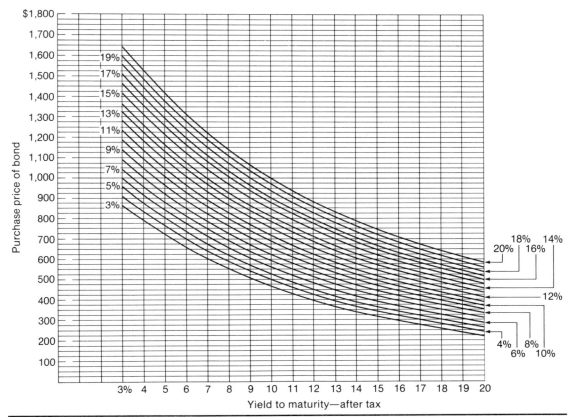

Graph 6–10
Bond Yield to Maturity: 10 Years/50 Percent Tax Bracket *(curves represent annual interest as a percentage of maturity value)*

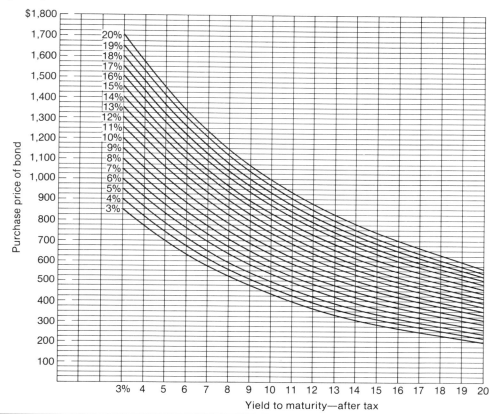

Graph 6–11
Bond Yield to Maturity: 11 Years/50 Percent Tax Bracket *(curves represent annual interest as a percentage of maturity value)*

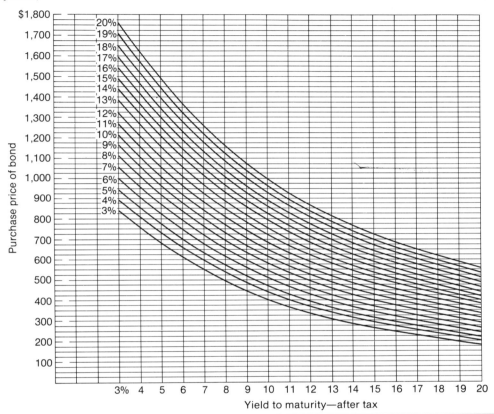

Graph 6–12
Bond Yield to Maturity: 12 Years/50 Percent Tax Bracket *(curves represent annual interest as a percentage of maturity value)*

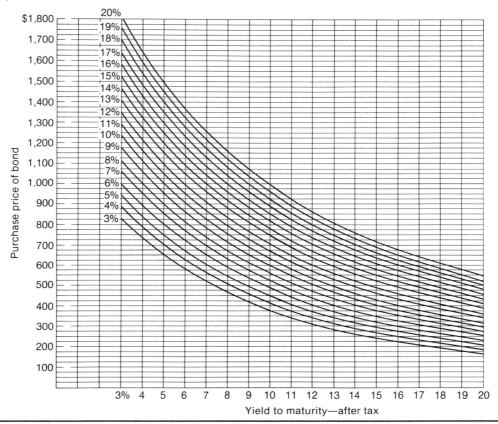

Graph 6–13
Bond Yield to Maturity: 13 Years/50 Percent Tax Bracket *(curves represent annual interest as a percentage of maturity value)*

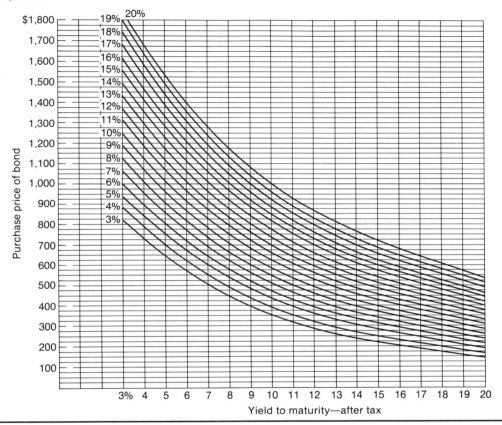

Graph 6–14
Bond Yield to Maturity: 14 Years/50 Percent Tax Bracket (*curves represent annual interest as a percentage of maturity value*)

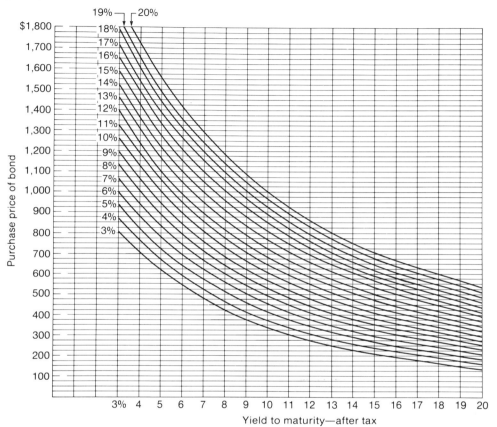

Graph 6–15
Bond Yield to Maturity: 15 Years/50 Percent Tax Bracket *(curves represent annual interest as a percentage of maturity value)*

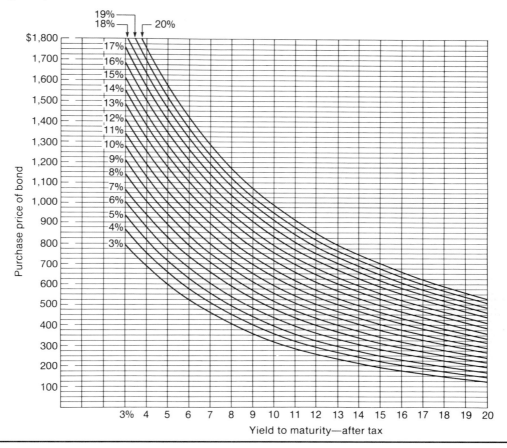

Graph 6–16
Bond Yield to Maturity: 16 Years/50 Percent Tax Bracket *(curves represent annual interest as a percentage of maturity value)*

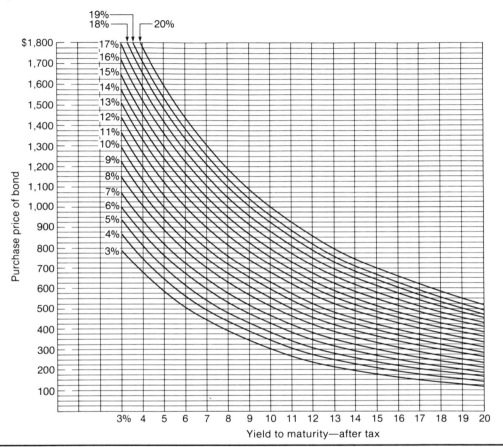

Graph 6–17
Bond Yield to Maturity: 17 Years/50 Percent Tax Bracket *(curves represent annual interest as a percentage of maturity value)*

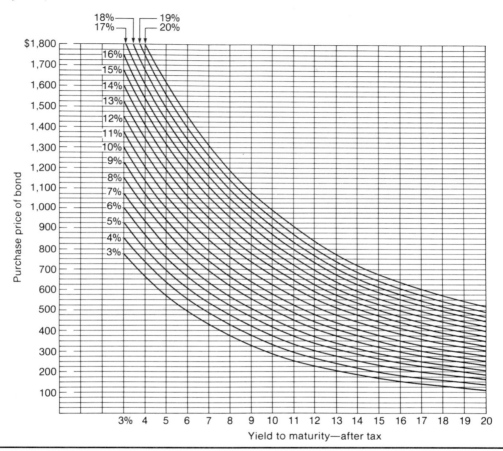

Graph 6–18
Bond Yield to Maturity: 18 Years/50 Percent Tax Bracket *(curves represent annual interest as a percentage of maturity value)*

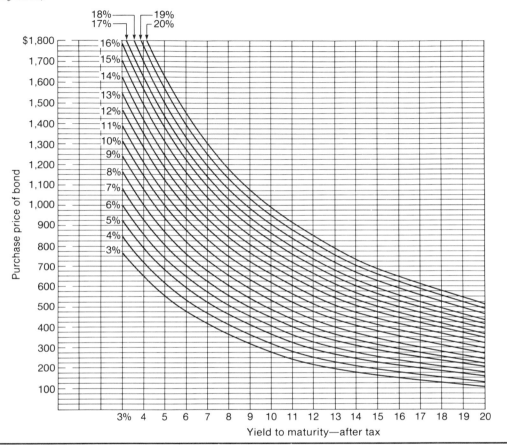

Graph 6–19
Bond Yield to Maturity: 19 Years/50 Percent Tax Bracket *(curves represent annual interest as a percentage of maturity value)*

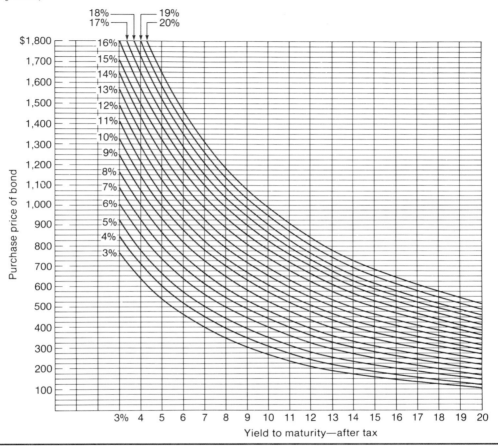

Graph 6–20
Bond Yield to Maturity: 20 Years/50 Percent Tax Bracket *(curves represent annual interest as a percentage of maturity value)*

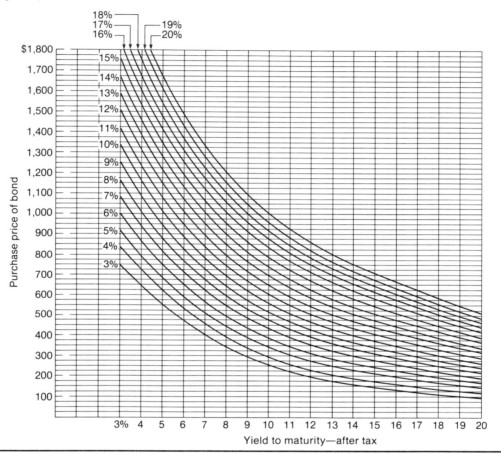

Graph 6–21
Bond Yield to Maturity: 21 Years/50 Percent Tax Bracket *(curves represent annual interest as a percentage of maturity value)*

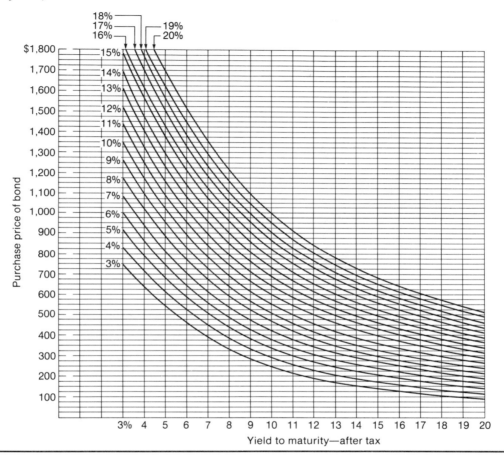

Graph 6–22
Bond Yield to Maturity: 22 Years/50 Percent Tax Bracket *(curves represent annual interest as a percentage of maturity value)*

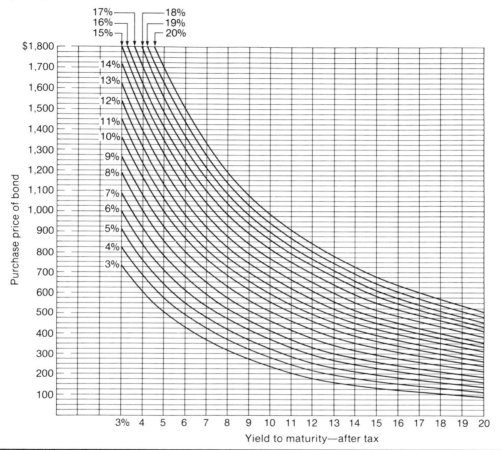

Graph 6–23
Bond Yield to Maturity: 23 Years/50 Percent Tax Bracket *(curves represent annual interest as a percentage of maturity value)*

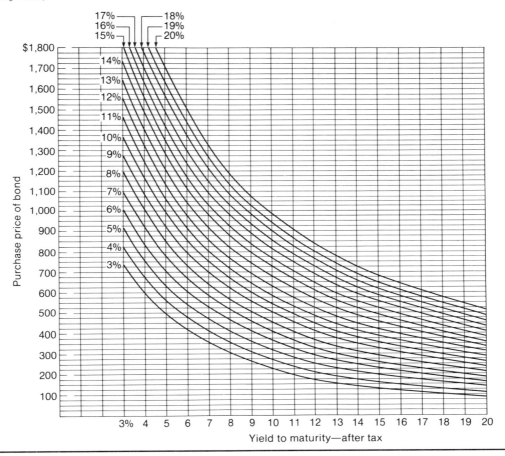

Graph 6–24
Bond Yield to Maturity: 24 Years/50 Percent Tax Bracket *(curves represent annual interest as a percentage of maturity value)*

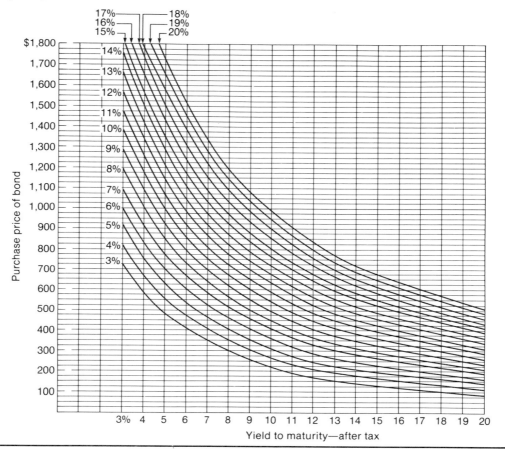

Graph 6–25
Bond Yield to Maturity: 25 Years/50 Percent Tax Bracket *(curves represent annual interest as a percentage of maturity value)*

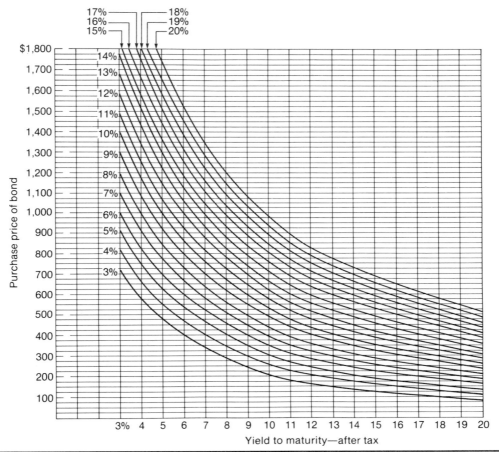

Graph 6–26
Bond Yield to Maturity: 26 Years/50 Percent Tax Bracket *(curves represent annual interest as a percentage of maturity value)*

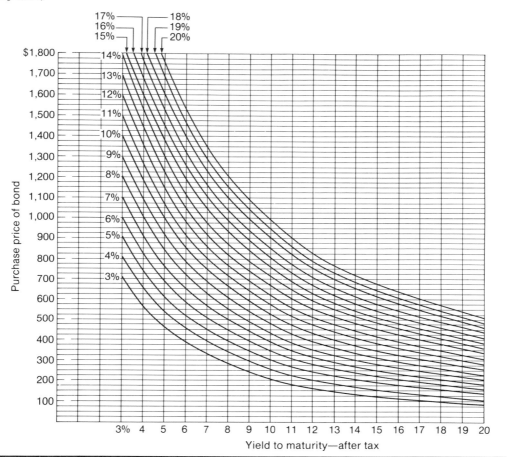

Graph 6–27
Bond Yield to Maturity: 27 Years/50 Percent Tax Bracket *(curves represent annual interest as a percentage of maturity value)*

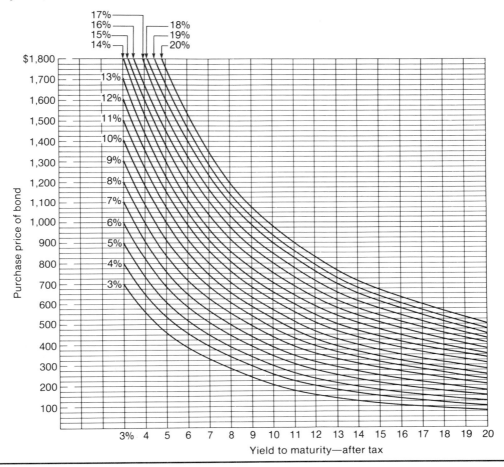

Graph 6–28
Bond Yield to Maturity: 28 Years/50 Percent Tax Bracket *(curves represent annual interest as a percentage of maturity value)*

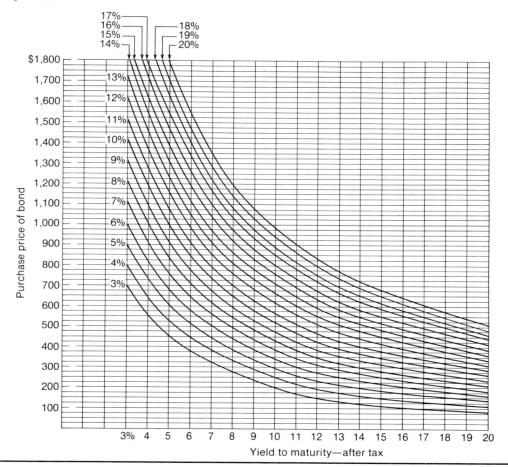

Graph 6–29
Bond Yield to Maturity: 29 Years/50 Percent Tax Bracket *(curves represent annual interest as a percentage of maturity value)*

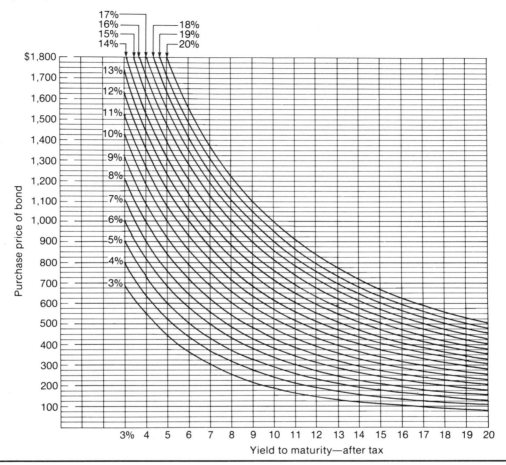

Graph 6–30
Bond Yield to Maturity: 30 Years/50 Percent Tax Bracket *(curves represent annual interest as a percentage of maturity value)*

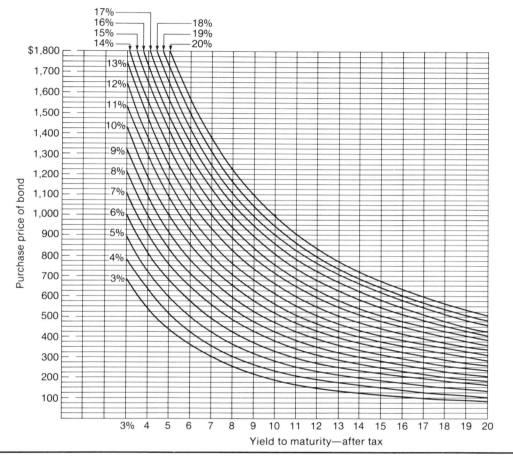

Graph 6–31
Bond Yield to Maturity: 1 Year/30 Percent Tax Bracket *(curves represent annual interest as a percentage of maturity value)*

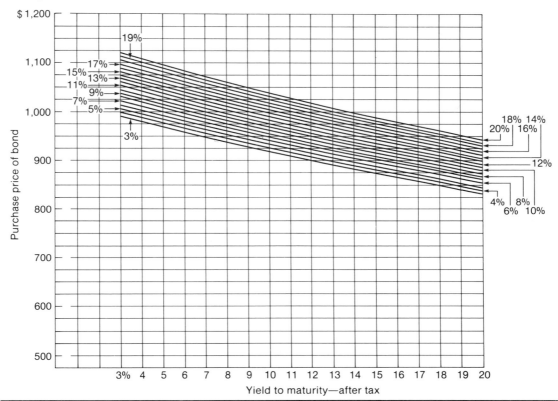

Graph 6–32
Bond Yield to Maturity: 2 Years/30 Percent Tax Bracket *(curves represent annual interest as a percentage of maturity value)*

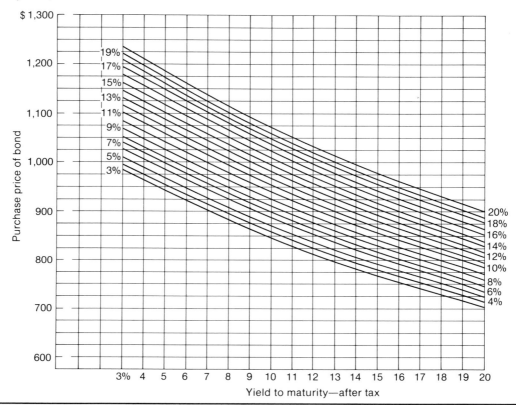

Graph 6–33
Bond Yield to Maturity: 3 Years/30 Percent Tax Bracket *(curves represent annual interest as a percentage of maturity value)*

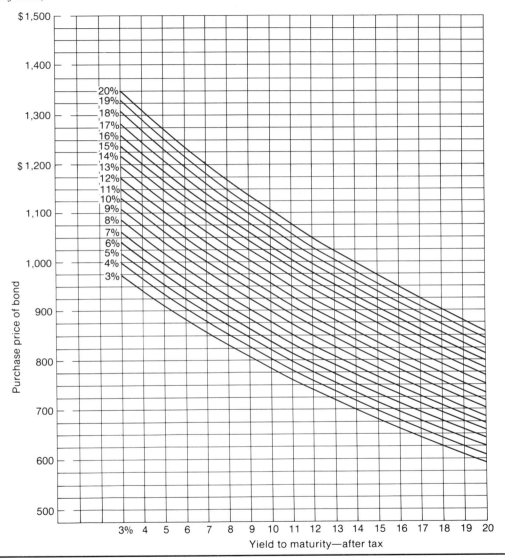

Graph 6–34
Bond Yield to Maturity: 4 Years/30 Percent Tax Bracket *(curves represent annual interest as a percentage of maturity value)*

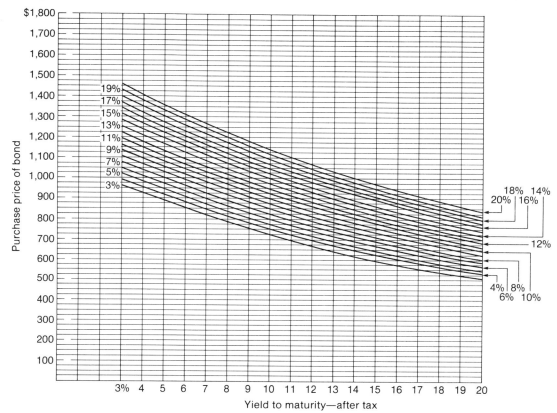

Graph 6–35
Bond Yield to Maturity: 5 Years/30 Percent Tax Bracket *(curves represent annual interest as a percentage of maturity value)*

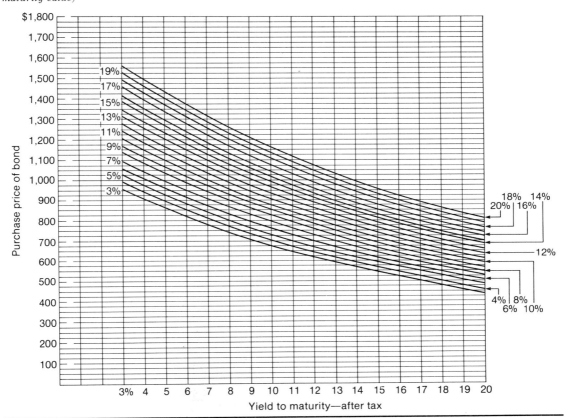

Graph 6–36
Bond Yield to Maturity: 6 Years/30 Percent Tax Bracket *(curves represent annual interest as a percentage of maturity value)*

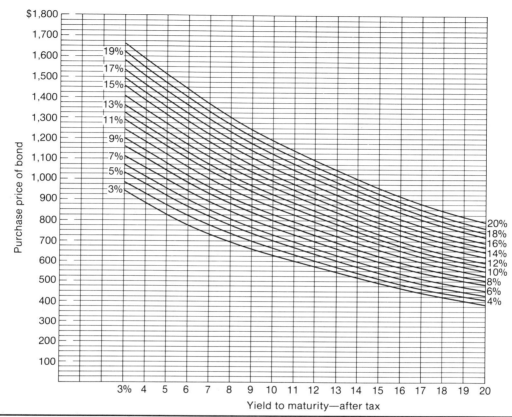

Graph 6–37
Bond Yield to Maturity: 7 Years/30 Percent Tax Bracket *(curves represent annual interest as a percentage of maturity value)*

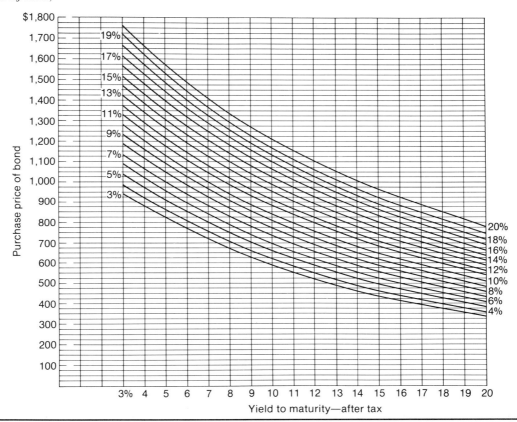

Graph 6–38
Bond Yield to Maturity: 8 Years/30 Percent Tax Bracket *(curves represent annual interest as a percentage of maturity value)*

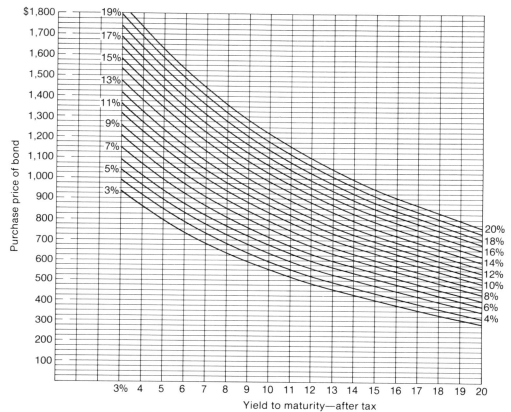

Graph 6–39
Bond Yield to Maturity: 9 Years/30 Percent Tax Bracket *(curves represent annual interest as a percentage of maturity value)*

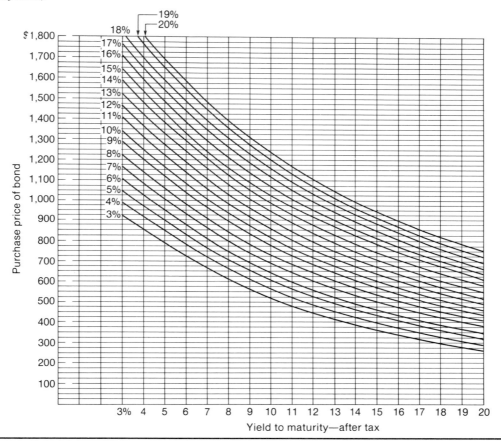

Graph 6–40
Bond Yield to Maturity: 10 Years/30 Percent Tax Bracket *(curves represent annual interest as a percentage of maturity value)*

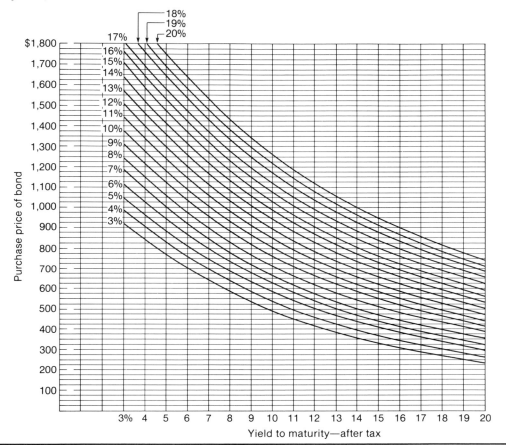

Graph 6–41
Bond Yield to Maturity: 11 Years/30 Percent Tax Bracket *(curves represent annual interest as a percentage of maturity value)*

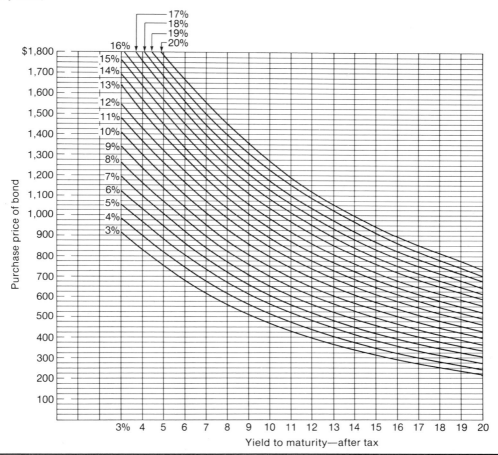

Graph 6–42
Bond Yield to Maturity: 12 Years/30 Percent Tax Bracket *(curves represent annual interest as a percentage of maturity value)*

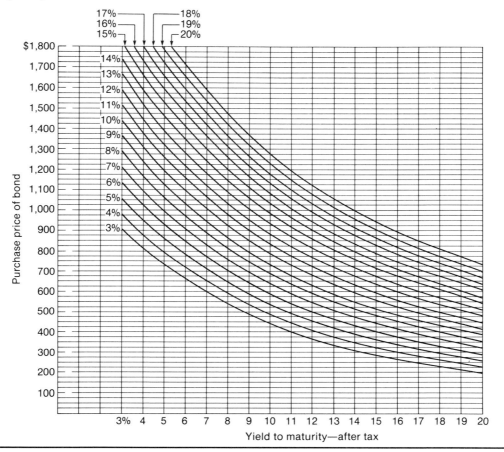

Graph 6–43
Bond Yield to Maturity: 13 Years/30 Percent Tax Bracket *(curves represent annual interest as a percentage of maturity value)*

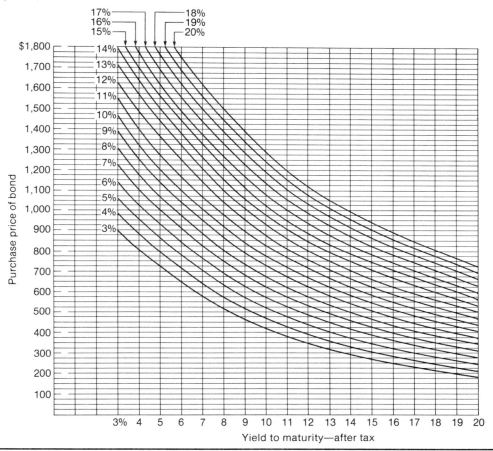

Purchase price of bond

Yield to maturity—after tax

Graph 6–44
Bond Yield to Maturity: 14 Years/30 Percent Tax Bracket *(curves represent annual interest as a percentage of maturity value)*

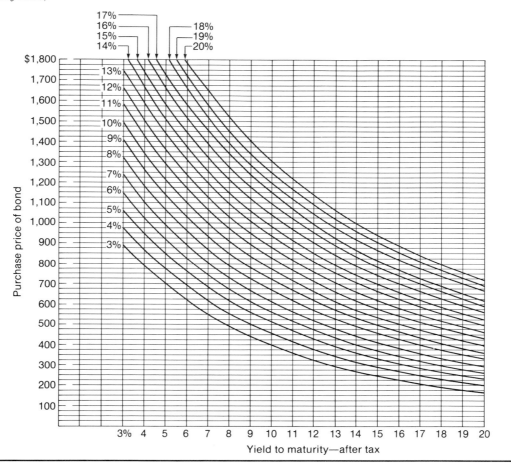

Graph 6–45
Bond Yield to Maturity: 15 Years/30 Percent Tax Bracket *(curves represent annual interest as a percentage of maturity value)*

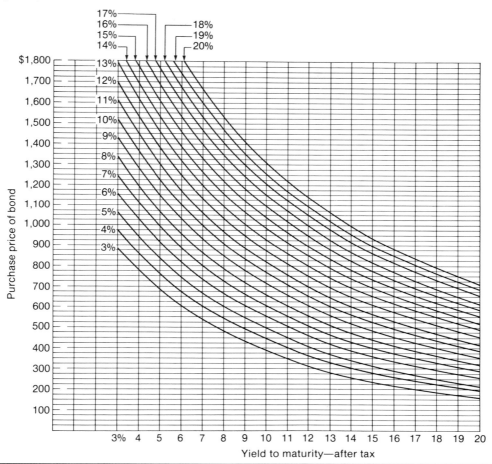

Graph 6–46
Bond Yield to Maturity: 16 Years/30 Percent Tax Bracket *(curves represent annual interest as a percentage of maturity value)*

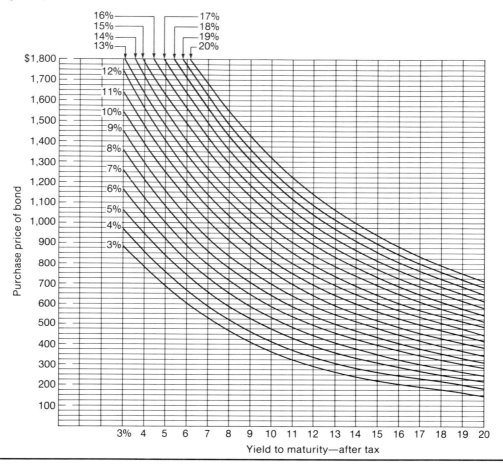

Graph 6–47
Bond Yield to Maturity: 17 Years/30 Percent Tax Bracket *(curves represent annual interest as a percentage of maturity value)*

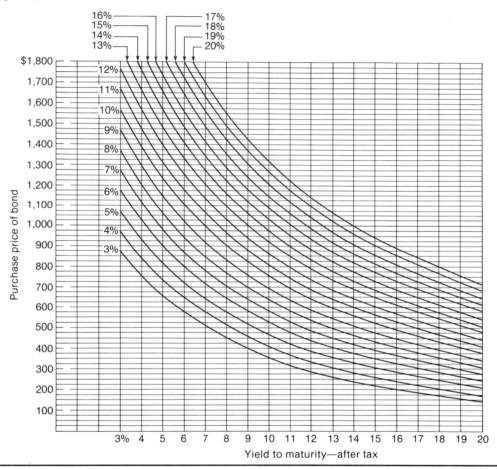

Graph 6–48
Bond Yield to Maturity: 18 Years/30 Percent Tax Bracket *(curves represent annual interest as a percentage of maturity value)*

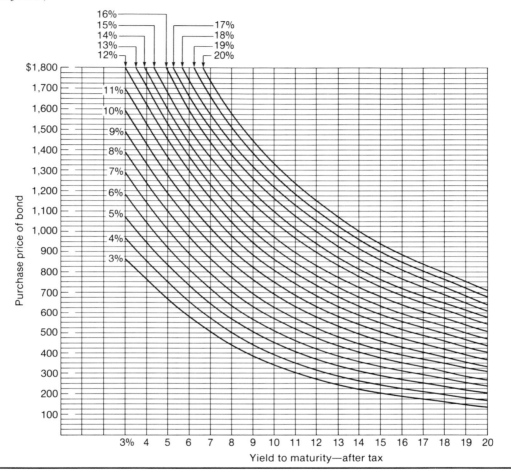

Graph 6–49
Bond Yield to Maturity: 19 Years/30 Percent Tax Bracket *(curves represent annual interest as a percentage of maturity value)*

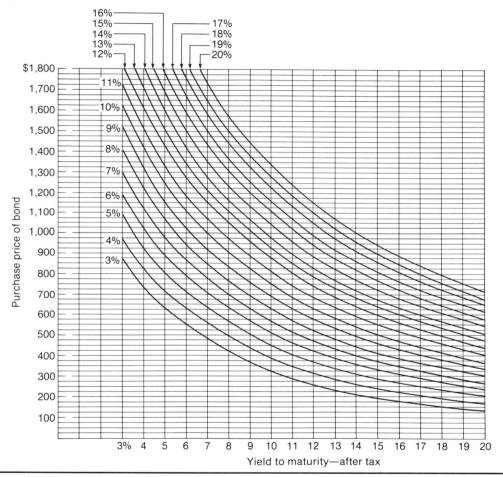

Graph 6–50
Bond Yield to Maturity: 20 Years/30 Percent Tax Bracket *(curves represent annual interest as a percentage of maturity value)*

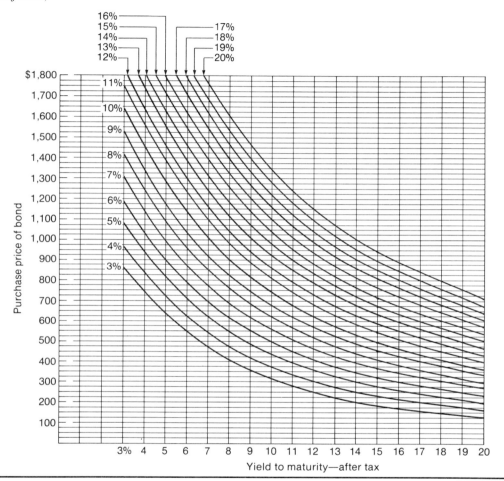

Graph 6–51
Bond Yield to Maturity: 21 Years/30 Percent Tax Bracket *(curves represent annual interest as a percentage of maturity value)*

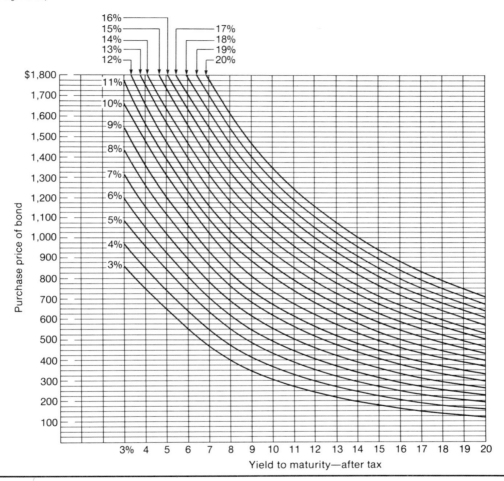

Graph 6–52
Bond Yield to Maturity: 22 Years/30 Percent Tax Bracket *(curves represent annual interest as a percentage of maturity value)*

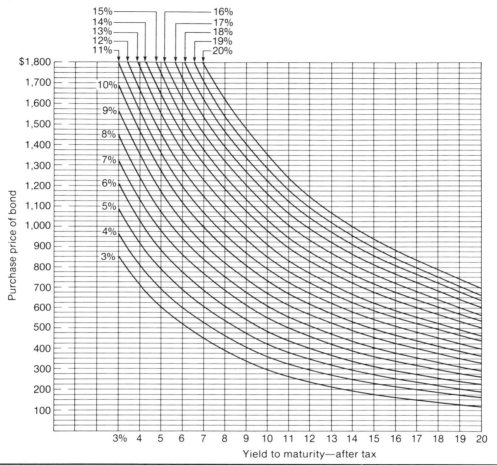

Graph 6–53
Bond Yield to Maturity: 23 Years/30 Percent Tax Bracket *(curves represent annual interest as a percentage of maturity value)*

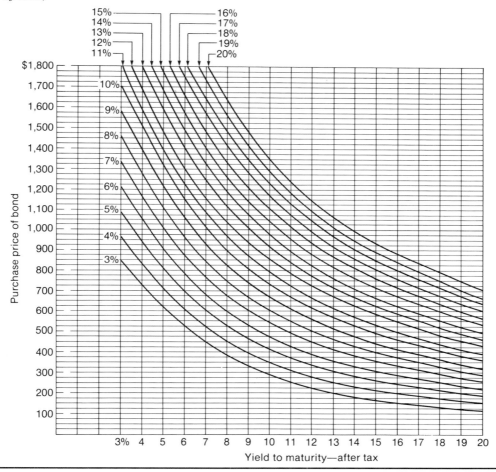

Yield to maturity—after tax

Graph 6–54
Bond Yield to Maturity: 24 Years/30 Percent Tax Bracket *(curves represent annual interest as a percentage of maturity value)*

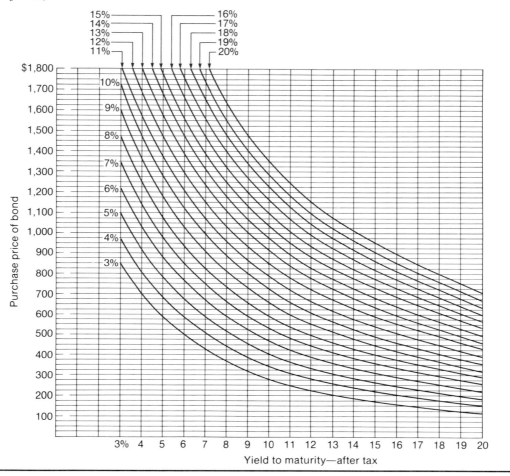

Graph 6–55
Bond Yield to Maturity: 25 Years/30 Percent Tax Bracket *(curves represent annual interest as a percentage of maturity value)*

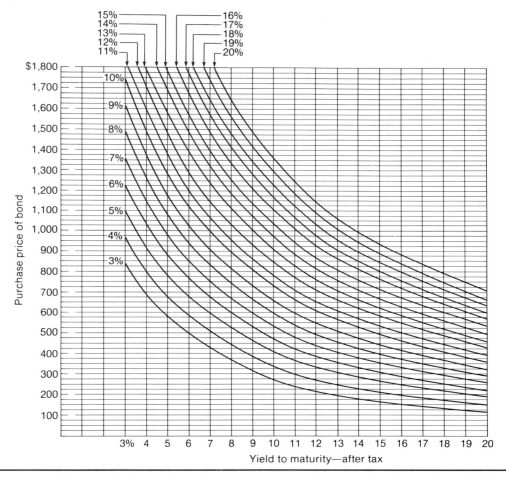

Graph 6–56
Bond Yield to Maturity: 26 Years/30 Percent Tax Bracket *(curves represent annual interest as a percentage of maturity value)*

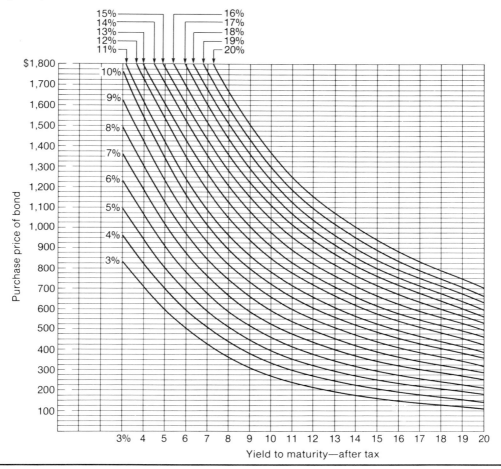

Graph 6–57
Bond Yield to Maturity: 27 Years/30 Percent Tax Bracket *(curves represent annual interest as a percentage of maturity value)*

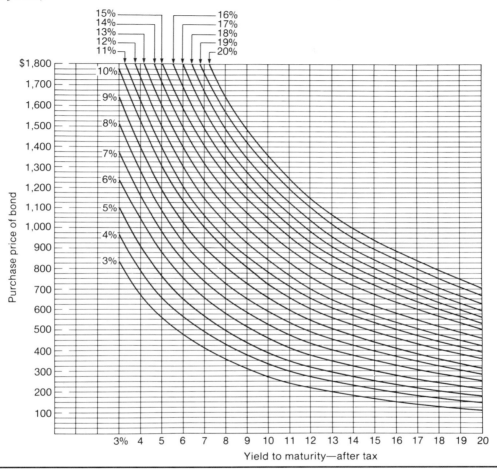

Graph 6–58
Bond Yield to Maturity: 28 Years/30 Percent Tax Bracket *(curves represent annual interest as a percentage of maturity value)*

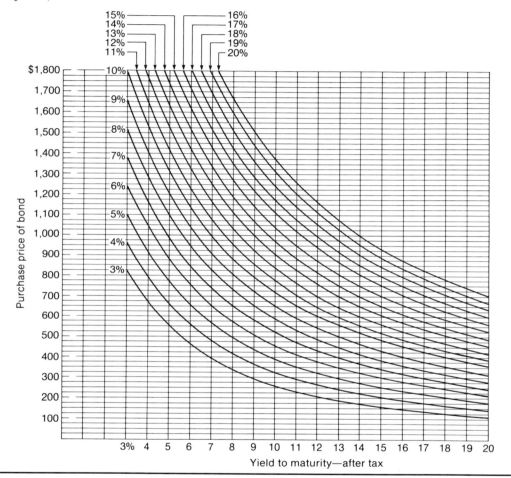

Graph 6–59
Bond Yield to Maturity: 29 Years/30 Percent Tax Bracket *(curves represent annual interest as a percentage of maturity value)*

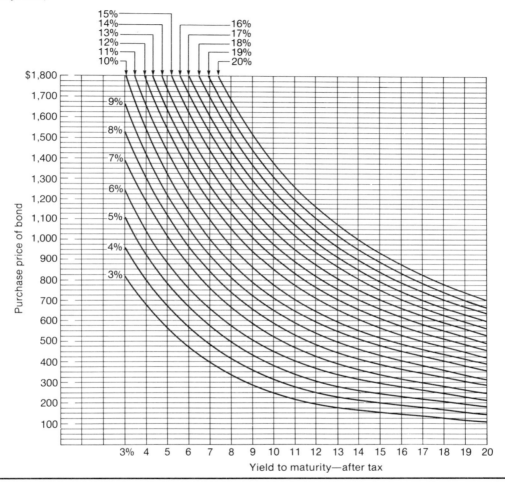

Graph 6–60
Bond Yield to Maturity: 30 Years/30 Percent Tax Bracket *(curves represent annual interest as a percentage of maturity value)*

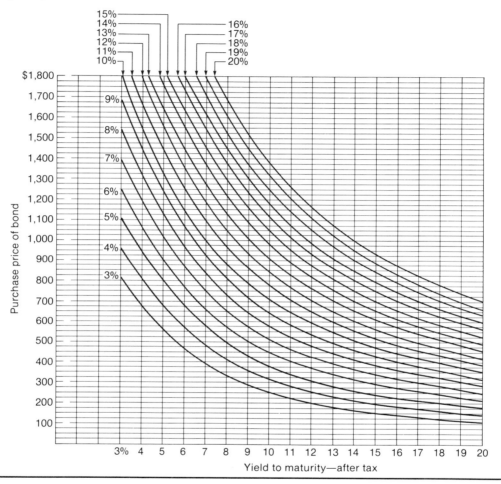

C H A P T E R   7

Real Estate Investing and IRR Analysis

Well selected real estate investments can be extremely rewarding. Nevertheless, real estate as an investment shares one major characteristic with all investments: risk. It is no panacea for the potential ills and difficulties of investing.

Generally, well-selected and properly purchased "income property" should provide owners with cash flow about equal to the yield on high-grade, long-term corporate bonds. Such yields fluctuate according to economic and political trends as illustrated in Graph 7–1. (Income property includes industrial buildings, shopping centers, apartment complexes, office buildings, and commercial buildings.) *Cash flow* is the excess of rental income over property operating expenses (excluding noncash charges such as depreciation and amortization) but including the cost of servicing principal and interest on mortgage loans). Let's look at cash flow another way. If you open a new bank account for your income property at the beginning of each year, deposit all receipts to it, and make all disbursements from it, then the balance in the account at the end of the year is the annual cash flow. The cash flow (as a percent of cash invested) from real estate investments, at the time of purchase, will tend to be closer to the annual yield from U.S. government issues shown on Graph 7–1 than to the higher-yielding, lower-quality corporate issues.

There is little information available about yields obtained by real estate investors. There is no Dow Jones Average of Real Estate Yields. In our business, the Larry Rosen Co., we devote substantial time to analyzing, selecting, negotiating, purchasing, and managing income property. In order to give you an idea of the actual financial results from income property investment, we have selected from our records all properties purchased prior to 1979 in which we were participants. Table 7–1 shows the annual cash flow (for each property for each year) divided by the initial cash investment. This ratio is commonly referred to as the *"cash-on-cash return on investment."*

Table 7–1
Percent Return from Cash Flow Divided by Cash Investment

		Year				
Type of Property	**Purchased**	**1978**	**1979**	**1980**	**1981**	**1982**
Factory building	Dec. 1978	—	12.5	8.9	−.6	11.5
Machine shop	May 1977	23.8	39.0	34.5	38.1	37.3
Industrial land and offices	Nov. 1977	18.5	18.1	19.9	19.6	29.1
Apartments	Dec. 1978	9.0	16.0	7.3	7.8	16.3
Office warehouses	Sept. 1978	26.3	9.9	14.9	20.7	17.2
Apartments	May 1978	10.0	10.2	11.5	11.7	15.5
Dental clinic*	Nov. 1977	50.1	50.1	50.1	50.1	50.1

*Entire investment was borrowed. Hence cash return is infinite. Property sold in 1982 for 180 percent of original purchase price.

Note: Cash flow is the excess of cash receipts over cash expenditures (including mortgage loan interest and principal repayments).

You may have noticed that cash expenditures as reflected in Table 7–1 included "mortgage loan principal payments." Such payments are direct reductions in the property owners outstanding mortgage loan balance. As they reduce the debt owed by the property owner, such payments are often said to increase the owner's "equity." **Equity**, in the real estate sense, is the excess of property market value over indebtedness. For example, consider the following:

At origin:	
Purchase price	$100,000
Initial loan	75,000
Cash investment	25,000
Five years later:	
Market value	$125,000
Loan outstanding	65,000
Equity	$ 60,000

For example, Sally Abelson buys a house for $100,000. She borrows $75,000 from a savings and loan association or other lender and invests $25,000 of her own money. Her initial equity is $25,000, which is equal to her initial cash investment. After some years, due to various factors including inflation, property maintenance, location, community economic factors, etc., the value of Sally's house has increased to

Graph 7–1
Long-Term Bond Yields

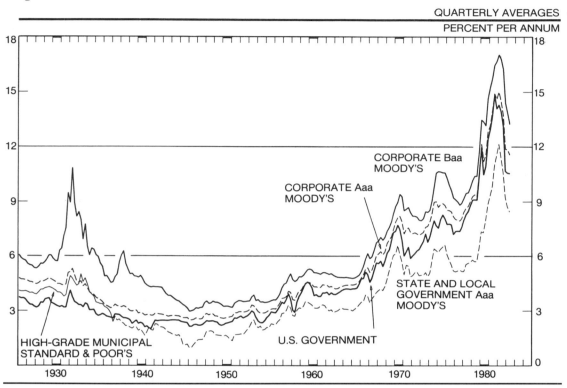

QUARTERLY AVERAGES
PERCENT PER ANNUM

Source: Board of Governors of the Federal Reserve System, *1983 Historical Chart Book*, p. 97.

$125,000. At this same time, her loan balance has been reduced from $75,000 to $65,000 as the result of her monthly payments of mortgage principal (and interest). At this point, Sally's equity is the difference between the market value of the house, $125,000, and her outstanding loan balance, $65,000; that is, she has $60,000 in equity. So Sally's home equity, or worth, has increased from $25,000 initially to $65,000.

Let's go back to our discussion of mortgage loan principal payments. Such payments reduced cash flow and thus reduced the cash-on-cash return percentage. But, some recognition, under most circumstances, should be given to such principal payments. *Such payments represent an increase in Sally's equity, provided the market value of the property has not diminished.* If the market value of Sally's home had not increased at all and still remained at $100,000 after five years, her equity would have increased by $10,000, the amount of the reduction in her debt. But if the market value decreases, such decrease would be offset against the equity increase from mortgage loan principal reduction.

To continue in the real world, let's look at each property in Table 7–1 from the point of view of increase in equity, or equity buildup resulting from loan principal payments. Table 7–2 shows the mortgage loan principal payments for each year divided by the owners' cash investment in the property. Assuming that each property's market value has not decreased, this ratio represents the *equity buildup* as a percentage of the original cash investment.

Table 7–2
Equity Buildup Divided by Cash Investment

Type of Property	Purchased	Year				
		1978	1979	1980	1981	1982
Factory building	Dec. 1978	—	2.0	2.6	2.4	2.7
Machine shop	May 1977	6.1	6.7	7.4	8.1	8.9
Industrial land and offices	Nov. 1977	4.7	5.6	6.2	6.8	7.4
Apartments	Dec. 1978	0.0	3.4	3.7	4.3	4.3
Office warehouses	Sept. 1978	2.6	− 3.7†	4.1	4.5	5.0
Apartments	May 1978	1.9	10.7	2.5	2.7	3.0
Dental clinic*	Nov. 1977	50.1	50.1	50.1	50.1	50.1

Note: Equity buildup percentage is the annual reduction of mortgage loan divided by the original cash investment.

*Entire investment was borrowed. Hence equity buildup is infinite. Loan was reduced by 17.5 percent during ownership.

†Loan was increased during the year to build an improvement to the property.

If we add the percentage returns from cash-on-cash to the equity buildup, does that give us the complete picture? Absolutely not, for two reasons. First, there are still tax effects, pro or con, to be considered. Second, the percentage returns on a year-by-year basis have not been weighted for the time factor of money. Remember, money due to be paid to you in the future is not worth as much as money you have in hand today. So we must take both taxes and time into consideration.

For the purpose of calculating U.S. taxes, buildings are assumed to depreciate in value every year. Therefore, after completing construction, the *theoretical depreciation* of a building may result in annual *losses* for income tax purposes. These losses may continue to shelter all or part of income (cash flow) for many years. Depreciation *deductions* from taxable income are *allowable* even though the property is, in fact, *appreciating* in value as a consequence of market conditions, good management, proper maintenance, etc. And, though the property may show a *tax loss,* it can have a *positive* cash flow, which the owners may spend, hold in reserve, or whatever.

To determine tax cost or tax savings and taxable income or loss from a real estate investment, several adjustments have to be made to cash flow as follows:

	Cash flow:		
(a)	Cash receipts	$1000	
(b)	Less: Cash expenditures	800	(includes mortgage loan principal payments)
(c)	Cash flow	200	(a) less (b)
(d)	Taxable income:		
(e)	Cash flow (as above)	$ 200	
(f)	Less: Depreciation	600	(depreciation was not included in cash expenditures)
(g)	Add: Mortgage loan principal payments	80	
(h)	Taxable income (loss)	($ 320)	(e) less (f) plus (g)
	Income tax:		
(i)	Taxable loss	($ 320)	
(j)	Tax bracket rate applicable	.5	(if in a 50 percent tax bracket)
(k)	Income tax savings	$ 160	(i) times (j)

Let's say Dr. David Markman, a 50 percent tax bracket investor, owned the above property. The taxable loss shown in (i) winds up on his income tax return as a deduction from income. A deduction only lessens his income, it doesn't directly reduce his tax owed in the amount of the deduction. After Dr. Markman's tax bracket rate is applied to the taxable loss, the resulting amount is the actual reduced income tax that he would pay as a result of the transaction. This is the amount shown in item (k), $160.

This simple example is not far, in terms of proportion, from actual situations. The important things to note are: *positive cash flow* and *negative taxable income.* As a result of the investment, Dr. Markman could spend, lend, or do whatever he wishes with the $200 cash flow. The negative taxable income of $320 in a 50 percent tax bracket produced $160 in tax savings. In other words, Dr. Markman, as a result of this investment, paid $160 less in income taxes and has $160 more to spend, invest, or lend. So the actual spendable cash from the investment above is $360; $200 in cash flow and $160 in tax savings. Thus cash flow after tax is $360; that is, item (c) plus (k).

Real estate investment has several potential pitfalls. First, there are the problems of evaluation, of selection, negotiation, and management. Second, the deduction generated by depreciation accumulates over the years and serves to reduce the tax basis of the property. If Dr. Markman's original cost for the entire property was a $2,000 cash investment and $8,000 loan, then his original basis was $10,000. But when he sells the property, the revised or adjusted basis that must be used to calculate his capital gain or loss is the original cost of $10,000 less all depreciation that he has deducted over the years. Let's say, those accumulated depreciation deductions amount to $4,000. Then his adjusted taxable basis is $10,000 less $4,000, or $6,000. If he sells the property for $10,000, his long-term capital gain ($4,000) is equal to the sales price ($10,000) less his taxable basis ($6,000). (Note: under present tax law, the entire gain at sale is taxed favorably as long-term capital gains if the owner has elected to use "straight-line" depreciation.[1] If "accelerated" methods of depreciation are used, the entire gain could instead be taxed at much higher ordinary income tax rates.)

So what's actually happened from the point of view of taxation? Over a period of years, Dr. Markman deducted $4,000 in depreciation from his taxable income. This saved him $2,000 in income taxes. He could spend or invest the $2,000 as the savings occurred.

When he sold the property, the $4,000 in deductions reduced his taxable basis and created a capital gain by the same amount. But capital gains are taxed more favorably than ordinary income. His tax on the capital gain may be determined as follows: 60 percent of the gain is ignored, forgotten, disregarded, abandoned; that leaves 40 percent of $4,000, or $1,600, with which to contend. The $1,600 is taxable at 50 percent, producing a tax at time of sale of $800. So Dr. Markman did well enough from the interplay between depreciation and taxable effects. He saved $2,000 in taxes in the early years when money is worth the most, and he paid for it in the final year, when money is worth the least, by incurring a tax liability or cost of $800.

Now let's see what the tax effects were of the properties we have looked at in Tables 7–1 and 7–2. For each property, Table 7–3 shows the tax cost or tax savings divided by the original cash investment.

Table 7–3
Tax Savings or Tax Cost Divided by Cash Investment

Type of Property	Purchased		Year			
		1978	1979	1980	1981	1982
Factory building*	Dec. 1978	50.1	3.9	5.0	44.3	− 3.4
Machine shop	May 1977	15.8	8.0	9.9	− 6.3	− 18.2
Industrial land and offices	Nov. 1977	13.1	14.2	13.0	12.8	− 10.3
Apartments	Dec. 1978	62.6	7.4	11.5	10.9	8.1
Office warehouses	Sept. 1978	2.4	2.2	− 1.5	− 7.8	− 7.0
Apartments	May 1978	4.7	3.1	2.6	2.4	0.4
Dental clinic[†]	Nov. 1977	− 2.1	− 2.1	− 2.1	− 2.1	− 2.1

Note: Tax cost or tax savings is the annual tax savings or cost divided by the original cash investment.

*Positive numbers indicate tax savings (as a percent of cash investment). Negative numbers, preceded by a "—", indicate tax cost.

†Entire investment was borrowed. Hence tax cost or savings as a percentage of cash invested is infinite.

---

[1]The capital gain is "long-term" if a minimum holding time period requirement is met.

Finally, let's put the results from all three components of return together, cash-on-cash return, equity buildup, and tax savings or cost. Table 7–4 is a summary of these actual investment experiences.

Table 7–4
Percent Combined Return from Cash, Equity Buildup, and Tax Savings or Cost

		Year				
Type of Property	**Purchased**	**1978**	**1979**	**1980**	**1981**	**1982**
Factory building	Dec. 1978	50.1	18.4	16.5	46.1	10.8
Machine shop	May 1977	45.7	53.7	51.8	39.9	28.0
Industrial land and offices	Nov. 1977	36.3	37.9	39.1	39.2	26.2
Apartments	Dec. 1978	71.6	26.8	22.5	23.0	28.7
Office warehouses	Sept. 1978	31.3	15.8	17.5	17.4	15.2
Apartments	May 1978	16.6	24.0	16.6	16.8	18.9
Dental clinic*	Nov. 1977	infinite return				

*Entire investment was borrowed. Hence the return is infinite.

In looking at Table 7–4, you *see the difficulty in determining which investments were better or worse* and by how much. It is now time to use our **magic number approach and determine the IRR** (internal rate of return) for each property. The IRR analysis is shown in Table 7–5. In order to calculate it, we must estimate an after-tax sales proceeds of each property for the final year of the analysis, together with projected combined after tax cash flow. The sales proceeds are estimated by dividing or capitalizing the 1982 cash-on-cash return by 10 percent. The combined, after tax, estimated sales proceeds and income for 1983 are shown in the column in Table 7–5 labeled "Est. 1983."

Table 7–5
Internal Rate of Return: All Factors Included

		Year					Est.	
Type of Property	**Purchased**	**1978**	**1979**	**1980**	**1981**	**1982**	**1983***	**IRR**
Factory building	Dec. 1978	50.1	18.4	16.5	46.1	10.8	122.80	31%
Machine shop	May 1977	45.7	53.7	51.8	39.9	28.0	346.40	55
Industrial land and offices	Nov. 1977	36.3	37.9	39.1	39.2	26.2	279.00	45
Apartments	Dec. 1978	71.6	26.8	22.5	23.0	28.7	179.10	44
Office warehouses	Sept. 1978	31.3	15.8	17.5	17.4	15.2	172.80	25
Apartments	May 1978	16.6	24.0	16.6	16.8	18.9	162.90	23
Dental clinic†	Nov. 1977	infinite return						∞

*Est. 1983 includes after tax proceeds of sale determined by capitalizing 1982 cash-on-cash return at 10 percent.

†Entire investment was borrowed. Hence the return is infinite.

Management

To maximize the benefits of real estate ownership of income property, managerial skill is required. Among the problems that management must address are the following:

Find suitable tenants.

Maintain high rates of occupancy.

Negotiate optimum rates.

Obtain favorable lease provisions such as tax and insurance escalators, default remedies, rental escalations, etc.

Collect rent due including late charges.

Maintain accurate accounting records.

Plan receipts and expenditures to obtain optimum tax advantages.

Prepare income tax information.

Purchase materials and hire labor at advantageous prices.

Keep the property in a reasonable state of repair.

Plan tax and fiscal matters to achieve desirable results.

The importance of buying property at advantageous prices cannot be overemphasized. The yield at which a property is purchased (cash-on-cash return on investment) will be a major factor in determining the price at which it can be resold. The difference between a cash-on-cash return of 6 percent and that of 8 percent may not seem very meaningful at first glance. However, let's consider the significance of purchasing a property at a 6 percent yield when the fair market value should have produced a 10 percent yield to the buyer.

For example, Mike McGrewder buys property for $1 million which yields $60,000, i.e., a 6 percent return on investment. If he overpaid, that is, bought at too high a price and too low a yield, then in order to resell the property to the new buyer to yield the required market rate of 10 percent, the price will have to be marked down to $600,000 for a loss to the first buyer of $400,000—40 percent of his investment. Thus a few percentage points of yield can greatly affect capital.[2]

Among the investment objectives that you should have when dealing with real estate are:

Preserve and protect your original investment capital. This may be achieved by buying structurally sound properties that have a proven earnings record or that are substantially preleased to experienced and responsible tenants.

---

[2]The loss, in this case, is 40% if the purchase were made "all cash." If half the purchase price was borrowed, then the loss represents 80% of the initial cash investment.

Provide capital gains through appreciation of your property's value. Through the years, well-selected property investments have yielded high profits to investors who bought and sold intelligently.

Shelter distributions of cash. Through the operation of the combined effects of mortgage financing and depreciation, tax shelter of all or part of the income from the property as well as other income may be generated.

Build up equity through reduction of mortgage loans on properties and appreciation of the market value.

Purchase property at below reproduction cost. Properties that can be bought at prices below reproduction cost include offerings from distressed sellers who desire a quick sale and properties that are producing less than market rates of income or that are older.

Select properties where the rentals are at below market rates. The main reason for this objective is that in the event that the tenant defaults or moves out and a replacement tenant must be found, the new rental under such circumstances should at least equal the old and hopefully exceed it.

Sell the property at the appropriate time based on changing market factors, available reinvestment opportunities, and tax considerations.

Summary

We have investigated many key concepts in this chapter, including: cash-on-cash return, equity buildup, tax savings or cost, combining all three return factors with estimated after tax proceeds of sale to determine an internal rate of return, investment management, and real estate investment objectives. In the next chapter, we develop *models* of real estate investment that will allow you to estimate internal rate of return for properties that you may be considering for investment or that you already own.

Real Estate,
IRR Models

The unique graphs contained in this chapter will allow you to compute the IRR for an extensive variety of income-producing real estate investments. Performing the calculations that were required to prepare these graphs, as well as performing the calculations to determine the IRR from a real estate investment, is an extremely complex and laborious task. **The beauty of these graphs is that they provide an accurate, yet simple, solution to the problem of determining the internal rate of return from a real estate investment.** To prepare each graph required in the neighborhood of *one quarter million calculations.* Thus for the 13 graphs in this chapter, about *3 million calculations* were involved.

The easiest way to familiarize yourself with finding the IRR for a real estate investment is to do it. Let's say that Rick Perly is considering acquiring an office building and his projections are as follows:

Rate of inflation	6%
Initial percent return—net operating income divided by the total investment	10%
Mr. Perly's tax bracket	40%
Loan as a percentage of the total investment	75%
Loan interest rate	10%
Years of loan amortization	25 years
Building cost divided by total investment cost	90%
Years of straight line depreciation	15 years
The property will eventually be sold in the nth year after purchase	15
The gross sales price will be determined by capitalizing the net operating income in the 15th year at a rate of n percent	10%

The above assumptions are all that are needed to find the graph that corresponds to (or comes closest to corresponding to) those assumptions. In this case, it is Graph 8–1. (Chart 8–1, **Match-up Worksheet,** allows you to quickly find the graph that matches the real estate situation you have at hand.) Please refer to Graph 8–1. The assumptions shown on the graph are identical to the characteristics of Mr. Perly's proposed investment.

Chart 8–1
Match-Up Worksheet

Assumptions	Graph Number												
	1	2	3	4	5	6	7	8	9	10	11	12	13
Rates of inflation 0–10%	yes	yes	yes	yes	yes	yes	yes	yes					yes
6									yes	yes	yes	yes	
Initial percent return:													
NOI/total invested 0 to 16%	yes	yes	yes	yes	yes	yes	yes	yes					yes
10									yes	yes	yes	yes	
Tax bracket 50%		yes	yes			yes			yes	yes			
40	yes						yes						
30				yes	yes						yes	yes	
0								yes					yes
Loan as a percent of total investment 75%	yes	yes		yes	yes	yes	yes	yes		yes		yes	
50									yes		yes		
0			yes										yes
Loan interest rate percentage 6–16%									yes	yes	yes	yes	
10	yes												
12		yes		yes	yes	yes	yes	yes					
0			yes										yes
Years of loan amortization 25 years	yes	yes		yes			yes	yes	yes	yes	yes	yes	
interest only					yes	yes							
not applicable			yes										yes
Building/Total investment 90%	yes	yes	yes	yes	yes	yes	yes	yes	yes	yes	yes	yes	yes
Years, straight line depreciation 15 years	yes	yes	yes	yes	yes	yes	yes	yes	yes	yes	yes	yes	yes
Year of sale, 15 years hence	yes	yes	yes	yes	yes	yes	yes	yes	yes	yes	yes	yes	yes
Capitalization rate at sale 10%	yes			yes					yes	yes	yes	yes	
12		yes	yes		yes	yes		yes					yes
16							yes						

To find the IRR, enter the graph on the vertical axis at the 10 percent point, which represents the initial net operating income (NOI) as a percentage of the total investment. Proceed horizontally until the 6 percent curve is reached, which represents the annual percentage of inflation assumed. At the intersection with the 6 percent curve, proceed toward the bottom of the graph until the bottom axis (horizontal line) is reached. The point of intersection is the IRR for this investment, 23.2 percent.

The same graph may be used to find the IRR for other rates of initial NOI to total investment and for other rates of inflation. For example, still referring to Graph 8–1, how would the IRR change if inflation were 10 percent instead of 6 percent? Entering the left axis at 10 percent for initial yield, proceed horizontally to the 10 percent curve, then descend to the bottom axis. The point of intersection is 28.8 percent, which is the new IRR. So if inflation, in this case, increases from 6 percent to 10 percent, the IRR increases from 23.2 percent to 28.8 percent.

Or, the same graph may be used to determine the IRR for varying levels of initial yield. If the initial yield is 7 percent (instead of 10 percent), what happens to the IRR? Enter the graph at the 7 percent point on the left axis, then go across to the 6 percent inflation curve, then descend to the bottom axis, where the IRR is about 14.4 percent. Thus the effect of a drop in the initial yield level from 10 percent to 7 percent is a decrease in IRR from 23.2 percent to 14.4 percent.

Following the graphs at the end of the Chapter are Tables 8–1 through 8–13 with printouts of the entire 15-year projection for **one point** on the graph. In order to understand the graphs and tables, several comments regarding the methodology may be helpful.

Inflation. The inflation rate is applied on an annual compound basis to increase the initial year's NOI divided by total investment. This is equivalent to increasing all items of rent and other income as well as all operating expenses (except depreciation and interest) by the inflation rate.

Loan principal and interest. This is the annual debt service amount including both principal and interest. It is calculated from the stated assumptions in terms of loan amount, years of amortization, and loan interest rate.

Initial depreciable assets. Land is not depreciable, but buildings are. Therefore a breakdown of the total investment amount is necessary between the two. Initial depreciable assets is determined by multiplying the fraction shown in "building divided by total investment" times the total investment.

Depreciation. Depreciation is determined by dividing the "initial depreciable assets" by the amount shown as "years, straight-line depreciation." The 15-year, straight-line depreciation under the asset cost recovery system does not subject the user to recapture of gains at sale as ordinary income.[1]

Sales proceeds and year of sale. The acquired property is assumed to be sold in the 15th year. The gross sales price is determined by

---

[1]The allowable depreciation period for most real estate investments (except low income housing) changed to 18 years in the 1984 Deficit Reduction Act, for property placed in service after March 15, 1984.

dividing the net operating income in the 15th year by the capitalization rate stated in the assumptions.

Capital gains tax on sale. The sales proceeds less the original cost of $1,000 less accumulated depreciation is the taxable long-term gain. Sixty percent of this gain is disregarded. The remaining 40 percent of the gain is multiplied by the tax bracket rate stated in the assumptions.

Cash from sale after tax and loan repayment. Both the outstanding loan balance remaining in the 15th year as well as capital gains tax are deducted from the sales proceeds to determine "cash from sale after tax and loan repayment."

Cash flow after tax. It is these amounts for each year that form the principal basis for the IRR determination. In the 15th year, the "cash flow after tax" also includes the "cash from sale after tax and loan repayment."

Internal rate of return. *This is the magic number that summarizes the results of the entire projection. It is an after tax amount including deduction of both ordinary income taxes and capital gains taxes. This rate equates the after tax cash flows of each year to the initial cash investment shown in the assumptions.*

Match-Up Worksheet

To find the graph you need to perform the IRR calculation you desire, first refer to the **match-up worksheet** (Chart 8–1). Select the graph that has the same characteristics as your proposed investment. If the worksheet doesn't contain exactly the same characteristics that you want, then select the graph that comes closest to having the desired characteristics. Then refer to the graph selected from the worksheet— to perform the IRR calculation.

That's all there is to it!

Sample IRR Calculations

Now refer to Chart 8–2. This contains one IRR calculation from each graph for the 13 Real Estate IRR graphs, using the assumptions stated for each such graph.

Several items worth noting from a study of Chart 8–2 are:

1. *Effect of reducing loan amount.* Compare the results of Graphs 8–2 and 8–3. Both are identical except that Graph 8–2 is based on a 75 percent loan (75 percent of the purchased price is borrowed and 25

Chart 8–2
Sample IRR Calculations

							Graph Number						
Assumptions	8–1	8–2	8–3	8–4	8–5	8–6	8–7	8–8	8–9	8–10	8–11	8–12	8–13
Rates of inflation	6%	6%	6%	6%	6%	6%	6%	6%	6%	6%	6%	6%	6%
Initial percent return: (NOI/Total investment)	10%	10%	10%	10%	10%	10%	10%	10%	10%	10%	10%	10%	11.5%
Tax bracket 50%	yes	yes	yes	yes	yes	yes	yes		yes	yes	yes	yes	
40								yes					
30													
0													yes
Loan as a percent of total investment 75%	yes	yes		yes	yes	yes	yes	yes					
50									yes	yes	yes	yes	
0			yes										yes
Loan interest rate percentage	10%	12%		12%	12%	12%	12%	12%	10%	10%	10%	10%	
Years of loan amortization	25	25		25	99	150	25	25	25	25	25	25	
Building/Total investment	90%	90%	90%	90%	90%	90%	90%	90%	90%	90%	90%	90%	90%
Years, straight line depreciation	15	15	15	15	15	15	15	15	15	15	15	15	15
Year of sale, x years hence	15	15	15	15	15	15	15	15	15	15	15	15	15
Capitalization rate at sale	10%	12%	12%	10%	12%	12%	16%	12%	10%	10%	10%	10%	12%
Key Results													
Loan principal + Interest per year	83	96		96	90	90	96	96	73	109	82	123	
Mortgage constant (Principal + Interest as percent of original loan)	11	12.8		12.8	12	12	12.8	12.8	14.5	14.5	16.4	16.4	
Sales proceeds after capital gains tax and payment of outstanding loan balance ($000)	1.4	1	1.5	1.5	0.9	0.8	0.7	1.3	1.4	1.3	1.6	1.4	2.4
Internal rate of return	23.2	20.6	11.4	21.2	21.2	22.0	18.8	19.7	15.4	20.0	15.2	23.3	17.5

percent is invested in cash). Graph 8–3 is an all-cash transaction. Note that the IRR *drops* from 20.6 percent for the leverage investment to only 11.4 percent for the all-cash transaction. (There are other circumstances where the reverse effect would be true—everything depends on the cost of the borrowed money.)

Also, see Graphs 8–9 and 8–10 for a similar comparison. With a 75 percent loan (Graph 8–10) the IRR is 20 percent, and when the loan is *reduced* to 50 percent (Graph 8–9), the IRR *drops* to 15.4 percent.

2. *Effect of differing tax brackets.* When the tax bracket is 50 percent (Graph 8–6), the IRR is 22 percent. At the lower bracket rate of 0 percent (Graph 8–8), the IRR drops to 19.7 percent. Here again there are multiple forces at work, and the situation could be reversed depending on the circumstances. Tax losses in the early years of ownership benefit the high bracket investor. But tax cost, when the investment is showing taxable income, benefits the lower tax bracket investor. For example, when the tax bracket decreases from 50 percent (Graph 8–10) to 30 percent (Graph 8–12), the IRR increases from 20 percent to 23.3 percent.

3. *Effect of altering the capitalization rate at sale.* When the capitalization rate is *increased* from 10 percent (Graph 8–4) to 12 percent (Graph 8–5), the IRR *stays unchanged* at 21.2 percent. However, if the years of loan amortization were the same for both situations, the IRR would *drop* to 20.17 percent at the higher 12 percent capitalization rate.

4. *Effect of increasing the number of years of loan amortization.* When the amortization time period is *increased* from 25 years (Graph 8–2) to 150 (equivalent to an interest-only loan with no amortization of principal—Graph 8–6), the IRR *increases* from 20.6 percent to 22 percent.

5. *Effect of changing loan interest rates.* When the loan interest rate *increases* from 10 percent (Graph 8–12) to 12 percent (Graph 8–4), the IRR *decreases* from 23.3 percent to 21.2 percent.

Summary

The following pages first show the 13 graphs for the determination of IRR.

It must be emphasized that the above results of comparison are not rules of thumb. The interplay of many, many variables is involved in determining the annual cash flow—and the IRR. The above effects are valid for the graphs involved and the inherent assumptions contained therein—nothing more.

Graph 8–1
After Tax IRR: 40 Percent Tax Bracket

Initial yield percent

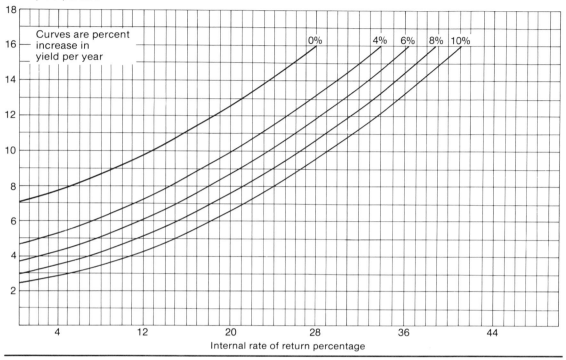

Internal rate of return percentage

Assumptions:	Rate of inflation	0–10%
	Initial percent return: (NOI/Total investment)	0–16%
	Tax bracket	40%
	Loan as percent of total investment	75%
	Loan interest rate percentage	10%
	Years of loan amortization	25
	Building/Total investment	90%
	Years straight line depreciation	15 yrs.
	Year of sale	15 yrs. hence
	Capitalization rate of sale	10%

Graph 8–2
After Tax IRR: 50 Percent Tax Bracket

Initial yield percent

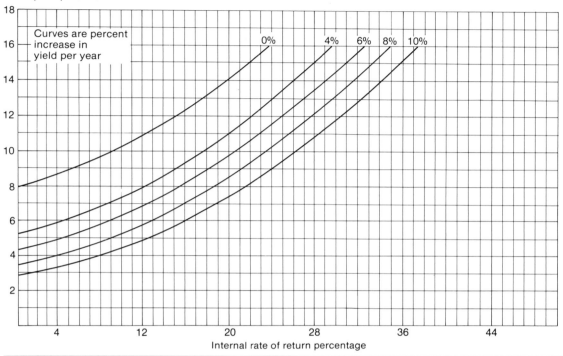

Internal rate of return percentage

Assumptions:		
	Rate of inflation	0–10%
	Initial percent return: (NOI/Total investment)	0–16%
	Tax bracket	50%
	Loan as percent of total investment	75%
	Loan interest rate percentage	12%
	Years of loan amortization	25
	Building/Total investment	90%
	Years straight line depreciation	15 yrs.
	Year of sale	15 yrs. hence
	Capitalization rate of sale	12%

Graph 8–3
After Tax IRR: 50 Percent Tax Bracket

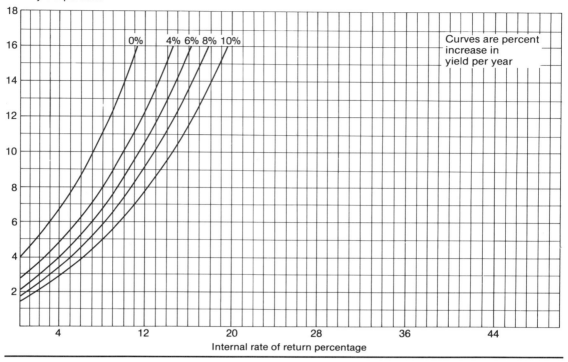

Initial yield percent

Internal rate of return percentage

Assumptions:

Rate of inflation	0–10%
Initial percent return: (NOI/Total investment)	0–16%
Tax bracket	50%
Loan as percent of total investment	0%
Loan interest rate percentage	0%
Years of loan amortization	NA
Building/Total investment	90%
Years straight line depreciation	15 yrs.
Year of sale	15 yrs. hence
Capitalization rate of sale	12%

Graph 8–4
After Tax IRR: 30 Percent Tax Bracket

Initial yield percent

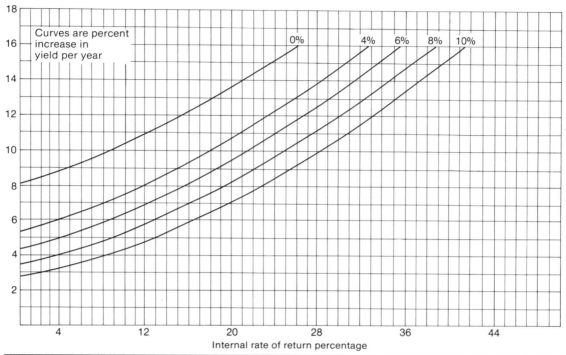

Internal rate of return percentage

Assumptions:	Rate of inflation	0–10%
	Initial percent return: (NOI/Total investment)	0–16%
	Tax bracket	30%
	Loan as percent of total investment	75%
	Loan interest rate percentage	12%
	Years of loan amortization	25
	Building/Total investment	90%
	Years straight line depreciation	15 yrs.
	Year of sale	15 yrs. hence
	Capitalization rate of sale	10%

Graph 8–5
After Tax IRR: 30 Percent Tax Bracket

Initial yield percent

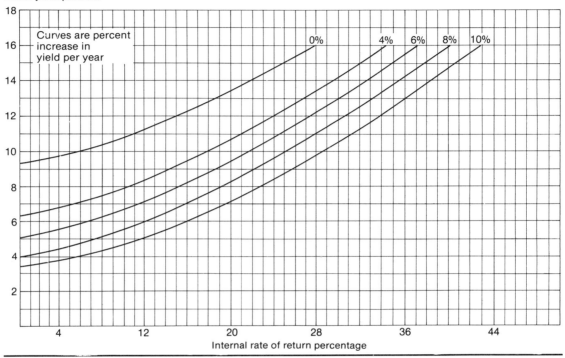

Internal rate of return percentage

Assumptions:	Rate of inflation	0–10%
	Initial percent return: (NOI/Total investment)	0–16%
	Tax bracket	30%
	Loan as percent of total investment	75%
	Loan interest rate percentage	12%
	Years of loan amortization	interest only
	Building/Total investment	90%
	Years straight line depreciation	15 yrs.
	Year of sale	15 yrs. hence
	Capitalization rate of sale	12%

Graph 8–6
After Tax IRR: 50 Percent Tax Bracket

Initial yield percent

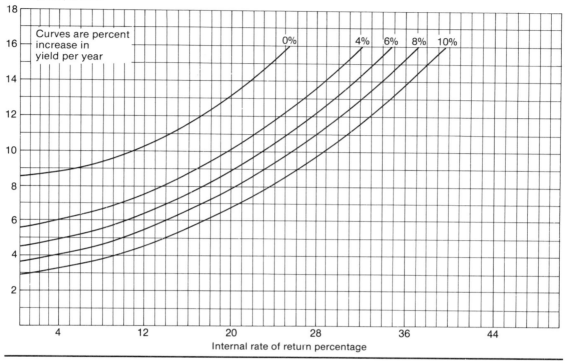

Internal rate of return percentage

Assumptions:		
	Rate of inflation	0–10%
	Initial percent return: (NOI/Total investment)	0–16%
	Tax bracket	50%
	Loan as percent of total investment	75%
	Loan interest rate percentage	12%
	Years of loan amortization	interest only
	Building/Total investment	90%
	Years straight line depreciation	15 yrs.
	Year of sale	15 yrs. hence
	Capitalization rate of sale	12%

Graph 8–7
After Tax IRR: 40 Percent Tax Bracket

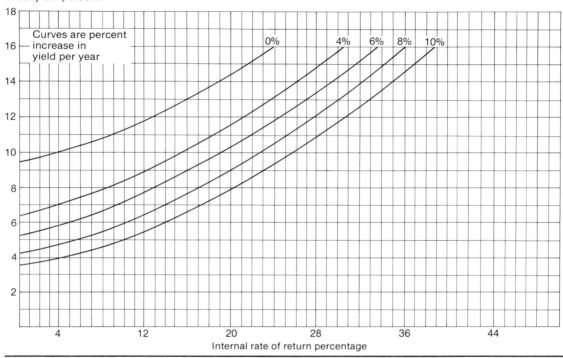

Initial yield percent

Internal rate of return percentage

Assumptions:
Rate of inflation	0–10%
Initial percent return: (NOI/Total investment)	0–16%
Tax bracket	40%
Loan as percent of total investment	75%
Loan interest rate percentage	12%
Years of loan amortization	25
Building/Total investment	90%
Years straight line depreciation	15 yrs.
Year of sale	15 yrs. hence
Capitalization rate of sale	16%

Graph 8–8
After Tax IRR: 0 Percent Tax Bracket

Initial yield percent

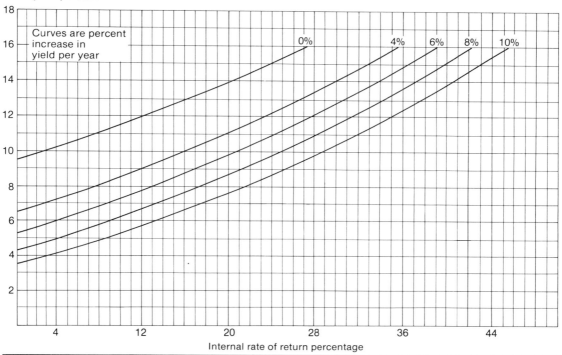

Internal rate of return percentage

Assumptions:	Rate of inflation	0–10%
	Initial percent return: (NOI/Total investment)	0–16%
	Tax bracket	0%
	Loan as percent of total investment	75%
	Loan interest rate percentage	12%
	Years of loan amortization	25
	Building/Total investment	90%
	Years straight line depreciation	15 yrs.
	Year of sale	15 yrs. hence
	Capitalization rate of sale	12%

Graph 8–9
After Tax IRR: 50 Percent Tax Bracket

Loan interest
rate percentage

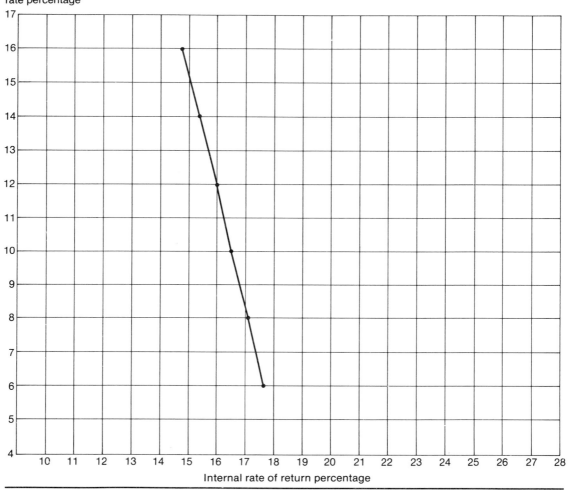

Internal rate of return percentage

Assumptions:	Rate of inflation	6%
	Initial percent return: (NOI/Total investment)	10%
	Tax bracket	50%
	Loan as percent of total investment	50%
	Loan interest rate percentage	6–16%
	Years of loan amortization	25
	Building/Total investment	90%
	Years straight line depreciation	15 yrs.
	Year of sale	15 yrs. hence
	Capitalization rate of sale	10%

Graph 8–10
After Tax IRR: 50 Percent Tax Bracket

Loan interest
rate percentage

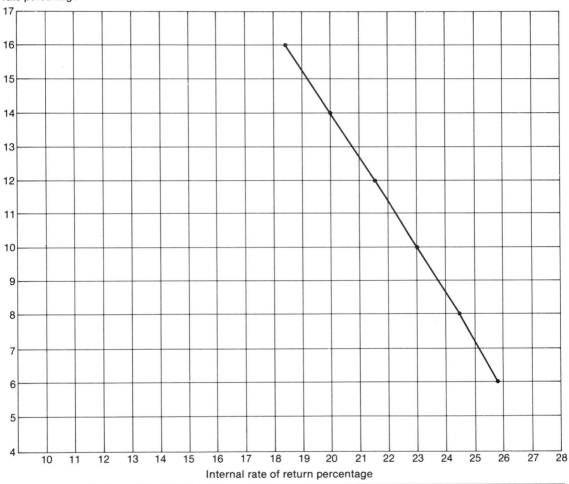

Internal rate of return percentage

Assumptions:	Rate of inflation	6%
	Initial percent return: (NOI/Total investment)	10%
	Tax bracket	50%
	Loan as percent of total investment	75%
	Loan interest rate percentage	6–16%
	Years of loan amortization	25
	Building/Total investment	90%
	Years straight line depreciation	15 yrs.
	Year of sale	15 yrs. hence
	Capitalization rate of sale	10%

Graph 8–11
After Tax IRR: 30 Percent Tax Bracket

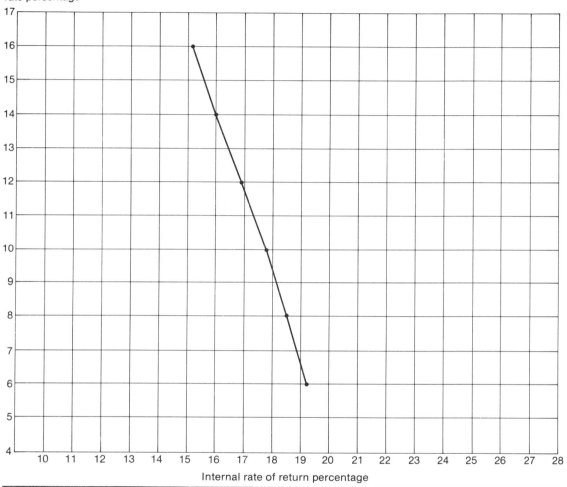

Loan interest
rate percentage

Internal rate of return percentage

Assumptions:	Rate of inflation	6%
	Initial percent return: (NOI/Total investment)	10%
	Tax bracket	30%
	Loan as percent of total investment	50%
	Loan interest rate percentage	6–16%
	Years of loan amortization	25
	Building/Total investment	90%
	Years straight line depreciation	15 yrs.
	Year of sale	15 yrs. hence
	Capitalization rate of sale	10%

Graph 8–12
After Tax IRR: 30 Percent Tax Bracket

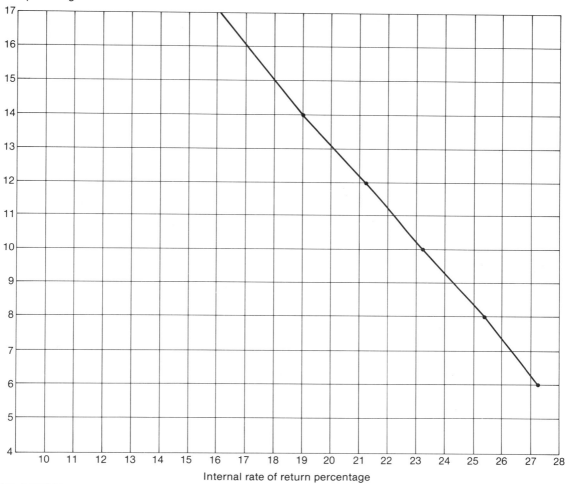

Loan interest
rate percentage

Internal rate of return percentage

Assumptions:	Rate of inflation	6%
	Initial percent return: (NOI/Total investment)	10%
	Tax bracket	30%
	Loan as percent of total investment	75%
	Loan interest rate percentage	6–16%
	Years of loan amortization	25
	Building/Total investment	90%
	Years straight line depreciation	15 yrs.
	Year of sale	15 yrs. hence
	Capitalization rate of sale	10%

Graph 8–13
After Tax IRR: 0 Percent Tax Bracket

Initial yield percent

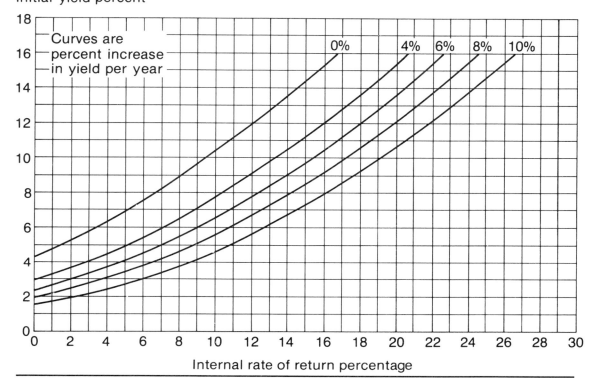

Internal rate of return percentage

Assumptions:	Rate of inflation	0-10%
	Initial percent return: (NOI/Total investment)	0-16%
	Tax bracket	0%
	Loan as percent of total investment	
	Loan interest rate percentage	
	Years of loan amortization	25
	Building/Total investment	90%
	Years straight line depreciation	15 yrs.
	Year of sale	15 yrs. hence
	Capitalization rate of sale	11%

Table 8–1

								Year								
	1	2	3	4	5	6	7	8	9	10	11	12	13	14	15	Totals
Loan (beginning)	750	742	734	725	715	703	691	678	663	646	628	609	587	563	537	
Interest, annual	75	74	73	72	71	70	69	68	66	65	63	61	59	56	54	997
Principal reduction	8	8	9	10	11	12	14	15	16	18	20	22	24	26	29	242
Loan (end)	742	734	725	715	703	691	678	663	646	628	609	587	563	537	508	
NOI/Investment*	0.10															
NOI	100	106	112	119	126	134	142	150	159	169	179	190	201	213	226	2,328
NOI/Total investment	0.10	0.11	0.11	0.12	0.13	0.13	0.14	0.15	0.16	0.17	0.18	0.19	0.20	0.21	0.23	
− Loan principal and interest	83	83	83	83	83	83	83	83	83	83	83	83	83	83	83	1,239
Cash flow before tax	17	23	30	36	44	51	59	68	77	86	96	107	119	131	143	1,088
Cash flow/Cash investment	0.07	0.09	0.12	0.15	0.17	0.20	0.24	0.27	0.31	0.35	0.39	0.43	0.47	0.52	0.57	
− Depreciation	60	60	60	60	60	60	60	60	60	60	60	60	60	60	60	900
+ Loan principal	8	8	9	10	11	12	14	15	16	18	20	22	24	26	29	242
Taxable income	−35	−28	−21	−13	−5	3	13	23	33	44	56	69	83	97	112	431
Income tax (− = Savings)	−14	−11	−8	−5	−2	1	5	9	13	18	22	28	33	39	45	172
Cash flow after tax, before sale	31	35	38	42	46	50	54	59	64	69	74	80	86	92	98	916
Sales proceeds and year of sale			15												2,261	2,261
Capital gains tax on sale															346	346
Cash from sale after tax and loan															1,407	1,407
Cash flow after tax	31	35	38	42	46	50	54	59	64	69	74	80	86	92	1,506	2,323
Internal rate of return								23.18%								

*NOI is net operating income. Investment is the total purchase price, including loan.

Assumptions:		
Tax bracket	40%	
Cash investment	$ 250	
Loan	$ 750	
Total investment	$1,000	
Years loan amortization	25 yrs.	
Loan interest	10%	
Loan principal and interest	$ 83	
Building/Total investment	0.90	
Initial depreciable assets	$ 900	
Years straight line depreciation	15 yrs.	
Year of sale	15 yrs.	
Capitalization rate at sale	10%	
Inflation	6%	
Mortgage constant	11.0168%	

Table 8–2

	Year															
	1	2	3	4	5	6	7	8	9	10	11	12	13	14	15	Totals
Loan (beginning)	750	744	738	731	723	714	704	693	681	667	651	634	614	592	568	
Interest, annual	90	89	89	88	87	86	85	83	82	80	78	76	74	71	68	1,225
Principal reduction	6	6	7	8	9	10	11	12	14	16	17	20	22	25	27	210
Loan (end)	744	738	731	723	714	704	693	681	667	651	634	614	592	568	540	
NOI/Investment*	0.10															
NOI	100	106	112	119	126	134	142	150	159	169	179	190	201	213	226	2,328
NOI/Total investment	0.10	0.11	0.11	0.12	0.13	0.13	0.14	0.15	0.16	0.17	0.18	0.19	0.20	0.21	0.23	
− Loan principal and interest	96	96	96	96	96	96	96	96	96	96	96	96	96	96	96	1,434
Cash flow before tax	4	10	17	23	31	38	46	55	64	73	83	94	106	118	130	893
Cash flow/Cash investment	0.02	0.04	0.07	0.09	0.12	0.15	0.18	0.22	0.26	0.29	0.33	0.38	0.42	0.47	0.52	
− Depreciation	60	60	60	60	60	60	60	60	60	60	60	60	60	60	60	900
+ Loan principal	6	6	7	8	9	10	11	12	14	16	17	20	22	25	27	210
Taxable income	−50	−43	−36	−29	−21	−12	−3	7	18	29	41	54	68	82	98	203
Income tax (− = Savings)	−25	−22	−18	−14	−10	−6	−1	4	9	14	20	27	34	41	49	101
Cash flow after tax, before sale	29	32	35	38	41	44	48	51	55	59	63	67	72	77	81	792
Sales proceeds and year of sale	15														1,884	1,884
Capital gains tax on sale															357	357
Cash from sale after tax and loan															987	987
Cash flow after tax	29	32	35	38	41	44	48	51	55	59	63	67	72	77	1,068	1,779
Internal rate of return									20.56%							

*NOI is net operating income. Investment is the total purchase price, including loan.

Assumptions:

Tax bracket	50%
Cash investment	$ 250
Loan	$ 750
Total investment	$1,000
Years loan amortization	25 yrs.
Loan interest	12%
Loan principal and interest	$ 96
Building/Total investment	90%
Initial depreciable assets	$ 900
Years straight line depreciation	15 yrs.
Year of sale	15 yrs.
Capitalization rate at sale	12%
Inflation	6%
Mortgage constant	12.7500%

Table 8–3

								Year								
	1	2	3	4	5	6	7	8	9	10	11	12	13	14	15	Totals
Loan (beginning)	0	0	0	0	0	0	0	0	0	0	0	0	0	0	0	0
Interest, annual	0	0	0	0	0	0	0	0	0	0	0	0	0	0	0	0
Principal reduction	0	0	0	0	0	0	0	0	0	0	0	0	0	0	0	0
Loan (end)	0	0	0	0	0	0	0	0	0	0	0	0	0	0	0	0
NOI/Investment*	0.10															
NOI	100	106	112	119	126	134	142	150	159	169	179	190	201	213	226	2,328
NOI/Total investment	0.10	0.11	0.11	0.12	0.13	0.13	0.14	0.15	0.16	0.17	0.18	0.19	0.20	0.21	0.23	
– Loan principal and interest	0	0	0	0	0	0	0	0	0	0	0	0	0	0	0	0
Cash flow before tax	100	106	112	119	126	134	142	150	159	169	179	190	201	213	226	2,328
Cash flow/Cash investment	0.10	0.11	0.11	0.12	0.13	0.13	0.14	0.15	0.16	0.17	0.18	0.19	0.20	0.21	0.23	
– Depreciation	60	60	60	60	60	60	60	60	60	60	60	60	60	60	60	900
+ Loan principal	0	0	0	0	0	0	0	0	0	0	0	0	0	0	0	0
Taxable income	40	46	52	59	66	74	82	90	99	109	119	130	141	153	166	1,428
Income tax (– = Savings)	20	23	26	30	33	37	41	45	50	54	60	65	71	77	83	714
Cash flow after tax, before sale	80	83	86	90	93	97	101	105	110	114	120	125	131	137	143	1,614
Sales proceeds and year of sale															1,884	1,884
Capital gains tax on sale															357	357
Cash from sale after tax and loan															1,527	1,527
Cash flow after tax	80	83	86	90	93	97	101	105	110	114	120	125	131	137	1,670	3,141
Internal rate of return								11.40%								

*NOI is net operating income. Investment is the total purchase price, including loan.

Assumptions:		
Tax bracket	50%
Cash investment	$1,000
Loan	$ 0
Total investment	$1,000
Years loan amortization	99 yrs.
Loan interest	0%
Loan principal and interest	$ 0
Building/Total investment	90%
Initial depreciable assets	$ 900
Years straight line depreciation	15 yrs.
Year of sale	15 yrs.
Capitalization rate at sale	12%
Inflation	6%
Mortgage constant	6%

Table 8–4

	Year																
	1	2	3	4	5	6	7	8	9	10	11	12	13	14	15	Totals
Loan (beginning)	750	744	738	731	723	714	704	693	681	667	651	634	614	592	568	
Interest, annual	90	89	89	88	87	86	85	83	82	80	78	76	74	71	68	1,225
Principal reduction	6	6	7	8	9	10	11	12	14	16	17	20	22	25	27	210
Loan (end)	744	738	731	723	714	704	693	681	667	651	634	614	592	568	540	
NOI/Investment*	0.10															
NOI	100	106	112	119	126	134	142	150	159	169	179	190	201	213	226	2,328
NOI/Total investment	0.10	0.11	0.11	0.12	0.13	0.13	0.14	0.15	0.16	0.17	0.18	0.19	0.20	0.21	0.23	
− Loan principal and interest	96	96	96	96	96	96	96	96	96	96	96	96	96	96	96	1,434
Cash flow before tax	4	10	17	23	31	38	46	55	64	73	83	94	106	118	130	893
Cash flow/Cash investment	0.02	0.04	0.07	0.09	0.12	0.15	0.18	0.22	0.26	0.29	0.33	0.38	0.42	0.47	0.52	
− Depreciation	60	60	60	60	60	60	60	60	60	60	60	60	60	60	60	900
+ Loan principal	6	6	7	8	9	10	11	12	14	16	17	20	22	25	27	210
Taxable income	−50	−43	−36	−29	−21	−12	−3	7	18	29	41	54	68	82	98	203
Income tax (− = Savings)	−15	−13	−11	−9	−6	−4	−1	2	5	9	12	16	20	25	29	61
Cash flow after tax, before sale	19	23	28	32	37	42	47	53	58	65	71	78	85	93	101	832
Sales proceeds and year of sale															2,261	2,261
Capital gains tax on sale															259	259
Cash from sale after tax and loan															1,461	1,461
Cash flow after tax	19	23	28	32	37	42	47	53	58	65	71	78	85	93	1,562	2,294
Internal rate of return								21.20%								

*NOI is net operating income. Investment is the total purchase price, including loan.

Assumptions:		
Tax bracket		30%
Cash investment	$	250
Loan	$	750
Total investment		$1,000
Years loan amortization		25 yrs.
Loan interest		12%
Loan principal and interest	$	96
Building/Total investment		90%
Initial depreciable assets	$	900
Years straight line depreciation		15 yrs.
Year of sale		15 yrs.
Capitalization rate at sale		10%
Inflation		6%
Mortgage constant		12.7500%

Table 8–5

	Year															
	1	2	3	4	5	6	7	8	9	10	11	12	13	14	15	Totals
Loan (beginning)	750	750	750	750	750	750	750	750	750	750	750	750	750	750	750	750
Interest, annual	90	90	90	90	90	90	90	90	90	90	90	90	90	90	90	1,350
Principal reduction	0	0	0	0	0	0	0	0	0	0	0	0	0	0	0	0
Loan (end)	750	750	750	750	750	750	750	750	750	750	750	750	750	750	750	0
NOI/Investment*	0.10															
NOI	100	106	112	119	126	134	142	150	159	169	179	190	201	213	226	2,328
NOI/Total investment	0.10	0.11	0.11	0.12	0.13	0.13	0.14	0.15	0.16	0.17	0.18	0.19	0.20	0.21	0.23	
− Loan principal and interest	90	90	90	90	90	90	90	90	90	90	90	90	90	90	90	1,350
Cash flow before tax	10	16	22	29	36	44	52	60	69	79	89	100	111	123	136	978
Cash flow/Cash investment	0.04	0.06	0.09	0.12	0.14	0.18	0.21	0.24	0.28	0.32	0.36	0.40	0.44	0.49	0.54	
− Depreciation	60	60	60	60	60	60	60	60	60	60	60	60	60	60	60	900
+ Loan principal	0	0	0	0	0	0	0	0	0	0	0	0	0	0	0	0
Taxable income	−50	−44	−38	−31	−24	−16	−8	0	9	19	29	40	51	63	76	78
Income tax (− = Savings)	−15	−13	−11	−9	−7	−5	−2	0	3	6	9	12	15	19	23	23
Cash flow after tax, before sale	25	29	34	38	43	49	54	60	67	73	80	88	96	104	113	954
Sales proceeds and year of sale	15														1,884	1,884
Capital gains tax on sale															214	214
Cash from sale after tax and loan															920	920
Cash flow after tax	25	29	34	38	43	49	54	60	67	73	80	88	96	104	1,033	1,874
Internal rate of return								21.20%								

*NOI is net operating income. Investment is the total purchase price, including loan.

Assumptions:

Tax bracket	30%
Cash investment	$ 250
Loan	$ 750
Total investment	$1,000
Years loan amortization	99 yrs.
Loan interest	12%
Loan principal and interest	$ 90
Building/Total investment	90%
Initial depreciable assets	$ 900
Years straight line depreciation	15 yrs.
Year of sale	15 yrs.
Capitalization rate at sale	12%
Inflation	6%
Mortgage constant	12.0002%

Table 8-6

	Year															
	1	2	3	4	5	6	7	8	9	10	11	12	13	14	15	Totals
Loan (beginning)	750	750	750	750	750	750	750	750	750	750	750	750	750	750	750	750
Interest, annual	90	90	90	90	90	90	90	90	90	90	90	90	90	90	90	1,350
Principal reduction	0	0	0	0	0	0	0	0	0	0	0	0	0	0	0	0
Loan (end)	750	750	750	750	750	750	750	750	750	750	750	750	750	750	750	750
NOI/Investment*	0.10															
NOI	100	106	112	119	126	134	142	150	159	169	179	190	201	213	226	2,328
NOI/Total investment	0.10	0.11	0.11	0.12	0.13	0.13	0.14	0.15	0.16	0.17	0.18	0.19	0.20	0.21	0.23	
− Loan principal and interest	90	90	90	90	90	90	90	90	90	90	90	90	90	90	90	1,350
Cash flow before tax	10	16	22	29	36	44	52	60	69	79	89	100	111	123	136	978
Cash flow/Cash investment	0.04	0.06	0.09	0.12	0.14	0.18	0.21	0.24	0.28	0.32	0.36	0.40	0.44	0.49	0.54	
− Depreciation	60	60	60	60	60	60	60	60	60	60	60	60	60	60	60	900
+ Loan principal	0	0	0	0	0	0	0	0	0	0	0	0	0	0	0	0
Taxable income	−50	−44	−38	−31	−24	−16	−8	0	9	19	29	40	51	63	76	78
Income tax (− = Savings)	−25	−22	−19	−15	−12	−8	−4	0	5	9	15	20	26	32	38	39
Cash flow after tax, before sale	35	38	41	45	48	52	56	60	65	69	75	80	86	92	98	939
Sales proceeds and year of sale		15													1,884	1,884
Capital gains tax on sale															357	357
Cash from sale after tax and loan															777	777
Cash flow after tax	35	38	41	45	48	52	56	60	65	69	75	80	86	92	875	1,716
Internal rate of return									21.95%							

*NOI is net operating income. Investment is the total purchase price, including loan.

Assumptions:

Tax bracket	50%
Cash investment	$ 250
Loan	$ 750
Total investment	$1,000
Years loan amortization	150 yrs.
Loan interest	12%
Loan principal and interest	$ 90
Building/Total investment	90%
Initial depreciable assets	$ 900
Years straight line depreciation	15 yrs.
Year of sale	15 yrs.
Capitalization rate at sale	12%
Inflation	6%
Mortgage constant	12.0000004968%

Table 8-7

										Year						
	1	2	3	4	5	6	7	8	9	10	11	12	13	14	15	Totals
Loan (beginning)	750	744	738	731	723	714	704	693	681	667	651	634	614	592	568	
Interest, annual	90	89	89	88	87	86	85	83	82	80	78	76	74	71	68	1,225
Principal reduction	6	6	7	8	9	10	11	12	14	16	17	20	22	25	27	210
Loan (end)	744	738	731	723	714	704	693	681	667	651	634	614	592	568	540	
NOI/Investment*	0.10															
NOI	100	106	112	119	126	134	142	150	159	169	179	190	201	213	226	2,328
NOI/Total investment	0.10	0.11	0.11	0.12	0.13	0.13	0.14	0.15	0.16	0.17	0.18	0.19	0.20	0.21	0.23	
− Loan principal and interest	96	96	96	96	96	96	96	96	96	96	96	96	96	96	96	1,434
Cash flow before tax	4	10	17	23	31	38	46	55	64	73	83	94	106	118	130	893
Cash flow/Cash investment	0.02	0.04	0.07	0.09	0.12	0.15	0.18	0.22	0.26	0.29	0.33	0.38	0.42	0.47	0.52	
− Depreciation	60	60	60	60	60	60	60	60	60	60	60	60	60	60	60	900
+ Loan principal	6	6	7	8	9	10	11	12	14	16	17	20	22	25	27	210
Taxable income	−50	−43	−36	−29	−21	−12	−3	7	18	29	41	54	68	82	98	203
Income tax (− = Savings)	−20	−17	−14	−11	−8	−5	−1	3	7	12	16	22	27	33	39	81
Cash flow after tax, before sale	24	28	31	35	39	43	47	52	57	62	67	73	79	85	91	812
Sales proceeds and year of sale			15												1,413	1,413
Capital gains tax on sale															210	210
Cash from sale after tax and loan															663	663
Cash flow after tax	24	28	31	35	39	43	47	52	57	62	67	73	79	85	754	1,475
Internal rate of return							18.83%									

*NOI is net operating income. Investment is the total purchase price, including loan.

Assumptions:	Tax bracket	40%
	Cash investment	$ 250
	Loan	$ 750
	Total investment	$1,000
	Years loan amortization	25 yrs.
	Loan interest	12%
	Loan principal and interest	$ 96
	Building/Total investment	90%
	Initial depreciable assets	$ 900
	Years straight line depreciation	15 yrs.
	Year of sale	15 yrs.
	Capitalization rate at sale	16%
	Inflation	6%
	Mortgage constant	12.7500%

Table 8-8

	Year															
	1	2	3	4	5	6	7	8	9	10	11	12	13	14	15	Totals
Loan (beginning)	750	744	738	731	723	714	704	693	681	667	651	634	614	592	568	
Interest, annual	90	89	89	88	87	86	85	83	82	80	78	76	74	71	68	1,225
Principal reduction	6	6	7	8	8	10	11	12	14	16	17	20	22	25	27	210
Loan (end)	744	738	731	723	714	704	693	681	667	651	634	614	592	568	540	
NOI/Investment*	0.10															
NOI	100	106	112	119	126	134	142	150	159	169	179	190	201	213	226	2,328
NOI/Total investment	0.10	0.11	0.11	0.12	0.13	0.13	0.14	0.15	0.16	0.17	0.18	0.19	0.20	0.21	0.23	
− Loan principal and interest	96	96	96	96	96	96	96	96	96	96	96	96	96	96	96	1,434
Cash flow before tax	4	10	17	23	31	38	46	55	64	73	83	94	106	118	130	893
Cash flow/Cash investment	0.02	0.04	0.07	0.09	0.12	0.15	0.18	0.22	0.26	0.29	0.33	0.38	0.42	0.47	0.52	
− Depreciation	60	60	60	60	60	60	60	60	60	60	60	60	60	60	60	900
+ Loan principal	6	6	7	8	9	10	11	12	14	16	17	20	22	25	27	210
Taxable income	−50	−43	−36	−29	−21	−12	−3	7	18	29	41	54	68	82	98	203
Income tax (− = Savings)	0	0	0	0	0	0	0	0	0	0	0	0	0	0	0	0
Cash flow after tax, before sale	4	10	17	23	31	38	46	55	64	73	83	94	106	118	130	893
Sales proceeds and year of sale		15													1,884	1,884
Capital gains tax on sale															0	0
Cash from sale after tax and loan															1,344	1,344
Cash flow after tax	4	10	17	23	31	38	46	55	64	73	83	94	106	118	1,474	2,237
Internal rate of return								19.70%								

*NOI is net operating income. Investment is the total purchase price, including loan.

Assumptions:		
Tax bracket	0%	
Cash investment	$ 250	
Loan	$ 750	
Total investment	$1,000	
Years loan amortization	25 yrs.	
Loan interest	12%	
Loan principal and interest	$ 96	
Building/Total investment	90%	
Initial depreciable assets	$ 900	
Years straight line depreciation	15 yrs.	
Year of sale	15 yrs.	
Capitalization rate at sale	12%	
Inflation	6%	
Mortgage constant	12.7500%	

Table 8–9

		Year														
	1	2	3	4	5	6	7	8	9	10	11	12	13	14	15	Totals
Loan (beginning)	500	495	489	483	476	469	461	452	442	431	419	406	391	375	358	
Interest, annual	50	49	49	48	48	47	46	45	44	43	42	41	39	38	36	665
Principal reduction	5	6	6	7	7	8	9	10	11	12	13	15	16	18	19	162
Loan (end)	495	489	483	476	469	461	452	442	431	419	406	391	375	358	338	
NOI/Investment*	0.10															
NOI	100	106	112	119	126	134	142	150	159	169	179	190	201	213	226	2,328
NOI/Total investment	0.10	0.11	0.11	0.12	0.13	0.13	0.14	0.15	0.16	0.17	0.18	0.19	0.20	0.21	0.23	
– Loan principal and interest	55	55	55	55	55	55	55	55	55	55	55	55	55	55	55	826
Cash flow before tax	45	51	57	64	71	79	87	95	104	114	124	135	146	158	171	1,501
Cash flow/Cash investment	0.09	0.10	0.11	0.13	0.14	0.16	0.17	0.19	0.21	0.23	0.25	0.27	0.29	0.32	0.34	
– Depreciation	60	60	60	60	60	60	60	60	60	60	60	60	60	60	60	900
+ Loan principal	5	6	6	7	7	8	9	10	11	12	13	15	16	18	19	162
Taxable income	–10	–3	3	11	19	27	36	45	55	66	77	89	102	116	130	763
Income tax (– = Savings)	–5	–2	2	5	9	13	18	23	28	33	39	45	51	58	65	381
Cash flow after tax, before sale	50	53	56	59	62	65	69	73	77	81	85	90	95	100	106	1,120
Sales proceeds and year of sale	15														2,261	2,261
Capital gains tax on sale															432	432
Cash from sale after tax and loan															1,490	1,490
Cash flow after tax	50	53	56	59	62	65	69	73	77	81	85	90	95	100	1,596	2,610
Internal rate of return								16.6%								

*NOI is net operating income. Investment is the total purchase price, including loan.

Assumptions:	Tax bracket	50%
	Cash investment	$ 500
	Loan	$ 500
	Total investment	$1,000
	Years loan amortization	25 yrs.
	Loan interest	10%
	Loan principal and interest	$ 55
	Building/Total investment	90%
	Initial depreciable assets	$ 900
	Years straight line depreciation	15 yrs.
	Year of sale	15 yrs.
	Capitalization rate at sale	10%
	Inflation	6%
	Mortgage constant	11.02%

Table 8–10

								Year								
	1	2	3	4	5	6	7	8	9	10	11	12	13	14	15	Totals
Loan (beginning)	750	742	734	725	715	703	691	678	663	646	628	609	587	563	537	
Interest, annual	75	74	73	72	71	70	69	68	66	65	63	61	59	56	54	997
Principal reduction	8	8	9	10	11	12	14	15	16	18	20	22	24	26	29	242
Loan (end)	742	734	725	715	703	691	678	663	646	628	609	587	563	537	508	
NOI/Investment*	0.10															
NOI	100	106	112	119	126	134	142	150	159	169	179	190	201	213	226	2,328
NOI/Total investment	0.10	0.11	0.11	0.12	0.13	0.13	0.14	0.15	0.16	0.17	0.18	0.19	0.20	0.21	0.23	
– Loan principal and interest	83	83	83	83	83	83	83	83	83	83	83	83	83	83	83	1,239
Cash flow before tax	17	23	30	36	44	51	59	68	77	86	96	107	119	131	143	1,088
Cash flow/Cash investment	0.07	0.09	0.12	0.15	0.17	0.20	0.24	0.27	0.31	0.35	0.39	0.43	0.47	0.52	0.57	
– Depreciation	60	60	60	60	60	60	60	60	60	60	60	60	60	60	60	900
+ Loan principal	8	8	9	10	11	12	14	15	16	18	20	22	24	26	29	242
Taxable income	–35	–28	–21	–13	–5	3	13	23	33	44	56	69	83	97	112	431
Income tax (– = Savings)	–17	–14	–11	–7	–3	2	6	11	17	22	28	34	41	48	56	215
Cash flow after tax, before sale	35	37	40	43	46	49	53	56	60	64	68	73	77	82	87	873
Sales proceeds and year of sale	15														2,261	2,261
Capital gains tax on sale															432	432
Cash from sale after tax and loan															1,321	1,321
Cash flow after tax	35	37	40	43	46	49	53	56	60	64	68	73	77	82	1,408	2,194
Internal rate of return								23.1%								

*NOI is net operating income. Investment is the total purchase price, including loan.

Assumptions:		
Tax bracket		50%
Cash investment		$ 250
Loan		$ 750
Total investment		$1,000
Years loan amortization		25 yrs.
Loan interest		10%
Loan principal and interest		$ 83
Building/Total investment		90%
Initial depreciable assets		$ 900
Years straight line depreciation		15 yrs.
Year of sale		15 yrs.
Capitalization rate at sale		10%
Inflation		6%
Mortgage constant		11.02%

Table 8–11

								Year								
	1	2	3	4	5	6	7	8	9	10	11	12	13	14	15	Totals
Loan (beginning)	500	495	489	483	476	469	461	452	442	431	419	406	391	375	358	
Interest, annual	50	49	49	48	48	47	46	45	44	43	42	41	39	38	36	665
Principal reduction	5	6	6	7	7	8	9	10	11	12	13	15	16	18	19	162
Loan (end)	495	489	483	476	469	461	452	442	431	419	406	391	375	358	338	
NOI/Investment*	0.10															
NOI	100	106	112	119	126	134	142	150	159	169	179	190	201	213	226	2,328
NOI/Total investment	0.10	0.11	0.11	0.12	0.13	0.13	0.14	0.15	0.16	0.17	0.18	0.19	0.20	0.21	0.23	
– Loan principal and interest	55	55	55	55	55	55	55	55	55	55	55	55	55	55	55	826
Cash flow before tax	45	51	57	64	71	79	87	95	104	114	124	135	146	158	171	1,501
Cash flow/Cash investment	0.09	0.10	0.11	0.13	0.14	0.16	0.17	0.19	0.21	0.23	0.25	0.27	0.29	0.32	0.34	
– Depreciation	60	60	60	60	60	60	60	60	60	60	60	60	60	60	60	900
+ Loan principal	5	6	6	7	7	8	9	10	11	12	13	15	16	18	19	162
Taxable income	–10	–3	3	11	19	27	36	45	55	66	77	89	102	116	130	763
Income tax (– = Savings)	–3	–1	1	3	6	8	11	14	17	20	23	27	31	35	39	229
Cash flow after tax, before sale	48	52	56	61	66	71	76	82	88	94	101	108	116	123	132	1,272
Sales proceeds and year of sale		15													2,261	2,261
Capital gains tax on sale															259	259
Cash from sale after tax and loan															1,663	1,663
Cash flow after tax	48	52	56	61	66	71	76	82	88	94	101	108	116	123	1,795	2,936
Internal rate of return								17.7%								

*NOI is net operating income. Investment is the total purchase price, including loan.

Assumptions:	Tax bracket	30%
	Cash investment	$ 500
	Loan	$ 500
	Total investment	$1,000
	Years loan amortization	25 yrs.
	Loan interest	10%
	Loan principal and interest	$ 55
	Building/Total investment	90%
	Initial depreciable assets	$ 900
	Years straight line depreciation	15 yrs.
	Year of sale	15 yrs.
	Capitalization rate at sale	10%
	Inflation	6%
	Mortgage constant	11.02%

Table 8–12

									Year							
	1	2	3	4	5	6	7	8	9	10	11	12	13	14	15	Totals
Loan (beginning)	750	742	734	725	715	703	691	678	663	646	628	609	587	563	537	
Interest, annual	75	74	73	72	71	70	69	68	66	65	63	61	59	56	54	997
Principal reduction	8	8	9	10	11	12	14	15	16	18	20	22	24	26	29	242
Loan (end)	742	734	725	715	703	691	678	663	646	628	609	587	563	537	508	
NOI/Investment*	0.10															
NOI	100	106	112	119	126	134	142	150	159	169	179	190	201	213	226	2,328
NOI/Total investment	0.10	0.11	0.11	0.12	0.13	0.13	0.14	0.15	0.16	0.17	0.18	0.19	0.20	0.21	0.23	
− Loan principal and interest	83	83	83	83	83	83	83	83	83	83	83	83	83	83	83	1,239
Cash before tax	17	23	30	36	44	51	59	68	77	86	96	107	119	131	143	1,088
Cash flow/Cash investment	0.07	0.09	0.12	0.15	0.17	0.20	0.24	0.27	0.31	0.35	0.39	0.43	0.47	0.52	0.57	
− Depreciation	60	60	60	60	60	60	60	60	60	60	60	60	60	60	60	900
+ Loan principal	8	8	9	10	11	12	14	15	16	18	20	22	24	26	29	242
Taxable income	−35	−28	−21	−13	−5	3	13	23	33	44	56	69	83	97	112	431
Income tax (− = Savings)	−10	−8	−6	−4	−2	1	4	7	10	13	17	21	25	29	34	129
Cash flow after tax, before sale	28	32	36	40	45	50	55	61	67	73	80	87	94	102	110	959
Sales proceeds and year of sale	15														2,261	2,261
Capital gains tax on sale															259	259
Cash from sale after tax and loan															1,494	1,494
Cash flow after tax	28	32	36	40	45	50	55	61	67	73	80	87	94	102	1,604	2,453
Internal rate of return								23.3%								

*NOI is net operating income. Investment is the total purchase price, including loan.

Assumptions:		
Tax bracket	30%	
Cash investment	$ 250	
Loan	$ 750	
Total investment	$1,000	
Years loan amortization	25 yrs.	
Loan interest	10%	
Loan principal and interest	$ 83	
Building/Total investment	90%	
Initial depreciable assets	$ 900	
Years straight line depreciation	15 yrs.	
Year of sale	15 yrs.	
Capitalization rate at sale	10%	
Inflation	6%	
Mortgage constant	11.02%	

Table 8–13

| | | | | | | | | | Year | | | | | | | |
	1	2	3	4	5	6	7	8	9	10	11	12	13	14	15	Totals
Loan (beginning)	0	0	0	0	0	0	0	0	0	0	0	0	0	0	0	0
Interest, annual	0	0	0	0	0	0	0	0	0	0	0	0	0	0	0	0
Principal reduction	0	0	0	0	0	0	0	0	0	0	0	0	0	0	0	0
Loan (end)	0	0	0	0	0	0	0	0	0	0	0	0	0	0	0	0
NOI/Investment*	0.11															
NOI	115	122	129	137	145	154	163	173	183	194	206	218	231	245	260	2,677
NOI/Total investment	0.12	0.12	0.13	0.14	0.15	0.15	0.16	0.17	0.18	0.19	0.21	0.22	0.23	0.25	0.26	
– Loan principal and interest	0	0	0	0	0	0	0	0	0	0	0	0	0	0	0	0
Cash flow before tax	115	122	129	137	145	154	163	173	183	194	206	218	231	245	260	2,677
Cash flow/Cash investment	0.12	0.12	0.13	0.14	0.15	0.15	0.16	0.17	0.18	0.19	0.21	0.22	0.23	0.25	0.26	
– Depreciation	60	60	60	60	60	60	60	60	60	60	60	60	60	60	60	900
+ Loan principal	0	0	0	0	0	0	0	0	0	0	0	0	0	0	0	0
Taxable income	55	62	69	77	85	94	103	113	123	134	146	158	171	185	200	1,777
Income tax (– = Savings)	0	0	0	0	0	0	0	0	0	0	0	0	0	0	0	0
Cash flow after tax, before sale	115	122	129	137	145	154	163	173	183	194	206	218	231	245	260	2,677
Sales proceeds and year of sale		15													2,364	2,364
Capital gains tax on sale															0	0
Cash from sale after tax and loan															2,364	2,364
Cash flow after tax	115	122	129	137	145	154	163	173	183	194	206	218	231	245	2,624	5,040
Internal rate of return								17.46%								

*NOI is net operating income. Investment is the total purchase price, including loan.

Assumptions:

Tax bracket	00%
Cash investment	$1,000
Loan	$ 0
Total investment	$1,000
Years loan amortization	25 yrs.
Loan interest	00%
Loan principal and interest	$ 0
Building/Total investment	0.90
Initial depreciable assets	$ 900
Years straight line depreciation	15 yrs.
Year of sale	15 yrs.
Capitalization rate at sale	11%
Inflation	6%
Mortgage constant	3.99838%

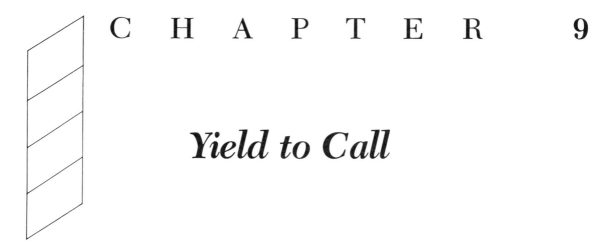

C H A P T E R 9

Yield to Call

Most bonds are callable by the issuer at a premium prior to the maturity date of the bonds. The reason that bonds include a callable provision is to allow the issuer to redeem the bonds (and perhaps issue new ones) in the event that interest rates drop materially after the original issuance of the bonds. Such a refinancing would reduce the issuer's interest costs.

Therefore investors who purchase bonds at a premium (over $1,000) MUST BEWARE of callable provisions.

For example, consider the following situation.

Bond purchase price	$1,103
Years to maturity	30
Coupon rate	10%
Yield to maturity (refer to Graph 9–1)	9%

The yield to maturity is 9 percent if the bond is held for 30 years and redeemed at maturity for $1,000. However if the bond is callable, then—in the event that the bond is called prior to maturity—the yield will not be 9 percent. Let us assume that the aforementioned bond is callable as follows:

Call date	5 years hence
Call price	$1,034

To determine the yield to call, several methods are available.

Graph 9–1
Bond Yield to Maturity: 30 Years

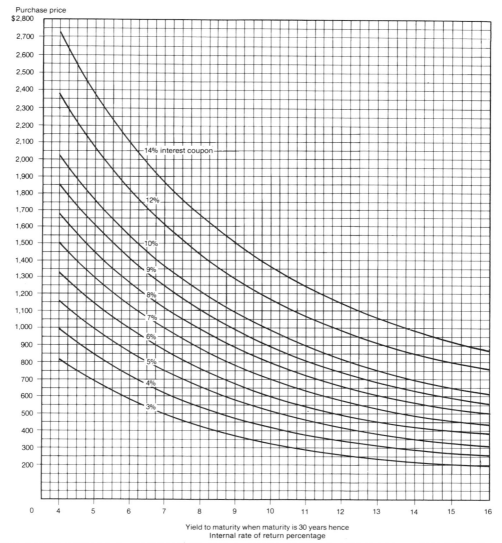

Yield to maturity when maturity is 30 years hence
Internal rate of return percentage

Formula

The formula is

$$A = R\left[\frac{1 - (1 + i)^{-n}}{i}\right] + S(1 + i)^{-n}$$

Where,

$$A = \text{purchase price of } \$1,103$$
$$R = \text{annual interest of } \$100$$
$$n = \text{years to call, } 5$$
$$S = \text{call price, } \$1,034$$
$$i = \text{yield to call.}$$

Then,

$$1,103 = 100\left[\frac{1 - (1 + i)^{-5}}{i}\right] + 1,034(1 + i)^{-5}$$

This equation may be solved by trial and error values for "i". The yield to call is only 8 percent. Thus if the bond is called, the investor's yield would be reduced by 100 basis points; i.e., from 9 percent to 8 percent.
    To summarize,

The 30-year yield to maturity is	9%
The 5-year yield to call is[1]	8%

Graphs or Tables

Bond yield to maturity graphs (or other published bond tables) may be used to determine yield to call if, and only if, adjustments are made by converting the call price to a $1,000 base as described below. First, determine the ratio of $1,000 to the call price.

$$\text{Maturity to call ratio} = \frac{1,000}{1,034} = 96.7117\%$$

Then, multiply the purchase price by this ratio.

$$\text{Revised purchase price} = 1,103 \times 0.967117 = 1,066.73$$

Then multiply the coupon rate by this ratio.

$$\text{Revised coupon} = 0.10 \times 0.967117 = 0.0967117 \text{ or } \$96.71$$

No adjustment is made to the number of years to call, which in this case remains at five.

Revised purchase price	$1,066.73
Revised coupon	0.0967117
Years to call	5

The above revisions convert the terms of the bond to a $1,000 base rather than $1,034 and the adjustment is such that the interest per

---

[1]The yield to call is less than the yield to maturity because the call date occurs sooner, and affords less time to amortize the "premium" at which the bond was purchased.

dollar invested ($0.090661) and the maturity value per dollar invested ($0.969317) remain the same. Prior to revision, the situation was:

$$\frac{100 \text{ interest}}{1{,}103 \text{ purchase price}} = .0907 \text{ interest per dollar of purchase price}$$

$$\frac{1{,}034 \text{ maturity (call) value}}{1{,}103 \text{ purchase price}} = 0.93744 \text{ maturity value per dollar of purchase}$$

After the revision, the relationship is unchanged.

$$\frac{96.7117 \text{ interest}}{1066.73 \text{ purchase price}} = 0.0907$$

$$\frac{1{,}000 \text{ revised maturity}}{1{,}066.73 \text{ revised purchase price}} = 0.93744$$

Using the revised coupon rate and revised purchase price, the yield to call (8 percent) may be determined from the graphs or from conventional bond yield tables. The revisions are necessary because both the graphs and yield tables are based on a $1,000 maturity value.[2]

Municipals and Call Provisions

At the time of underwriting a municipal issue, call features or special redemption features are one of the items negotiated between the issuers and the underwriters. Naturally, the municipal issuer wants to have as short (e.g., sooner-in-time) a call provision as possible so that if rates fall, it can refund the higher rate issue with the proceeds of a lower rate borrowing. Conversely, the bond purchasers want to have call protection for as long as possible. Typically, buyers have been protected against calls, in recent issuances, for 10 years from the date of original issue.

Extraordinary calls—beware! Some bonds, particularly single-family housing finance issues, contain extraordinary call provisions that allow the issuer to use "unloaned funds" to call bonds *at par* by random lot. Unloaned funds in this context means the portion of the bond issue that the finance authority was unable to lend (to home buyers to fi-

---

[2]The original yield to maturity, or IRR, may be determined by using Graph 5–30. Enter the graph on the vertical axis at the $1,103 purchase price; proceed horizontally to the $100, or 10 percent coupon rate curve; then descend to the bottom axis. The point of intersection is the IRR, 9 percent. The yield to call, or IRR to the projected call date 5 years hence, is obtained from graph 5–5. Enter the graph on the vertical axis with the *revised purchased price*, $1066.73; proceed horizontally to the approximate location of a 9.671 curve (6/10 of the distance from the 9 percent curve toward the 10 percent curve). Then descend to the bottom axis where the yield to call is seen to be about 8 percent. The foregoing IRR's are for a zero tax bracket. For other than a zero tax bracket, the comparable graphs in Chapter 6 are applicable if the bond is purchased at a discount or at par; if purchased at a premium, the graphs in Chapter 5 must be used.

nance home purchases) and may also include the proceeds of prepaid (prior to maturity) home mortgages. Thus beware of buying issues of this nature at a premium as you may find yourself obliged to sell back a bond you bought for $1,200 at its *par value* of $1,000.

Sinking-fund calls—beware! Many revenue bonds also have "sinking funds" that are, in effect, reserves set aside annually from which debt is retired by a sinking-fund call, through random lot selection, *at or near par.* These calls can and do often occur prior to the first ordinary call provision date. Stover Glass & Co.'s July 26, 1983, newsletter states: "If you buy a *new* issue bond at par that is subject to a sinking-fund call, it is sort of like playing Russian roulette. If your bond is called when rates are low, you will be forced to reinvest at the low rates and if called when rates are high, you'll be able to cash your bond in early and get a higher yielding bond." [The real risk here is that the bond you bought for $1,000 may be trading at $1,200 when you are forced to sell to the sinking fund at or near $1,000.] If you buy a secondary market bond that is subject to a sinking-fund call and selling at a premium, be sure you know how active the sinking fund is because if it [the bond] is suddenly called on you, it could result in a loss. If you buy a bond at a discount you can only gain from a sinking-fund call, and the sooner the sinking-fund call occurs, the more substantial your gain will be."

Pre-refunding calls. We spoke earlier of refunding bond issues when the borrower can issue new debt at a lower rate than that being paid on the old debt. But if the old bonds have call protection for some years into the future, the issuer can bring out a new issue at the current lower tax-free rates and invest the proceeds in higher yielding taxable U.S. Treasury issues to be held in an escrowed account for the purpose of paying off the old issue at the earliest possible call date.

This process is called *pre-refunding.* The debtor benefits from the higher yield it receives on the Treasuries than it pays on the new bond issue. Bondholders may benefit by a higher market price resulting from a higher credit rating for the issue. The credit ranking for the bond is likely to be increased to an AAA issue due to the escrowed funds reserved for bond repayment. Also to be considered from the bondholders view, for better or worse, is the shortened maturity, in effect, to the call date.

Refunded but not called. Debtors can follow almost the same process as described in "pre-refunding calls" even when the original bond issue is not callable. In this case, the new issue proceeds are escrowed until maturity. Here the bondholder benefits by an increase in credit rating to AAA without the potential detriment of a shortened maturity.

Broker practice. Bond brokers, as a matter of business ethics and customary procedure, quote the lesser yield to maturity of (a) the yield to call; or, (b) yield to maturity; or else both yields, if the yield to call is below the yield to maturity.

Why yield to call may be lower than yield to maturity. When a bond is purchased at a premium, the coupon interest is partially offset by the premium, that is the excess of the purchase price over the $1,000 maturity value. Since the call date occurs sooner than the maturity date, there is less time to amortize the premium to the call date. Thus, the yield to call date will be lower than the yield to date of maturity.

Beware of mortgage backed bonds bought at a premium. Such mortgage backed bonds as Ginnie-Maes or Freddie-Macs provide cash flow comprised of both interest and repayment of the underlying mortgage loan. Such bonds are usually quoted on a yield basis based on a historical "average" life or duration of the bond, frequently 12 years (even though the underlying mortgage loans may have durations of 20 or 30 years). The 12 year average life is based upon experience. People sell their homes and pay off their house mortgages before maturity of the loan in many or most instances. However, such bonds purchased at a premium with a high coupon rate will be likely to be paid off early by the borrowers (to refinance at a lower rate). Thus, the average life may be less than normal. There will be less time to amortize the premium at which the bond was purchased, and the yield to maturity will be less than that quoted at purchase, since the yield at purchase was based on a 12 year life.

Sinking funds. The existence of a sinking fund may be of concern when a bond is purchased at a premium. A sinking fund bond is one which requires an annual sinking fund "call" of a portion of the bonds outstanding. The bonds which are called are then retired, normally at par value of $1,000. The result of a sinking fund call for an investor in a premium bond will be a lower yield to the sinking fund call date than the investor would have received (and was expecting to receive) if the bonds were held to maturity. Conversely, the purchaser of a discount bond would realize a higher yield if the bonds are called.

Investigate. Investors ought to obtain full details of sinking fund and call provisions before investing. If your broker thinks a "call date" is when you are expecting the broker to telephone you, or if the broker thinks a "sinking fund" is a mutual fund that is declining in price, then find yourself a bond broker who is knowledgeable.

C H A P T E R   10

IRR and Beyond

Even though the IRR concept is terribly useful and informative, it doesn't eliminate the need for thoughtful consideration on the part of investors. IRR is subject to even further refinement to fine-tune the decision-making process. Two additional refinements are possible: *partitioning* the IRR and determining the *marginal* IRR.

Consider the alternative investments presented in Table 10–1. Both have the same IRR, 39.08 percent. Yet in the case of Dr. Markman's property, there are no before tax cash flow benefits; the entire return is derived from tax benefits (interest expense on loan and depreciation) and the projected sales proceeds in the fifth year. On the other hand, Mr. McClintock's property projects a strong annual before tax cash flow, has normal tax benefits, and is not expected to show significant after tax proceeds at sale. Even though both Dr. Markman's property and Mr. McClintock's property have the same projected IRR, which would you rather buy?

Certainly, the IRR that is ultimately realized (as opposed to projected) for Mr. McClintock's property is much more likely to equal or exceed stated projections than Dr. Markman's. Consider the following breakdown of the IRR composition (after first obtaining the net present value of each cash flow stream discounted at the overall IRR rate of 39.08 percent):

As a percentage of total benefit:	Dr. Markman	Mr. McClintock
Before tax cash flow	0.00%	59.94%
Tax benefits	38.51	7.50
Subtotal	38.51	67.45
Sales proceeds, after tax	61.49	32.55
Total	100.00%	100.00%

Table 10–1
Partitioning IRR

Seller	Year 0	1	2	3	4	5	Total	Percent of Total	Present Value at IRR Rate	Present Value as Percent of Total
Dr. Markman:										
Cash investment	100,000						0	0.00%	0	0.00%
Cash flow before tax	0	20,000	19,000	18,000	17,000	16,000	90,000	21.95	38,511	38.51
Subtotal		20,000	19,000	18,000	17,000	16,000			38,511	38.51
Sales proceeds (after tax and loan)						320,000	320,000	78.05	61,489	61.49
Cash flow (after tax)	–100,000	20,000	19,000	18,000	17,000	336,000	410,000	100.00	100,000	100.00
Internal rate of return						39.08%				
Mr. McClintock:										
Cash investment	100,000									
Cash flow before tax	0	29,000	29,000	29,000	29,000	29,000	145,000	44.02	59,943	59.94
Tax benefits (cost)		5,000	4,000	3,000	2,000	1,000	15,000	4.55	7,504	7.50
Subtotal		34,000	33,000	32,000	31,000	30,000			67,447	67.45
Sales proceeds (after tax and loan)						169,425	169,425	51.43	32,553	32.55
Cash flow (after tax)	–100,000	34,000	33,000	32,000	31,000	199,425	329,425	100.00	100,000	100.00
Internal rate of return						39.08%				

Since projected cash flow and tax benefits are much more likely to be accurately predicted than are sales proceeds five years down the road, the intelligent choice would be Mr. McClintock's property, where 67.45 percent of the IRR (compared to 38.51 percent for Dr. Markman) results from the more predictable stream of cash flows (see Graph 10–1).

The problem in real estate investing, like investing in anything, is to identify the risks. And what better way is there to intelligently choose among alternative investments than by partitioning the IRR?

Graph 10–1
Partitioned IRR: Percent of IRR Resulting from Cash Flow, Tax Benefits, Resale

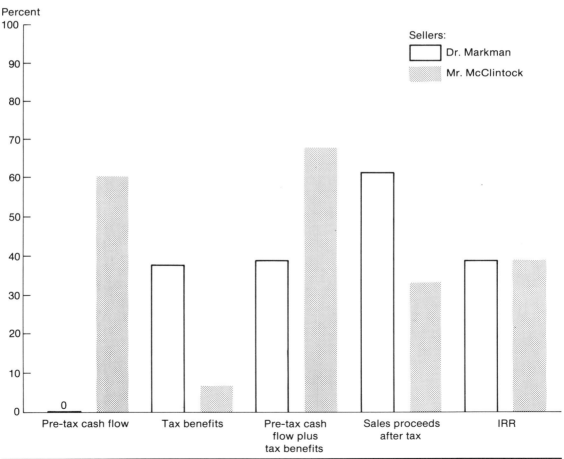

Ranked in order of security or safety, the components to partition are:

1. Initial or guaranteed before tax cash flow (such as base rent on a retail lease that also has a percentage or overage rent. Include future rent increases that are contractually binding in existing leases).

2. Tax benefits (subject to the risk of change in tax laws and a change in the investor's marginal tax rate).

3. Growth in cash flow above initial or base level (such as income from percentage rents or future increases in rent that are not contractually binding).

4. Sales proceeds, including equity buildup through loan amortization—to the extent of the original equity investment.

5. Sales proceeds—resulting from expected future appreciation in the value of the property.

When to Sell the Investment

When the rate of return to be gained by holding the investment is less than the rate of return that is obtainable by investing the after tax sales proceeds in a different investment, then it is time to sell. Because of the diminishing nature of tax benefits that result from finite depreciation, replacement investments eventually become an alluring possible alternative.

Please refer to Table 10–2, **Marginal Internal Rate of Return.** This presents a 15-year analysis for a hypothetical investment with $250 cash invested and a $750 loan for a 40 percent tax bracket investor. The 15-year IRR is 23.17 percent. However, the lower section of the table proceeds to determine cash flows for holding periods of 1 to 14 years, as well. Notice that the element that changes is the after tax proceeds of sale which increases with the length of the holding period. (Gross sales proceeds are determined by capitalizing at a stated rate, 10 percent in the example, the net operating income in the year of sale. For example, in year 10, the NOI is $169, and the sales proceeds are 169 ÷ .10, or $1,690.)

Look at the heading near the bottom entitled **Average IRR: Holdings of 1 to 15 Years.** This shows the IRR for varying holding periods. It increases each year until it peaks in the sixth year, then slightly diminishes each year thereafter. However, from year 2 through year 15, it is never less than 21.66 percent. Bear in mind that this is an AVERAGE IRR in that it always includes the results from the first year to the last year of the desired holding period. If the first 4 years' results were particularly beneficial, they will still affect the results for a 10- or 12-year analysis favorably.

Assumptions:

Tax bracket	40%
Cash investment	$250
Loan	$750
Total investment	$1,000
Years loan amortization	25
Loan interest	10%
Loan principal and interest	$83
Building/Total investment	90%
Initial depreciable assets	$900
Years straight line depreciation	15
Year of sale	15
Capitalization rate at sale	10%
Inflation	6%
Mortgage constant	11.017%

Table 10–2
Marginal IRR

	Year															Totals
	1	2	3	4	5	6	7	8	9	10	11	12	13	14	15	
Loan (beginning of year)	750	742	734	725	715	703	691	678	663	646	628	609	587	563	537	
Annual interest	75	74	73	72	71	70	69	68	66	65	63	61	59	56	54	997
Principal reduction during year	8	8	9	10	11	12	14	15	16	18	20	22	24	26	29	242
Loan (end of year)	742	734	725	715	703	691	678	663	646	628	609	587	563	537	508	
Net operating income (NOI)/Cash investment**	10.00%															
Net operating income	100	106	112	119	126	134	142	150	159	169	179	190	201	213	226	2,328
NOI/Total investment	10.00%	10.60%	11.24%	11.91%	12.62%	13.38%	14.19%	15.04%	15.94%	16.89%	17.91%	18.98%	20.12%	21.33%	22.61%	
Less: Loan principal and interest	83	83	83	83	83	83	83	83	83	83	83	83	83	83	83	1,239
Cash flow before tax	17	23	30	36	44	51	59	68	77	86	96	107	119	131	143	1,088
Cash flow/Cash investment	6.95%	9.35%	11.89%	14.59%	17.45%	20.48%	23.69%	27.09%	30.70%	34.53%	38.58%	42.88%	47.44%	52.27%	57.39%	
Less: Depreciation	60	60	60	60	60	60	60	60	60	60	60	60	60	60	60	900
Plus: Loan principal repayment during year	8	8	9	10	11	12	14	15	16	18	20	22	24	26	29	242
Taxable income	−35	−28	−21	−13	−5	3	13	23	33	44	56	69	83	97	112	431
Income Tax (− indicates savings in tax)	−14	−11	−8	−5	−2	1	5	9	13	18	22	28	33	39	45	172

Table 10–2 (continued)

	Year															Totals
	1	2	3	4	5	6	7	8	9	10	11	12	13	14	15	
Cash flow after tax, before sale	31	35	38	42	46	50	54	59	64	69	74	80	86	92	98	916
Sales proceeds in year of sale		15													2,261	2,261
Capital gains tax on sale															346	346
Cash from sale after tax and loan repayment															1,407	1,407
Cash flow after tax	31	35	38	42	46	50	54	59	64	69	74	80	86	92	1,506	2,323
Internal rate of return								23.17%								
Marginal IRR based on sale at each year-end:																
Sales proceeds	1,000	1,060	1,124	1,191	1,262	1,338	1,419	1,504	1,594	1,689	1,791	1,898	2,012	2,133	2,261	
Capital gains tax on sale	10	29	49	69	90	112	134	157	181	206	232	259	287	316	346	
Cash from sale after tax and loan repayment	248	297	350	407	469	535	607	683	766	855	950	1,052	1,162	1,281	1,407	
Cash flow if sale in year 1	279															
Cash flow sale in year 2	31	332														
Cash flow sale in year 3	31	35	388													
Cash flow sale in year 4	31	35	38	449												
Cash flow sale in year 5	31	35	38	42	515											
Cash flow sale in year 6	31	35	38	42	46	585										
Cash flow sale in year 7	31	35	38	42	46	50	661									
Cash flow sale in year 8	31	35	38	42	46	50	54	742								
Cash flow sale in year 9	31	35	38	42	46	50	54	59	830							
Cash flow sale in year 10	31	35	38	42	46	50	54	59	64	923						
Cash flow sale in year 11	31	35	38	42	46	50	54	59	64	69	1,024					
Cash flow sale in year 12	31	35	38	42	46	50	54	59	64	69	74	1,132				
Cash flow sale in year 13	31	35	38	42	46	50	54	59	64	69	74	80	1,248			
Cash flow sale in year 14	31	35	38	42	46	50	54	59	64	69	74	80	86	1,372		
Cash flow sale in year 15	31	35	38	42	46	50	54	59	64	69	74	80	86	92	1,506	
Average IRR: Holdings of 1 to 15 years	11.76%	21.66%	24.29%	25.12%	25.32%	25.25%	25.05%	24.81%	24.55%	24.29%	24.04%	23.80%	23.58%	23.37%	23.17%	

Table 10–2 (*concluded*)

		Year															Totals
		1	2	3	4	5	6	7	8	9	10	11	12	13	14	15	
Marginal IRR: Percent return from holding 1 more year		11.76%	33.81%	30.69%	28.27%	26.33%	24.76%	23.44%	22.33%	21.37%	20.54%	19.81%	19.16%	18.58%	18.07%	17.60%	
Proof that no reinvestment is needed to achieve the stated IRR 15 year analysis										23.17%							Totals
	Total																
Outstanding (unrecovered) cash investment		$250	$277	$306	$339	$375	$417	$463	$517	$578	$648	$729	$824	$ 936	$1,067	$1,222	
Cash flow (after tax) for year		31	35	38	42	46	50	54	59	64	69	74	80	86	92	1,506	2,323
IRR × outstanding cash investment		58	64	71	78	87	97	107	120	134	150	169	191	217	247	283	2,073
Reduction in outstanding investment (recovery)		−27	−29	−33	−37	−41	−47	−53	−61	−70	−82	−95	−111	−131	−155	1,223	250
Outstanding cash investment at end of year		277	306	339	375	417	463	517	578	648	729	824	936	1,067	1,222	0	

How can we avoid this "average" syndrome? By using the "marginal return concept." Freshman economics says that the marginal return is that obtained from adding one more unit to what you already have. It is the return on "that one more unit," not the average for all the units. The marginal concept·is often thought of in terms of taxation. The important consideration in looking at tax cost or tax savings is the marginal rate of tax, how much tax am I going to pay by adding or subtracting $1 of income to what I already have?

In this case, we want to know when to sell the investment. We have already set forth the proposition that the time to sell is when the return for holding is less than the return obtainable by investing the after tax sales proceeds in an alternate investment. To determine the rate obtained by continuing to hold the investment, the marginal IRR is an accurate measure. *The marginal IRR for year n is a measure of how much more cash the investor will have by selling in year n compared to what he or she would have from selling the previous year, year n − 1.* The increase in cash by selling in year *n* is divided by the cash that would have resulted from a sale in year *n* − 1.

A. The increase in cash by selling in year *n* is the cash from the sale after tax and loan plus, the cash flow after tax, before sale in that year; less, the cash from sales proceeds after tax and loan repayment at the end of year *n* − 1.

B. The cash that would have resulted from a sale in year *n* − 1 is the cash from sales proceeds after tax and loan repayment at the end of year *n* − 1.

The marginal IRR is simply A divided by B. For a sale in year 6, this would be ($50 + $535 − $469) ÷ $469, or 24.8 percent. **In other words, the marginal return is the percent return from holding the investment one more year.** The marginal return so obtained is thus directly comparable to IRR's obtainable from alternative investments.

Note that in Table 10–2, the marginal return is greater than the average IRR for holdings of 1–5 years and is less than the average IRR for holdings of 6 years or more.

If, in year 8, an investment is obtainable with an IRR of 25 percent, then the existing investment should be considered for sale to obtain the alternate, because the marginal return for continuing to hold the existing investment for year 8 is only 22.3 percent. (Naturally, another possibility would be to obtain both by refinancing the existing investment and using the proceeds of the loan to acquire the alternate.)

The Real McCoy

You may be thinking, "All these illustrations are so farfetched. Where can you buy a property for $1,000 with $250 cash? What I want to see is an analysis of a real situation." OK. But if you are adverse to detail, you aren't going to be happy with what follows.

Presented in Table 10–3 is a real pro forma analysis that I prepared for an actual property that my clients and I purchased recently. It is a freestanding retail store of 3,000 square feet in Louisville. The lot is 75' x 200'. The property is leased to a national firm that, together with franchisees, sells about $500 million per year. In addition to a base rent of $6,000 per year, the tenant pays a percentage rent equal to 1 percent of sales in excess of $375,000 per year. Last year the store sold $614,000, so percentage rents are already being paid. Sales are assumed to increase at the rate of inflation, which I projected at 6 percent per year. Loan financing is at prime plus ½ percent, interest only.

The real estate analysis program, which I constructed, allows any of the assumptions to be changed and the results instantly (almost) recomputed. For example, analyzing the effect of varying assumptions in the following areas are useful—tax bracket, inflation rate, size of loan, interest rate, and capitalization rate upon resale. Analysis of Table 10–3 shows that 25 to 30 percent interest would be required for a fully taxed investment to be equal to the return from this property (see equivalent return on a fully taxed investment). The *after tax* IRR is projected to be almost 15 percent. The *marginal* IRR peaks in the third year at 17.48 percent but remains above 15 percent for holdings of anywhere from 2 to 15 years.

Table 10–4 depicts the results of *partitioning* the IRR of the investment depicted in Table 10–3. In this instance, I have used the five-year holding period, wherein the average IRR was 14.77 percent. (Remember these are after tax results.)

The results of the partitioning show that:

Source	IRR Percentage
Cash flow before tax	37.88%
Tax benefits (cost)	6.89
Subtotal	44.76
Sales proceeds, after tax	55.24
Total	100.00

What Reinvestment Percent Rate Is Needed to Achieve IRR?

Alice Ann Brown is thinking of making a real estate investment, and she has studied the projected financial results including the IRR, which is estimated to be 20 percent. She realizes that the IRR is an after tax result. But, she ponders, is it necessary to reinvest the cash flow each year at a rate equal to the IRR in order to wind up with true results equal to the IRR at purchase?

This is a very significant question. If the answer is yes, Alice Ann, you must reinvest at a reinvestment rate equal to the IRR, then it means that a reinvestment rate that is lower than the initial IRR rate will result in a true IRR that is less than the initial estimate, etc. There is a lot of confusion over this point, and few knowledgeable investors are aware of the correct answer. If you doubt this, ask your stockbroker, banker, and real estate broker and see what reply you receive.

The answer is NO REINVESTMENT OF CASH FLOW IS REQUIRED TO ACHIEVE THE IRR! Alice Ann can spend every penny she receives from her real estate without reinvesting at all, and her IRR will be as originally calculated (if the projections hold true). Proof of this is contained in the last seven lines at the bottom of Table 10–2.

To best understand this concept, let's *consider all cash flows* related to this investment *deposited to or withdrawn from a bank* account. *The bank pays interest annually on the balance at a rate equal to the IRR of 23.17 percent.* In the table, consider that the descriptive terms in the left margin are analogous to the following

> Outstanding (unrecovered) cash investment—Beginning bank balance.
> Cash flow (after tax) for year—Withdrawals from the account.
> IRR × outstanding cash investment—Deposits to the account.
> Reduction in outstanding investment (recovery)—Simply deposits less withdrawals. If deposits less withdrawals is a positive number, it is added to the outstanding investment (bank) balance; if negative, it is deducted.

Then what we have is an *initial deposit* of $250 (the cash investment in the property) from which we *subtract annual withdrawals* equal to the cash flow and to which we *add annual deposits* at the rate of IRR times the outstanding or current balance in the account.

Inspect the year by year transactions in the account. The totals at the end of the period show that the withdrawals, including proceeds of sale ($2,323), were exactly equal to the sum of deposits or earnings ($2,073) and the return of the original deposit ($250).

Thus it is apparent that *no reinvestment of earnings was necessary to achieve a return equal to the IRR.* In fact, *if reinvestment at any percentage rate other than zero is assumed, each annual cash flow would increase as would the overall IRR.*

Assumptions:

Sales, starting	$614,000 (present annualized amount)
Tax bracket	50.00%
Cash investment	$46,800
Loan	$31,200
Total investment	$78,000
Total investment includes leases of	$16,260
Years amortization, leases	3.50
Total investment includes personal property	$0
Years amortization, personal property	0.00 (whole years)
Purchase price of land	$7,500 (per contract)
Years loan amortization	99.00 (interest only, no amortization)
Loan interest	10.00%
Loan principal and interest	$3,120
Fixed or minimum rental per year	$6,000
Initial depreciable assets	$54,240
Years straight line depreciation	15.00 (whole years)
Year of future sale of property	15.00 (from year of purchase)
Capitalization rate at sale	10.00%
Inflation rate	6.00% (applies to most expenses)
Mortgage constant	10.0008% (principal and interest)
Annual sales increase	6.00%
Sales breakpoint for percent rent	$375,000
Additional rent percent of sales greater than breakpoint	1.000%
Maximum real estate tax paid by owner	$0
Maximum insurance paid by owners	$0
Building square feet	3,000

Table 10–3
Pro Forma Analysis

		1	2	3	4	5	6	7	8	9	10	11	12	13	14	15	Totals
Income:																	
Sales		$614,000	650,840	689,890	731,284	775,161	821,671	870,971	923,229	978,623	1,037,340	1,099,580	1,165,555	1,235,489	1,309,618	1,388,195	14,291,445
Fixed or minimum rent		6,000	6,000	6,000	6,000	6,000	6,000	6,000	6,000	6,000	6,000	6,000	6,000	6,000	6,000	6,000	90,000
Percentage rent additional		2,390	2,758	3,149	3,563	4,002	4,467	4,960	5,482	6,036	6,623	7,246	7,906	8,605	9,346	10,132	86,664
Total rent		8,390	8,758	9,149	9,563	10,002	10,467	10,960	11,482	12,036	12,623	13,246	13,906	14,605	15,346	16,132	176,664
Vacancy allowance	0.00%	0	0	0	0	0	0	0	0	0	0	0	0	0	0	0	0
Effective gross income (EGI)		8,390	8,758	9,149	9,563	10,002	10,467	10,960	11,482	12,036	12,623	13,246	13,906	14,605	15,346	16,132	176,664
Expenses:																	
Management fee	6.00%	503	526	549	574	600	628	658	689	722	757	795	834	876	921	968	10,600
Utilities		0	0	0	0	0	0	0	0	0	0	0	0	0	0	0	0
Real estate tax		617	654	694	735	779	826	876	928	984	1,043	1,106	1,172	1,242	1,317	1,396	14,371
Proceeds from limit on owner tax		−617	−654	−694	−735	−779	−826	−876	−928	−984	−1,043	−1,106	−1,172	−1,242	−1,317	−1,396	−14,371
Insurance		0	0	0	0	0	0	0	0	0	0	0	0	0	0	0	0

Table 10–3 (*continued*)

	Year 1	2	3	4	5	6	7	8	9	10	11	12	13	14	15	Totals
Proceeds from limit on insurance	0	0	0	0	0	0	0	0	0	0	0	0	0	0	0	0
Repairs and maintenance	0	0	0	0	0	0	0	0	0	0	0	0	0	0	0	0
Professional fees	125	133	140	149	158	167	177	188	199	211	224	237	252	267	283	2,909
Advertising	0	0	0	0	0	0	0	0	0	0	0	0	0	0	0	0
Roof reserve or allowance	0	0	0	0	0	0	0	0	0	0	0	0	0	0	0	0
Asphalt reserve or allowance	0	0	0	0	0	0	0	0	0	0	0	0	0	0	0	0
Other expenses	0	0	0	0	0	0	0	0	0	0	0	0	0	0	0	0
Total Expenses	628	658	689	723	758	795	835	877	921	969	1,019	1,072	1,128	1,187	1,251	13,509
Loan (beginning balance)	31,200	31,200	31,199	31,199	31,199	31,198	31,198	31,198	31,197	31,197	31,196	31,195	31,195	31,194	31,193	
Interest per year	3,120	3,120	3,120	3,120	3,120	3,120	3,120	3,120	3,120	3,120	3,120	3,120	3,120	3,119	3,119	46,796
Principal of loan reduction per year	0	0	0	0	0	0	0	0	1	1	1	1	1	1	1	8
Loan (ending balance)	31,200	31,199	31,199	31,199	31,198	31,198	31,198	31,197	31,197	31,196	31,195	31,195	31,194	31,193	31,192	
Net operating income (NOI)	7,762	8,100	8,460	8,840	9,244	9,671	10,125	10,605	11,115	11,655	12,227	12,834	13,477	14,159	14,881	163,155
NOI/Total investment	9.95%	10.39%	10.85%	11.33%	11.85%	12.40%	12.95%	13.60%	14.25%	14.94%	15.68%	16.45%	17.28%	18.15%	19.08%	
Less: loan principal and interest	3,120	3,120	3,120	3,120	3,120	3,120	3,120	3,120	3,120	3,120	3,120	3,120	3,120	3,120	3,120	46,804
Cash flow before income tax	4,641	4,980	5,339	5,720	6,123	6,551	7,005	7,485	7,995	8,535	9,107	9,714	10,357	11,039	11,761	116,351
Cash flow/cash investment	9.92%	10.64%	11.41%	12.22%	13.08%	14.00%	14.97%	15.99%	17.08%	18.24%	19.46%	20.76%	22.13%	23.59%	25.13%	
Less: depreciation	3,616	3,616	3,616	3,616	3,616	3,616	3,616	3,616	3,616	3,616	3,616	3,616	3,616	3,616	3,616	54,240
Plus: loan principal reduction	0	0	0	0	0	0	0	0	1	1	1	1	1	1	1	8
Less: amortization of leases	4,646	4,646	4,646	2,323	0	0	0	0	0	0	0	0	0	0	0	16,260
Less: amortization of personal property	0	0	0	0	0	0	0	0	0	0	0	0	0	0	0	0
Taxable income	−3,620	−3,281	−2,922	−219	2,508	2,936	3,389	3,870	4,379	4,919	5,492	6,098	6,742	7,423	8,146	45,859
Income tax (− = Tax Savings)	−1,810	−1,641	−1,461	−109	1,254	1,468	1,695	1,935	2,190	2,460	2,746	3,049	3,371	3,712	4,073	22,930
Cash flow after tax (pre sale)	6,451	6,621	6,800	5,829	4,870	5,083	5,310	5,550	5,805	6,075	6,361	6,664	6,986	7,327	7,688	93,422
Sales proceeds in year 15															148,814	148,814
Capital gains tax on sale in year 15																
Cash from sale after tax and loan repayment															89,359	89,359
Cash flow after tax	6,451	6,621	6,800	5,829	4,870	5,083	5,310	5,550	5,805	6,075	6,361	6,664	6,986	7,327	97,047	182,781
Assessed value for real estate tax	$61,740	65,444	69,371	73,533	77,945	82,622	87,579	92,834	98,404	104,308	110,567	117,201	124,233	131,687	139,588	
Real estate tax rate	1.000%	1.000%	1.000%	1.000%	1.000%	1.000%	1.000%	1.000%	1.000%	1.000%	1.000%	1.000%	1.000%	1.000%	1.000%	
Annual rent per square foot	$2.80	2.92	3.05	3.19	3.33	3.49	3.65	3.83	4.01	4.21	4.42	4.64	4.87	5.12	5.38	
Annual sales per square foot	$204.67	216.95	229.96	243.76	258.39	273.89	290.32	307.74	326.21	345.78	366.53	388.52	411.83	436.54	462.73	

Table 10–3 (*concluded*)

								Year							
	1	2	3	4	5	6	7	8	9	10	11	12	13	14	15
Return on cash investment of $46,800 is:															
Before tax cash flow/cash investment	9.92%	10.64%	11.41%	12.22%	13.08%	14.00%	14.97%	15.99%	17.08%	18.24%	19.46%	20.76%	22.13%	23.59%	25.13%
Tax savings or cost (−)/cash investment	3.87%	3.51%	3.12%	0.23%	−2.68%	−3.14%	−3.62%	−4.13%	−4.68%	−5.26%	−5.87%	−6.52%	−7.20%	−7.93%	−8.70%
Equity—Loan principal/cash investment	0.00%	0.00%	0.00%	0.00%	0.00%	0.00%	0.00%	0.00%	0.00%	0.00%	0.00%	0.00%	0.00%	0.00%	0.00%
Total return on cash investment	13.79%	14.15%	14.53%	12.46%	10.41%	10.86%	11.35%	11.86%	12.41%	12.98%	13.59%	14.24%	14.93%	15.66%	16.43%
Equivalent return on fully taxed investment	27.57%	28.30%	29.06%	24.91%	20.81%	21.73%	22.69%	23.72%	24.81%	25.96%	27.19%	28.48%	29.86%	31.31%	32.86%
The internal rate of return for this property is									14.97%						
Marginal internal rate of return															
Sales proceeds at end of each year	$77,616	81,004	84,595	88,402	92,437	96,714	101,248	106,054	111,148	116,548	122,272	128,339	134,771	141,588	148,814
Capital gains tax on sale	1,576	3,905	6,276	8,225	9,755	11,334	12,964	14,648	16,390	18,194	20,062	21,998	24,008	26,094	28,263
Cash from sale after tax and loan	44,841	45,899	47,120	48,978	51,483	54,182	57,086	60,208	63,561	67,158	71,015	75,146	79,569	84,301	89,359
Cash flow, sale in year 1	51,292														
Cash flow, sale in year 2	6,451	52,520													
Cash flow, sale in year 3	6,451	6,621	53,920												
Cash flow, sale in year 4	6,451	6,621	6,800	54,807											
Cash flow, sale in year 5	6,451	6,621	6,800	5,829	56,353										
Cash flow, sale in year 6	6,451	6,621	6,800	5,829	4,870	59,266									
Cash flow, sale in year 7	6,451	6,621	6,800	5,829	4,870	5,083	62,397								
Cash flow, sale in year 8	6,451	6,621	6,800	5,829	4,870	5,083	5,310	65,759							
Cash flow, sale in year 9	6,451	6,621	6,800	5,829	4,870	5,083	5,310	5,550	69,366						
Cash flow, sale in year 10	6,451	6,621	6,800	5,829	4,870	5,083	5,310	5,550	5,805	73,233					
Cash flow, sale in year 11	6,451	6,621	6,800	5,829	4,870	5,083	5,310	5,550	5,805	6,075	77,376				
Cash flow, sale in year 12	6,451	6,621	6,800	5,829	4,870	5,083	5,310	5,550	5,805	6,075	6,361	81,811			
Cash flow, sale in year 13	6,451	6,621	6,800	5,829	4,870	5,083	5,310	5,550	5,805	6,075	6,361	6,664	86,555		
Cash flow, sale in year 14	6,451	6,621	6,800	5,829	4,870	5,083	5,310	5,550	5,805	6,075	6,361	6,664	6,986	91,627	
Cash flow, sale in year 15	6,451	6,621	6,800	5,829	4,870	5,083	5,310	5,550	5,805	6,075	6,361	6,664	6,986	7,327	97,047
IRR—Sale at end of each year	9.60%	13.05%	14.32%	14.72%	14.77%	14.82%	14.85%	14.88%	14.90%	14.92%	14.94%	14.95%	14.96%	14.97%	14.97
Marginal IRR—Percent return from holding 1 more year	9.60%	17.13%	17.48%	16.31%	15.06%	15.12%	15.16%	15.19%	15.21%	15.22%	15.21%	15.20%	15.18%	15.15%	15.12%

Table 10–4
Partitioning IRR

	Year						Total	Percent of Total	Present Value at IRR Rate	Present Value as Percent of Total
	0	1	2	3	4	5				
Cash investment	$46,800									
Cash flow before tax		4,641	4,980	5,339	5,720	6,123	26,803	32.67%	$17,727	37.88%
Tax benefits (cost)		1,810	1,641	1,461	109	−1,254	3,767	4.59	3,222	6.89
Subtotal		6,451	6,621	6,800	5,829	4,869	30,570	37.26%	$20,949	44.76%
Sales proceeds (after tax and loan)						51,483	51,483	62.74%	25,851	55.24%
Cash flow (after tax)	−46,800	6,451	6,621	6,800	5,829	56,352	82,053	100.00%	46,800	100.00%
Internal rate of return			14.77%							

C H A P T E R   11

Bond Selection,
Tax Considerations,
and Price Volatility

Discount bonds, premium bonds, or par bonds—which should one buy? A bond may be purchased at a *discount* from its maturity value; e.g., a $1,000 bond may be purchased for $600; or a *premium* from its maturity value; e.g., a $1,000 bond may be purchased at $1,200; or a bond may be bought at *par;* e.g., a $1,000 bond may be acquired for that amount, $1,000.

Income Tax Effects

Income tax effects of the alternative purchases must be considered. Different or varying tax treatment applies to premium taxable bonds, premium municipal (tax-free) bonds, discount bonds, and convertible bonds.

Taxable Premium Bonds

You can elect to amortize the premium you pay to buy taxable bonds. If you make the choice to amortize, the owner would reduce the basis (original cost) of the bonds by a part of the premium each year amortized over the life of the bonds. The investor may deduct the amount by which the investor reduces the basis for each year as a *miscellaneous deduction from taxable income*. The choice applies for the year he or she makes the election and for all later years. It applies to all similar bonds you own in the year the election is made and to similar bonds you acquire in later years. The method of amortization employed may be the one customarily used by the taxpayer if it is deemed to be reasonable. The two most commonly used methods of amortizing premiums are (*a*) straight-line, and (*b*) formula methods.

The portion of the premium that should be allocated to a particular year, called the "amortizable bond premium" of such year, is determined by spreading the premium (cost less maturity value less amount paid, if any, for convertible feature) over the period from the date of purchase to the maturity (or earlier call date, if applicable). If the bond is called prior to maturity, the then unamortized portion of the premium is deductible in the year of call. The adjustment to taxable basis of the bond is made by reducing the basis each year, beginning with the date of acquisition or with a later year in which the election is made, by the amortizable bond premium for such year. At call or maturity, any unamortized premium (attributable to the period prior to amortization) will constitute a capital loss to the investor.

When the bond is sold, the difference between sale price and the adjusted basis (cost price less amortization) will represent a capital gain or loss—long-term or short-term depending upon the holding period.

For example, a new taxable bond is bought for $1,200, at issuance, and has a 20-year maturity. The premium is $200 ($1,200 − $1,000 maturity value). The annual amortization (deductible from both taxable income and basis) is $10 ($200 ÷ 20 years).

Tax-Exempt Bonds

You must amortize the premium and reduce the basis of tax-exempt bonds. However, you may *not* deduct the amortized premium from taxable income. *And if the investor buys tax-exempt bonds at a discount, the gain when the bond is sold for more than cost is a "taxable gain."* That is, the amount of the market discount is *not* tax-exempt interest. For example, a municipal (tax-free) bond is bought for $600 and later sold for $900. The $300 difference is a taxable capital gain.

Premium on Convertible Bonds

If you paid a premium to buy a convertible bond, the portion of the premium that relates to the conversion feature of the bond may not be amortized or deducted. Amortization is not allowed for any part of a premium that is paid for the conversion feature of a convertible bond. To find the value of the conversion feature, first determine the market value of a bond that has no conversion feature and that is of the same character and grade as the convertible issue. Second, determine the yield to maturity of this similar bond. Third, find the theoretical cost of the convertible issue that would produce the same yield to maturity as that of the similar nonconvertible issue. The difference between the latter and the cost of the convertible is the value of the conversion feature.

Taxable Discount Bonds

The coupon income is reported each year as interest income. No effect is given to the discount until the bond is sold. At such time of sale, the investor realizes a capital gain or loss based on the difference between the sale price and the original cost. Thus it is apparent that a discount bond, if held to maturity, will automatically create a capital gain for the investor. The ultimate payment of tax on that capital gain ought to be considered in comparing the relative merits of bonds that might be purchased at premiums, par, or discounts.

For example, a taxable discount bond is purchased at $833 and pays $80 per year interest and is held until it matures in 20 years. Each year the $80 interest is included in taxable interest income of the owner and upon receiving $1,000 at maturity, the investor will owe tax on the capital gain. The gain is $167 ($1,000 maturity value less the $833 original cost). Assuming that the tax is $33.40, then the maturity value may be treated or regarded as $966.60; i.e., $1,000 less the estimated tax of $33.40. The yield to maturity, ignoring income and capital gains tax, is 10 percent (Graph 5–20). The after tax yield to maturity (in a 50 percent tax bracket) is reduced to 5.25 percent (Graph 6–20).

Income Tax Considerations

After tax return on investment should be the primary concern of the investor. Assume that Shirley Pigeon pays 50 percent tax on ordinary income and 20 percent tax on long-term gains. She is considering the purchase of one of the following three bonds. Based only on after tax yield to maturity, which bond should be purchased?

	Purchase Cost	Coupon	Years to Maturity	Conventional Before Tax, Yield to Maturity
Premium bond	$1,170	12%	20	10%
Par bond	1,000	10	20	10
Discount bond	830	8	20	10

Premium Bond

The after tax results of buying the premium bond may be determined by treating the annual $120 in interest as reduced by the annual amortization of the premium. The annual amortization is calculated by dividing the $170 premium by the 20 years to maturity, which is $8.50 per year. The after tax annual interest will then be:

a.	Interest coupon	$120.00
b.	Less amortization	8.50
c.	Subtotal	111.50
d.	Less: 50 percent tax	55.75
e.	After tax interest (*a*)–(*d*)	$ 64.25

The after tax yield to maturity is 5.05 percent, determined by use of Graph 5–20 (with 6.425% as the interest coupon) or trial and error as follows:

After Tax Yield to Maturity	Purchase Price
5%	$1,178
5.1	1,164
5.05	1,171

With respect to the premium bond, no capital loss will be recognizable at maturity since the annual amortization of premium reduces the cost basis, which at maturity will have been reduced to $1,000. Thus the quoted or conventional yield drops from 10 percent before tax to only 5.05 percent after tax or, if the premium is not amortized over the ownership period, the after tax yield to maturity is about 4.76 percent (Graph 6–20). Thus Shirley should definitely elect to amortize the premium, because to do so results in a *significant increase in the IRR*.

Discount Bond

The after tax results of the discount bond may be determined by treating the long-term capital gains tax, payable at maturity, as a reduction in the maturity value.

Maturity value	$1,000
Less: purchase cost	830
Capital gain	170
Tax at 20 percent	34
Adjusted maturity value	$ 966

The after tax yield to maturity is 5.3 percent, determined by the use of Graph 6–20 or trial and error as follows:

After Tax Yield to Maturity	Purchase Price
4%	$984
5	862
5.3	830

Recognizing both the taxability of annual interest, which reduces the annual interest to $40, and the capital gains tax at maturity, which reduces the maturity value to $966 after tax, the investor's after tax yield is reduced from the conventional before tax 10 percent to only 5.3 percent *after tax*.

Par Bond

The after tax yield of the par bond may be determined by reducing the annual interest income of $100 by tax of $50. No adjustment is required to the $1,000 maturity value. Thus for a $1,000 bond purchased for the same amount with an after tax yield of $50 per year and a 20-year maturity, the after tax yield to maturity is 5 percent. Thus the before tax yield to maturity of 10 percent drops to 5 percent after income taxes.

Summary

The following table summarizes the before and after tax yields of the premium bond, discount bond, and par bond discussed in the preceding text.

Comparison After Tax: 20 Years to Maturity

	Purchase Cost	Coupon	Before Tax Yield to Maturity	After Tax Yield to Maturity
Premium bond (amortized)	$1,170	12%	10%	5.1%
Premium bond (unamortized)	1,170	12	10	4.8
Discount bond	830	8	10	5.3
Par bond	1,000	10	10	5.0

Thus in the foregoing examples, the discount bond would be a superior purchase to the alternatives.

Municipals

In the municipals market place, it would be unlikely that the 20-year premium, par, and discount bonds would be priced to each yield 10 percent before tax. Discount bonds usually offer the highest yield to maturity (IRR), followed by premium bonds, and then par bonds. The saying "DIscover PRetty PAstures" can be an aid to remembering the normal pattern of yields—from high to low—for the three categories of bonds (having equal lengths until maturity and credit ratings).

One reason why discount bonds tend to have the highest yields is that banks and other corporations or institutions are important purchasers. And they are subject to a much higher corporate capital gains tax (say 46 percent) than are private individuals (say 15 to 20 percent). The price on discount municipals must be set low enough so that the after capital gains tax yield to such corporations will be attractive. (Corporations would pay no capital gains tax on a muni bought at par or a premium.)

Premium municipal bonds almost always yield more than comparable par bonds. This may be due to one or more factors including the following: First, the psychological factor invoked by the word *premium*. Many investors demand a premium yield to induce them to buy a bond at a price higher than par. Second, a bond bought at a premium may have a greater risk than expected that future results will be achieved, due to an early call or redemption for sinking fund requirements.

Bond Price Volatility

It is well known that as economic conditions change the yields to maturity and thus the prices of bonds fluctuate. Volatility measures the percentage price fluctuations of bonds, and relative volatility is a comparison of such fluctuations between different bonds. Volatility varies according to

Coupon rate—*low* coupon issues are *more* volatile than those with high coupons.

Maturity—the *more distant* the maturity the higher the volatility.

Initial yield to maturity—issues with *higher* yields to maturity at time of purchase are more volatile than issues with lower yields to maturity at time of purchase.

The following table summarizes the factors that influence volatility.[1]

Price Volatility

Bond Feature	Characteristics of Low Volatility	Characteristics of High Volatility
Coupon rate	higher coupons	lower coupons
Maturity	near or short	distant
Initial yield to maturity	lower	higher

---

[1]The slope of the curves in the graphs in Chapters 5 and 6 may be compared to determine relative volatility. When any two bond purchases are compared (e.g. short-term maturities versus long), that which has the *steeper* curve is the *more* volatile.

Bond Price Volatility—Short versus Long Maturities

A given change in the yield to maturity of a bond has a progressively greater effect on the bond price as the time until maturity lengthens. For example, consider a 6 percent coupon, $1,000 bond, bought at par to yield 6 percent until maturity. The following table shows the change in bond price for various maturities that results from an increase in yield to maturity from 6 percent to 9 percent.

Maturity Effect on Volatility

Years to Maturity	Yield to Maturity			Bond Price		
	Original	Revised	Percent Change	Original	Revised*	Percent Change
5	6%	9%	50%	$1,000	$883	−11.7%
10	6	9	50	1,000	807	−19.3
15	6	9	50	1,000	758	−24.2
20	6	9	50	1,000	726	−27.4
25	6	9	50	1,000	705	−29.5
30	6	9	50	1,000	692	−30.8

*Revised price after yield to maturity increases from 6 percent to 9 percent.

While the price volatility generally increases with longer maturities, the incremental increases lessen as maturity lengthens. Nevertheless, a 50 percent increase in yield to maturity results in an 11.7 percent drop in bond price for a 5-year maturity versus a 30.8 percent drop for a 30-year maturity as shown in the table.

Bond Price Volatility—High versus Low Coupons

The lower the coupon rate of a bond, the greater is the change in the bond price that takes place from a given change in yield to maturity. For example, consider a 6 percent coupon, $1,000 bond, bought at par to yield 6 percent until maturity. The table that follows shows the

Coupon Effect on Volatility

Coupon	Yield to Maturity			Bond Price		
	Original	Revised	Percent Change	Original	Revised*	Percent Change
12%	6%	9%	50%	$1,688	$1,274	−24.5%
10	6	9	50	1,459	1,091	−25.2
8	6	9	50	1,229	909	−26.1
6	6	9	50	1,000	726	−27.4
4	6	9	50	771	544	−29.5
2	6	9	50	541	361	−33.3

*Revised after yield increases from 6 percent to 9 percent.

change in bond price for various coupon rates that results from an increase in yield to maturity from 6 percent to 9 percent for a bond with a 20-year maturity.

Thus with a $120 coupon (12 percent), a 50 percent increase in yield to maturity results in a price drop of 24.5 percent, but with a $20 coupon (2 percent), the price decreases by 33.3 percent from the same yield change.

Bond Price Volatility—Magnitude of Yield to Maturity at Purchase

Is volatility greater if the yield to maturity at the time of purchase is *low*, e.g., 2 percent, as compared to *high*, e.g., 8 percent? The answer is emphatically YES. The *higher* the yield to maturity at time of purchase, the *greater* is the bond price volatility. This principle is evidenced by the following table.

Volatility and Yield at Purchase

Yield to Maturity			Bond Price*		
Initial	Revised	Percent Change	Initial	Revised[†]	Percent Change
2%	3%	50%	$1,654	$1,446	−12.6%
4	6	50	1,272	1,000	−21.4
6	9	50	1,000	726	−27.4
8	12	50	804	552	−31.3

*Bond Price based on $60 coupon, 20 years to maturity with interest paid annually.
[†]Price for revised yield to maturity.

Thus the table shows that a 50 percent increase in yield to maturity results in only a 12.6 percent drop in bond price at a 2 percent yield at purchase, but results in a much larger (31.3 percent) drop at an 8 percent yield at purchase level. In other words, the higher the yield to maturity at purchase, the greater is the volatility.

Summary

The volatility, that is, the percentage price change of a bond, is a function of three factors: maturity, coupon rate, and the starting level of yields. *The longer the maturity, the lower the coupon rate, and the higher the initial yield to maturity, the lower the price volatility.*

Is Yield to Maturity the True Yield?

Is a buyer of a bond with a yield to maturity of 10 percent assured that 10 percent will actually be earned? In answering this question, assume that interest and principal are paid by the debtor on schedule. The answer is YES! However, the actual yield to maturity will vary according to whether interest is reinvested and, if reinvested, the rate earned on such reinvestment. *Bond yield to maturity calculations contain an implicit assumption that the periodic receipts of interest by the bond-holder will not be reinvested upon receipt.* If future reinvestments of interest receipts are made, then the cash flow is greater than that presumed in the initial yield to maturity calculation; and the higher the rate earned on the sums reinvested, the higher the *new* yield to maturity becomes.

For example, the owner of a $1,000 bond with 10-year maturity, purchased at par with 10 percent annual interest coupons, would actually experience a varying yield to maturity depending on the "reinvestment rate," the rate at which the $100 annual interest receipts are reinvested. The following table illustrates the foregoing:

Effect of Interest Reinvestment Rate on Yield to Maturity

Interest Reinvestment Rate	Interest without Reinvestment	Interest Including Reinvestment at Reinvestment Rate	Total Value Including Principal	Interest Reinvestment ÷ Total Interest	Yield to Maturity or IRR *(Before Tax)*
0%	$1,000	$1,000	$2,000	0%	10.00%
10	1,000	1,594	2,594	37	14.36
12	1,000	1,755	2,755	43	15.49
15	1,000	2,030	3,030	51	17.00

Notes: Stated yield to maturity at purchase 10%
       Purchase price $1,000
       Annual interest $ 100
       Years to maturity   10

Thus it is evident that the yield to maturity, though stated at 10 percent, will actually be equal to or greater than 10 percent, e.g., 10 to 17 percent in the table; depending on the rate at which reinvestment of earnings takes place. A similar effect of the investment rate on yield will be experienced if the bonds are originally purchased at a discount or premium rather than at par.

Interest Reinvestment and Bond Maturity

Interest reinvestment proceeds compared to total interest earned varied from 0 percent to 51 percent in the preceding table. As the rate at which interest reinvestment increases, so does the importance or effect of the interest reinvestment component of total return.

As the time period until maturity of a bond lengthens, e.g., a 20-year maturity versus a 5-year maturity, the percentage of total return represented by interest reinvestment also increases as shown in the following table.

Interest Reinvestment and Maturity

Maturity	Interest Paid until Maturity without Reinvestment	Interest Earned Including Reinvestment of Interest at 10 Percent	Interest from Reinvestment only	Interest Reinvestment ÷ Total Interest
1 year	$ 100	$ 100	0	0%
10	1,000	1,594	$ 594	37
20	2,000	5,728	3,728	65

Notes: Interest rate   10% coupon
       Purchase price $1,000
       Interest reinvestment rate 10%

The table shows that the longer the period to maturity, other factors being equal, the larger the importance of interest reinvestment earnings.

Practical Significance

A bond buyer expects interest rates in future years to average less than the rates at the time of purchase. Should the investor buy discount bonds, bonds at par, or bonds at a premium? If the investor is *not* planning to reinvest interest receipts and expects lower rates in the future, then the characteristics of high volatility—to maximize capital appreciation—are appropriate including low coupon and distant maturity. But if interest is to be reinvested, then the investor should buy premium bonds because the yield to maturity, considering reinvestment, is higher. As the table shows, with 5 percent interest on reinvested amounts, the yield to maturity for the premium bond is 22.44 percent versus 21.68 percent for the discount bond.

Future Reinvestment Rate Effect on Par, Discount, or Premium Purchase

Price at Purchase	Coupon	At Maturity, Sum of Cash Flows Including Interest, Interest Reinvestment, and Principal at Reinvestment Rate of			Yield to Maturity with Reinvestment Rate of		
		0%	5%	15%	0%	5%	15%
$1,170	12%	$3,400	$4,968	$13,293	10.0%	13.76%	22.44%
1,000	10	3,000	4,307	11,244	10.0	13.60	22.13
830	8	2,600	3,645	9,195	10.0	13.38	21.68

Notes: Yield to maturity at purchase 10%
       Maturity   20 years

Conversely, an investor expects interest rates in future years to rise. He, too, will find that par or premium bonds, as compared to discount bonds, will provide a higher yield to maturity.

Thus it is evident from the preceding table that if the future reinvestment rate (5 percent) is less than the initial yield to maturity at purchase (10 percent), the *premium* bond provides the *best* yield to maturity (13.76 percent). And if the future reinvestment rate (15 percent) is greater than the yield to maturity at purchase (10 percent), then again, the *premium* bond provides the *best* yield to maturity (22.44 percent). Finally, any bond purchased, whether premium, par, or discount—without reinvesting interest—produces a 10 percent yield to maturity.

Price Patterns of Bonds Based on Ratings

Assume that for a group of bonds, the quality rating and years until maturity of each bond are the same. All such bonds would normally trade a price that, irrespective of their differing coupon rates, will provide approximately equal yields to maturity.

The following table shows utility bond issues that are all rated equally (Aaa, A, or Bbb −) by Standard & Poor's and all mature in the same year, 20 years hence. Their coupons and market closing prices (on the same day) and yields to maturity and current yields at such prices are shown. The bonds in each rating category are listed in the order of magnitude of price from high to low.

Bond Yields and Ratings

Description	Price	Current Yield	Yield to Maturity
Aaa rated bonds:			
Dallas Power and Light 9⅜%	$863	10.87%	11.10%
Texas Power and Light 8⅞	813	10.92	11.24
Texas Electric Service 8⅞	813	10.92	11.24
American Tel and Tel 6	615	9.76	10.70
Mountain States Tel & Tel 5	521	9.59	10.99
New Jersey Bell Tel 4⅞	506	9.63	11.01
Southern Bell 4¾	494	9.62	11.09
Pacific Northwest Bell Tel 4½	471	9.55	11.10
New York Telephone Co. 4¼	464	9.16	10.98
Average			11.05
A rated bonds:			
Dayton Power & Light 9½	819	11.60	11.89
Empire Dist. Elect. 9½	806	11.78	12.09
Central Louisiana Elect 9⅛	791	11.53	11.90
Kansas City Power & Lt. 9⅛	790	11.55	11.90
Consolidated Edison, N.Y. 9⅜	788	11.90	12.23
Carolina Power & Lt. 8¾	764	11.46	11.89
Consolidated Edison, N.Y. 8.90	763	11.67	12.09

Bond Yields and Ratings (*concluded*)

Description	Price	Current Yield	Yield to Maturity
Pennsylvania Power Co. 9¼	755	12.25	12.65
Virginia Electric & Pwr 9s	755	11.92	12.34
Delmarva Pwr & Light 8¾	751	11.65	12.10
Virginia Electric & Pwr 8⅞	744	11.93	12.35
Public Service Colorado 1st 8¾	743	11.78	12.21
General Tel Fla. 8⅝	741	11.64	12.10
Mississippi Power Co. 8⅛	701	11.59	12.10
Gulf States Utilities 7⅞	683	11.54	12.10
Iowa Electric Lt. & Pwr. 7⅞	670	11.75	12.33
Pacific Tel & Tel 4⅝	460	10.05	11.68
Average			12.11
Bbb – rated bonds:			
Portland General Electric 9⅞	784	12.60	12.90
Arkansas Power & Lt. 1st 9⅝	781	12.32	12.65
Boston Edison 1st 9⅜	764	12.27	12.64
Jersey Central Pwr. & Lt. 10s	750	13.33	13.68
Louisiana Power & Lt. 9⅜	735	12.76	13.14
Alabama Power 1st 9s	718	12.54	12.97
Jersey Central Pwr. & Lt. 8¾	685	12.77	13.25
Average			13.03

Yields to maturity *within* each rating category do not seem to vary significantly either from high to low or from the average for the group. The following table summarizes the yield variations.

Comparison of Yield Variations by Ratings

Group	Yield to Maturity		
	Average	Highest	Lowest
Aaa	11.05%	11.24%	10.70%
A	12.11	12.65	11.68
Bbb –	13.03	13.68	12.64

However, although the difference in yield to maturity in the Aaa category from lowest to highest (10.7 percent to 11.24 percent) does not seem great, $100,000 in bonds purchased today at the higher yield to maturity, with reinvestment at the purchase yield, would produce $49,800 more interest over the 20-year life of the bonds.

The higher priced, higher coupon bonds do not seem to trade at yields to maturity that vary greatly from those of the lower priced, lower coupon bonds. See the following table. However, in general, discount bonds are normally priced at slightly higher yields to maturity.

Yield to Maturity by Price

	Yield to Maturity		
Group	Highest Priced Bond	Average Yield	Lowest Priced Bond
Aaa	11.10%	11.05%	10.98%
A	11.89	12.11	11.68
Bbb –	12.90	13.03	13.25

Note: *Years to maturity: 20*

Higher Yields, Lower Ratings

The higher the rating of a bond for quality, the lower one may expect its yield to maturity to be and the lower the rating of a bond, the higher one may expect its yield to maturity to be. It is, of course, assumed that the bonds have equal times until maturity. This relationship is shown in the following table.

Ratings and Yields to Maturity *(for bonds with the same maturity)*

Standard and Poor's Quality Rating	Issue	Yield to Maturity
Aaa	Dallas Power & Lt. 9⅜	11.10%
Aa +	General Tel Illinois 8½	11.39
Aa	Public Service E & G 9⅛	11.39
Aa –	Utah Power & Lt. 9¼	11.70
A +	Atlantic City Elect. 8⅞	11.89
A	Central Louisiana Elect. 9⅛	11.90
A –	Rochester Gas & Elect. 9⅛	12.34
Bbb +	Mississippi Pwr & Lgt. 9¼	12.35
Bbb	Public Service New Hampshire 9's	12.90
Bbb –	Jersey Central Pwr & Lt. 8¾	13.25
Bb +	Public Service New Hampshire 14½	14.27

Analysis of the above information indicates that *conventional bond yields to maturity increase as the bond ratings decline* but that there is not absolute uniformity in the rate of increase. Thus investors should investigate alternatives before purchasing and should consider such factors as: (*a*) *earlier refund terms*—determine earliest call price and date; (*b*) *sinking fund call price*—amounts to be called, years of call, and sliding scale of call prices and year when sinking fund starts; (*c*) *yield to maturity;* (*d*) *current yield;* (*e*) *rating;* (*f*) *where traded* and *liquidity;* (*g*) *volatility;* (*h*) *after tax results;* and (*i*) *effect of reinvestment rates.*

The yields to maturity in the foregoing table and the tables which follow are all pre-tax. It is noteworthy that in comparing such pre-tax yields to maturity of premium bonds to discount bonds that the Premium bonds generally sell at lower yields to maturity. The reason is:

(*a*) the interest on the higher coupon bonds (premium bonds) is taxable as ordinary income; and there is no capital gain at maturity from a premium bond;

(*b*) thus, such bonds are marked down in price to provide a higher pre-tax yield to maturity, because their after tax yields will be reduced more than those of a discount or par bond due to the effect of taxes.

Municipal Bond Quality

Municipal bonds, in general, have demonstrated a good record of paying interest and principal when due. However, there have been defaults, and one should not rely blindly on a credit rating by Moody's, Standard & Poor's, or other rating services. Municipals may be categorized for safety into four general categories, in order of safety, as follows:

1. U.S. government-backed tax-exempt bonds. Public Housing Authority bonds (PHAs) are unconditionally guaranteed by the U.S. Department of Housing and Urban Development (HUD). Also enjoying the highest degree of safety are bonds that have been "pre-refunded in governments" or "escrowed until maturity in governments."

2. General obligations backed by the full faith and credit of the issuer and essential service revenue bonds such as water, sewer, and electric bonds.

3. Housing Finance Agency Bonds and revenue bonds for roads, tunnels, bridges, and airports.

4. Industrial revenue bonds and bonds for hospitals, nursing homes and extended-care facilities.

In addition, the quality or safety of a bond may be judged by the existing condition of the issuer. The rankings, in this regard, from higher to lower degrees of quality, are as follows:

1. Issues of an existing fully operational facility as, for example, a highway authority.

2. Issues of successful revenue producers that are expanding as, for example, a hospital adding some additional beds.

3. Issues for totally new projects, which rely upon engineering and accountants estimates of projected financial results.

The Dangers of Bonds

Refer to Graph 11–1, which shows yields and prices of long-term U.S. government bonds from 1973–83. The two curves on the graph represent the high and low of the bonds yield for each year. For example, yields peaked in 1981 at over 15 percent and the lowest yield was in 1973 at about 5.75 percent. The left axis of the graph depicts the yield to maturity, and the right vertical axis shows the approximate bond price for a 30-year issue with an 8 percent coupon.

Graph 11–1
Yields of Long-Term U.S. Government Bonds

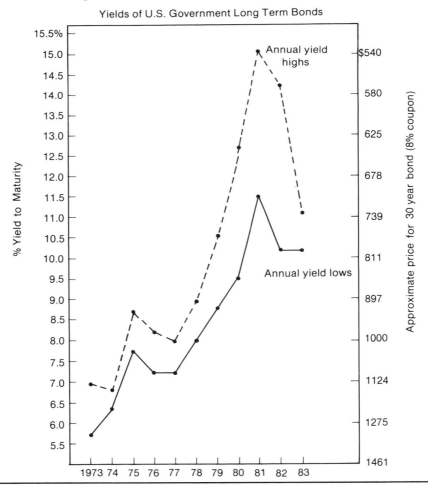

The following observations may be made from studying the graph.

1. Most of the time yields were rising and prices were falling.

2. Prices are volatile. A purchase in 1973 at the yield low, would have been about $1,275 per bond. Similar bonds purchased in 1981 could have been bought for about $540 at their low.

However, for some nonactive investors who are not seeking to maximize their investment returns, the volatility of bonds may not be of too much importance. For example, a bond buyer who purchases a bond with the intention of holding it until maturity would have little cause to worry about its ups and downs in the intervening years.

Bond Yield Compared to Stock Dividend Yields

Bond yields, in recent years, have been higher than dividend yields. This has not always been the case, however, as shown in Graph 11–2. The rationale for bond yields exceeding stock dividend yields is that bonds lack the opportunity for appreciation that stocks might provide.

Graph 11–2
Stock and Bond Yields

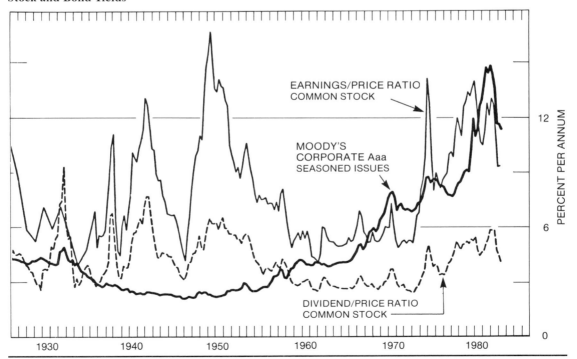

Source: 1983 Historical Chart Book; Federal Reserve Board of Governors.

Historically, the common view was that stocks were riskier and therefore stock investors deserved higher yields than bond investors.

Long-Term Bond Yields versus Short-Term Interest Rates

Long-term and short-term rates tend to follow the same trend, up or down, but the short-term rates are considerably more volatile during short time periods as shown in Graph 11–3. Yields for AAA corporate bonds are the annual averages for selected bonds of all types of corporations rated AAA by Standard and Poor's. Yields are for 30-year bonds, as compiled by the National Bureau of Economic Research, Inc., and Scudder, Stevens and Clark. The commercial paper rates are the annual average of monthly figures.

Graph 11–3
Long- and Short-Term Interest Rates

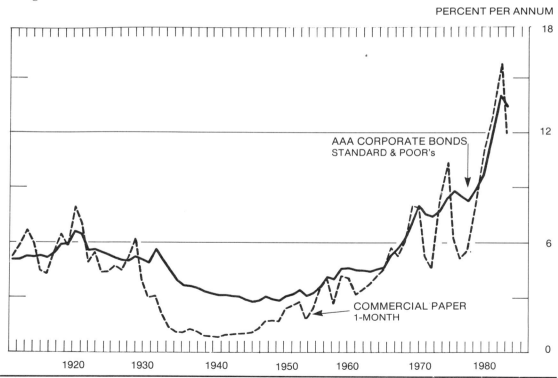

Source: 1983 Historical Chart Book; Federal Reserve Board of Governors.

Trading Bonds

Long-term bond yields have been rising most of the time in recent years. *If yields are rising, prices are falling.* If you think many people, including institutions, have lost a lot of money in the bond market, you would be absolutely correct. They have. But that doesn't mean there isn't money to be made in bonds.

The most successful investment strategy in the past 15 years or so would have been to buy bonds when yields were high, then sell after a relatively small decrease in yields, say 14 to 20 percent, then wait for a much larger percentage increase in yields, say 40 percent or more, before buying again. Please don't interpret this as a formula to follow. Use the charts to develop your own method. But in the past, it seems that the best results in bond investing would have been achieved by holding for a small drop in yields and waiting for a large rise in yields before buying again.

Why would such a difference in the percentages trigger buying or selling? The mathematics of percentages partially account for this wide variance; the rest is accounted for by the fact that the bond market has been a falling price market since the 1940s. Consider the example of a bond that first increases by 100 basis points in yield and then drops by the same 100 points.

	Start Level	End Level	Percent Change	Points Change
Rise	100	200	100%	+100
Fall	200	100	50%	−100

Thus in rising from 100 to 200, by 100 points, the increase was 100 percent, but to return to the start level required a drop of only 50 percent to decrease by the same 100 points.

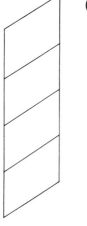

Earnings Reinvestment— Misconceptions and the Reality of IRR Assumptions

Any combination of cash investment(s) and future cash flows may be analyzed by the IRR method. The IRR may be calculated for a stock investment, a bond investment, or a real estate holding. The after tax IRR is an exceedingly accurate measure of true investment performance.

Think of any investment in the following terms. A bank account is opened for that investment and that investment only. The initial cash investment is the deposit that opens the account. Annual interest is deposited to the account. The rate of annual interest is the IRR for the investment. The investment earns each year at the rate of IRR determined at the time of purchase. And the amount of interest deposited to the account is the product of the IRR times the unrecovered investment or bank account balance. The change in the unrecovered investment (bank) balance is the difference between the cash flow for the year and the product of the IRR times the unrecovered investment (bank balance). (For a par bond the annual deposit will be equal to the product of IRR times the purchase price.) Withdrawals are made from the account. The amount of the withdrawals each year are equal to the "cash flow" projected for the investment in the IRR calculation.

For a bond, the purchase price is the opening deposit to the investment bank account. The periodic (e.g. annual) interest deposit is the product of the account balance multiplied by the yield to maturity or IRR. The withdrawals equal the annual bond coupon, e.g. $30 for a

3 percent bond, $75 for a 7.5 percent issue. Withdrawals in the final
year of the account also include the maturity value of the bond. Each
year the appropriate credit for interest (deposits) and charge for cash
flow (withdrawals) are made to the account. If the account winds up
with a zero balance in the final year (the year of the bond's maturity),
it is apparent that the account has earned interest at a rate equal to the
IRR without reinvesting one penny of the income.[1]

The foregoing principle is not generally recognized even in the
more sophisticated financial circles. Consider some of the following
quotes from *Inside the Yield Book* by Sidney Homer and Martin L.
Leibowitz, Ph.D., published jointly by Prentice-Hall, Inc., and New
York Institute of Finance in 1972. Sidney Homer was a general partner
in charge of Salomon Brothers bond market research department and
is the author of several other books and numerous articles on the bond
market.

> Interest on Interest. While conventional yield book calculations are
> entirely correct mathematically, they do not and cannot take account of
> the rate at which bond coupons may be reinvested to earn "interest-on-
> interest" by the investor who wishes his investment to be fully com-
> pounded. [A true statement.] Furthermore, for long-term bonds, this
> missing link of "interest-on-interest" often amounts to over half the total
> return. [This can be true if interest from the bonds is reinvested.] As a
> result, his total realized compound yield *may turn out to be far above—
> or far below—the yield book yield.* [See comments below.]
>
> *The investor will achieve a fully compounded yield equal to the
> bond's stated yield to maturity at the time of purchase only if he can
> reinvest all coupons at his purchase yield.* [This statement can very
> easily be misinterpreted. The accuracy of this statement depends en-
> tirely on the definition of "a fully compounded yield." The investor
> achieves a return equal to the yield to maturity or IRR without rein-
> vesting at all. If he reinvests all receipts at a reinvestment rate equal to
> the yield to maturity at purchase, the yield to maturity at purchase
> (i.e., revised IRR) increases significantly.]
>
> *However, some investors mistakenly expect that a bond purchased
> at a given yield will always produce that rate as a realized compound
> yield over the whole life of the bond. If future reinvestment rates dur-
> ing the life of the bond are less than the purchase yield, then the
> realized compound yield for the whole life of the bond will be less than
> the purchase yield; if future rates are higher than the purchase yield,
> then the realized compound yield will be more than the purchase yield.*

---

[1]The "unrecovered investment" for a bond is the initial investment adjusted
during the life of the bond so that it equals the maturity value, at maturity. For a
discount bond, the unrecovered investment balance must increase each year; for a
premium bond, the unrecovered investment balance decreases each year; and for a
par bond, the balance remains constant. The change in "unrecovered investment
balance" is the difference between the product of the IRR times the balance and the
actual cash flow for each year.

[Again, Mr. Homer's definition of "realized compound yield" cannot be the internal rate of return (IRR) or yield to maturity, because if it is the statement is wrong. On page 64 of his book, Mr. Homer says: ". . . the term 'realized compound yield' was used to describe the total effective compound yield obtained from a bond purchased at a given price when the coupon income is reinvested and thus compounded at a specified 'reinvestment rate' over the entire life of the bond. Only when the reinvestment rate equals the yield-to-maturity at purchase, does the realized compound yield coincide with the yield book's yield-to-maturity."]

Please refer to Table 12–1 for the details of a discount bond, Table 12–2 for a par bond, and Table 12–3 for a premium bond. In all cases, the cash flows do not contain a single penny of income from reinvestment of interest. The annual proceeds from coupon revenue are withdrawn as they are received. In other words, to achieve a return equal to the IRR or yield to maturity at purchase, no reinvestment of coupon revenues is required.

If coupon revenues were reinvested, the annual cash flows would increase and the IRR would be higher, as was demonstrated in the previous chapter.

Table 12–1
Discount Bond

Years to maturity	5
Purchase price (original investment)	$800
Coupon (annual interest or annual cash flow)	$30
Maturity value (proceeds of sale of investment)	$1,000
Yield to maturity (IRR)	8%
Tax bracket	0%

	Year 1	2	3	4	5	Total
Investment balance (beginning)	800	834	871	911	954	
Plus: IRR × Investment balance (deposits)	64	67	70	73	76	350
Less: Cash flow for period (withdrawals)	30	30	30	30	1,030	1,150
Investment balance (ending)	834	871	911	954	0	

Summary:	
Investment balance (beginning)	800
Plus: Sum IRR × cash investment balance (interest deposits)	350
Less: Sum of cash flows (withdrawals)	1,150
Investment balance (ending)	0

Table 12–2
Par Bond

Years to maturity		5
Purchase price (original investment)		$1,000
Coupon (annual interest or annual cash flow)		$100
Maturity value (proceeds of sale of investment)		$1,000
Yield to maturity (IRR)		10%
Tax bracket		0%

	Year					
	1	2	3	4	5	Total
Investment balance (beginning)	1,000	1,000	1,000	1,000	1,000	
Plus IRR × cash investment balance (deposits)	100	100	100	100	100	500
Less: Cash flow for period (withdrawals)	100	100	100	100	1,100	1,500
Investment balance (ending)	1,000	1,000	1,000	1,000	0	
Summary:						
Investment balance (beginning)						1,000
Plus: Sum IRR × cash investment balance (interest depositits)						500
Less: Sum of cash flows (withdrawals)						1,500
Investment balance (ending)						0

Table 12–3
Premium Bond

Years to maturity		5
Purchase price (original investment)		$1,200
Coupon (annual interest or annual cash flow)		$100
Maturity value (proceeds of sale of investment)		$1,000
Yield to maturity (IRR)		5.34%
Tax bracket		0.00%

	Year					
	1	2	3	4	5	Total
Investment balance (beginning)	1,200	1,164	1,126	1,086	1,044	
Plus: IRR × investment balance (deposits)	64	62	60	58	56	300
Less: Cash flow for period (withdrawals)	100	100	100	100	1,100	1,500
Investment balance (ending)	1,164	1,126	1,086	1,044	0	
Summary:						
Investment balance (beginning)						1,200
Plus: Sum IRR × Investment balance (interest deposits)						300
Less: Sum of cash flows (withdrawals)						1,500
Investment balance (ending)						0

Terminal Value and Reinvestment of Cash Flows

Assume that cash flows from an investment are reinvested at any arbitrarily chosen rate of interest. Each cash flow compounds at this reinvestment rate until a stated future terminal date. The "terminal value" is the sum accumulated at that point from all cash flows and the reinvested interest thereon, as well as the proceeds from sale of the investment. You can think of the *terminal value* in terms of a bank account. You make an investment and all the proceeds from that investment including cash flows and sales proceeds are deposited into the account. Each deposit (i.e., the account balance) earns interest at the reinvestment rate. The value of the bank account at the end of the time period is the terminal value. If the reinvestment rate is 0 percent, then the terminal value would simply be the sum of the periodic cash flows added to the proceeds of sale.

Assume that Mrs. Abelson is comparing two proposed investments, as follows:

	Proposal A	Proposal B
Initial investment	10,000	10,000
Annual cash flows:		
Year 1	1,000	0
Year 2	1,000	0
Year 3	1,000	0
Year 4	1,000	0
Year 5	11,000	16,105
Total annual cash flows	15,000	16,105

The internal rate of return in both cases is the same—10 percent. Which is the more attractive investment (assuming risks of achieving the cash flows are comparable)? Note that the cash flows of Proposal A amount to $15,000 compared to $16,105 for Proposal B. But the entire cash flow for Proposal B is at the maturity of the investment. If no reinvestment of annual cash flows takes place, then are the proposals equivalent since the IRR is the same for both proposals? We shall determine the answer to that question in a moment.

But if the cash flows are to be reinvested, then the IRRs for the two proposals change. Let's say Mrs. Abelson determines that she wants to reinvest the cash flows but she is not sure at what reinvestment rate. She wants to know which proposal is the better investment at the following reinvestment rates: 0, 5, 8, 10, and 15 percent. The results of her analysis are shown in Table 12–4 and Graph 12–1.

The moment reinvestment takes place, the IRR for that investment is increased from its original 10 percent to a higher amount. This results from the fact that reinvestment, to whatever extent, increases

Table 12–4
Revised IRRs Resulting from Reinvestment of Cash Flow

(Yield to maturity) IRR before reinvestment: 10%

	Proposal A Reinvestment Rate					Proposal B Reinvestment Rate				
	0%	5%	8%	10%	15%	0%	5%	8%	10%	15%
Cash flow:										
Year 1	1,000	1,000	1,000	1,000	1,000	0	0	0	0	0
Year 2	1,000	1,050	1,080	1,100	1,150	0	0	0	0	0
Year 3	1,000	1,103	1,166	1,210	1,323	0	0	0	0	0
Year 4	1,000	1,158	1,260	1,331	1,521	0	0	0	0	0
Year 5	11,000	11,216	11,360	11,464	11,749	16,105	16,105	16,105	16,105	16,105
Terminal value	15,000	15,526	15,867	16,105	16,742	16,105	16,105	16,105	16,105	16,105
Revised IRR (after reinvestment)	10.00%	10.94%	11.54%	11.95%	13.03%	11.95%	11.95%	11.95%	11.95%	11.95%
Interest rate to equate initial investment to terminal value	8.45%	9.20%	9.67%	10.00%	10.86%	10.00%	10.00%	10.00%	10.00%	10.00%

the annual cash flows, and increased cash flows cause the IRR to increase. At a reinvestment rate of 8 percent, the revised IRR jumps to 11.54 percent; and at a reinvestment rate of 15 percent, the revised IRR becomes 13.03 percent. For Proposal B, the revised IRR increases to 11.95 percent because the entire cash flow occurs at the end of the fifth year. The original $10,000 investment has compounded during the five years at the initial 10 percent IRR. This is equivalent to a $10,000 investment, with 10 percent coupon, reinvested at a rate of 10 percent.

The reinvestment proposal that will be the best choice is the one that will result in the higher revised IRR; that is, the IRR computed on the basis of cash flow after considering any reinvestment of earnings. If the original investments were equal, as in the case of Proposals A and B, and were for the same period of time, the best choice would also be the proposal with the higher terminal value. Now let's address the question raised a moment ago: If no reinvestment occurs, are Proposals A and B equivalent since they both have an IRR of 10 percent?

As to terminal values, the answer is no, except under one circumstance. Refer to Graph 12–1, **Terminal Value Breakeven Point.** The terminal value of Proposal B remains a constant $16,105, as a 10 percent reinvestment rate is "locked-in" from the start. However, the higher the rate at which cash flows are reinvested, the higher the terminal value of Proposal A. Note that Proposal A has a terminal value of $15,000 at a 0 percent reinvestment rate and a terminal value of $16,742 at a 15 percent reinvestment rate. The point where the two curves cross, the 10 percent reinvestment rate, is the breakeven point

Graph 12–1
Terminal Value Break-even Point

Terminal value
(values of cash
flows compounded
to maturity at
the reinvestment
rate percentage)

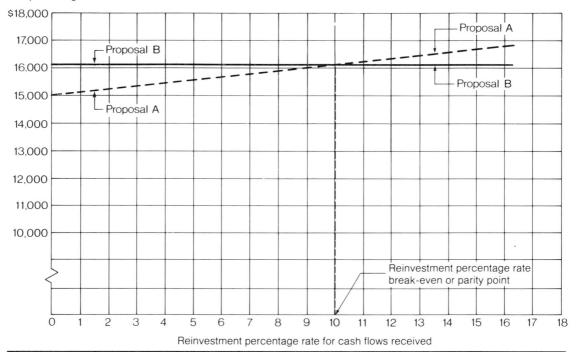

Reinvestment percentage rate for cash flows received

when the terminal values of Proposal A and Proposal B are equivalent to each other. At all reinvestment rates greater than 10 percent (which was the initial IRR prior to reinvestment), Proposal A's terminal value is greater than that of Proposal B. Conversely, at all reinvestment percentage rates below 10 percent, the terminal value of Proposal A is less than Proposal B.

Terminal Values Are Not the Solution: Use Revised IRRs

Merely computing and comparing terminal values for various series of cash flows does *not* adequately account for two inherent investment characteristics: (*a*) initial investments which are unequal and (*b*) periods of time that are not the same. In order to properly compare alternative investment proposals, assuming that all or a portion of earnings are reinvested, the *best method* is to calculate the **revised IRR.**

The first step in determining the revised IRR is to calculate the annual cash flows, after reinvestment of earnings at a stipulated percentage rate and then compute the revised IRR for those cash flows. The *revised IRR* is the percentage rate that equates the original investment to the future cash flows, including the proceeds of reinvesting, taking into consideration the timing of such cash flows. Thus it eliminates the problems that arise from simply considering terminal values.

However, a single investment such as the $10,000 investment of Proposal B, is equivalent to investing $10,000 in a bond at par; receiving annual cash returns equal to the IRR times the investment ($10,000 × 0.1 = $1,000 per year), and reinvesting such "imputed cash flows" at the IRR rate (10 percent for Proposal B). The revised IRR of the "imputed cash flows" is 11.95 percent for Proposal B. See Table. 12–4 for the calculations.

Let's return to the evaluation of Proposals A and B. Please refer to Table 12–4. The entire cash flow from Proposal B is at its terminus. The investment is equivalent to $10,000 initially, with both a 10 percent coupon and reinvestment rate. The revised internal rate of return is 11.95 percent, as compared to its original IRR of 10 percent. No other reinvestment rate, hence no other revised IRR, is possible.

But the situation is quite different for Proposal A. As the percentage rate at which earnings are reinvested increases, so too does the revised IRR. For example, at a reinvestment of earnings rate of 15 percent, Proposal A's revised IRR jumps to 13.03 percent. As you will deduce by studying Table 12–4, *Proposal A is the superior investment in all cases where there is reinvestment of earnings at rates higher than 10 percent.* Note that the revised IRR method produces the same conclusion that you obtain from considering only the terminal values.

More Misconceptions

A basic tenet of Homer and Leibowitz's bond analysis in *Inside the Yield Book* is based on the following reasoning and approach.

1. Take into account the proceeds of reinvestment of cash flows (interest-on-interest cash flows). (Note: I agree with this.)

2. Determine the terminal value which they call "future value."

3. Determine the compound rate of interest that equates the bond purchase price to the single sum, future value. This rate, Homer calls "fully-compounded yield to maturity," or "realized compound yield." And this same rate, we call (see Table 12–14) "interest rate to equate initial investment to terminal value." (I disagree with Step 3, as explained hereafter.)

The key measure of actual and relative performance should be the Revised IRR. Homer and Leibowitz say it should be "realized compound yield." The two measures are *not* the same. Consider Table 12–4, Proposal A, and you will note substantial differences as follows:

Reinvestment Percentage Rate	Rosen's Revised Internal Rate of Return	Interest Rate to Equate Initial Investment to Terminal Value (*Homer's realized compound yield*)
0.00%	10.00%	8.45%
5.00	10.94	9.20
8.00	11.54	9.67
10.00	11.95	10.00
15.00	13.03	10.86

For Proposal A, when the reinvestment percentage rate is 10.00 percent, then 11.95 percent is the rate that equates the initial investment to the future cash flows. And 10.00 percent is the compound rate that equates the initial investment ($10,000) to the terminal value ($16,105). Obviously 11.95 percent is not the same or even remotely close to 10.00 percent. So which is correct?

Let's study Proposal A when the annual cash flows are reinvested at a reinvestment return rate of 10 percent (in other words, when each dollar of cash flow is reinvested to earn at a compound rate of 10 percent).

Is the revised internal rate of return (or, if you like, revised yield to maturity) really 11.95 percent? If the present value of the future cash flows discounted to the present at 11.95 percent is equal to $10,000, the initial investment, then we are indeed correct in stating that the revised IRR is 11.95 percent. As the following table shows, at a discount rate of 11.95 percent, the present value of the cash flows is indeed, $10,000.

But what about Sidney Homer's method? Does he obtain only 10 percent as the compound realized yield when the reinvestment rate is 10 percent? He does, as shown below.

1. The terminal value is the value of $10,000 at maturity plus an annuity of $1,000 per year reinvested at 10 percent compound. The value of the annuity is $6,105.10.[2]

---

[2]Where V = Value of the account after n investments of R, and i is the rate of interest after the last investment is made:

$$V = R\left[\frac{(1 + i)^n - 1}{i}\right] = 1000\left[\frac{(1.1)^5 - 1}{.1}\right] = \frac{1000 \times .6105}{.1} = 6,105.$$

2. The terminal value is the sum of the maturity value, $10,000, plus the annuity value, $6,105, that is $16,105.

3. Then, the question is: $10,000 (the initial investment) compounds at what rate to become $16,105 in five years? The answer is 10 percent.[3]

Thus by Mr. Homer's method, the realized compound return is 10 percent (as opposed to the author's revised IRR of 11.95 percent). (Remember, 10 percent was the IRR before any reinvestment of cash flows.) Who is correct?

The author says he is correct! Why? Granted that the amount of money accumulated in both cases will be the same at maturity value, $16,105. Mr. Homer's method in step 3 above can be further analyzed to determine the imputed annual cash flows that result from compounding $10,000 at 10 percent to obtain $16,105 after five years, as shown below:

Year	Balance at Beginning of Year	Interest Earned During Period (*Cash Flows*)	Balance at End of Year	Present Values of Cash Flows Discounted at 10 Percent IRR	Present Values of Cash Flows Discounted at 11.95 Percent IRR
0			10,000		
1	10,000	1,000	11,000	909.09	893.26
2	11,000	1,100	12,100	909.09	877.70
3	12,100	1,210	13,310	909.09	862.41
4	13,310	1,331	14,641	909.09	847.39
5	14,641	1,464	16,105	909.09	832.57
Totals		6,105		4,545.45	4,313.33
Plus: Present value of $10,000 at maturity				6,209.21	5,686.95
Total present value				10,754.66	10,000.20

It is clear that the cash flows generated in each year for this par bond are the same in both Homer's method and the authors. The sum accumulated at maturity with reinvestment at 10 percent is also the same, $16,150. But discounting the cash flows to the present at Mr. Homer's compound realized yield rate of 10 percent produces a value of $10,754.66; that is, $754.66 more than the original $10,000 investment. *It is clear from the information presented in the foregoing table that 11.95 percent is the rate that equates the future cash flows to the initial investment of $10,000.* Mr. Homer's 10 percent compound realized return rate does not. Homer's compound realized return (CRR) is

[3]Where FV is the Future Value, PV is the Present Value, *n* is the number of years, and *i* is the compound interest rate:

$$FV = PV(1 + i)^5; 16105 = 10000(1 + i)^5; 1.6105 = (1 + i)^5;$$
$$1.6105^{(1/5)} = (1 + i); i = 1.1000 - 1 = 0.1, \text{ or } 10\%$$

comparable to an initial investment ($10,000) with a theoretical coupon of the CRR rate (10%), which is reinvested at that same CRR rate (10%), and a maturity value equal to the initial investment ($10,000).

Now, let's compare the three types of bonds: par, discount, and premium. Each bond pays $100 per year interest, which is reinvested to earn 10 percent. The bonds mature in five years. Please refer to Table 12–5. The columns under the heading **No Reinvestment** show the cash flows when interest is not reinvested; and the columns under the heading **Reinvestment** show the results of reinvesting cash flows at 10 percent compound.

The usual pattern of IRR relationships is evident. (*a*) With reinvestment, the revised IRR is greater than the original IRR, and (*b*) the revised IRR is greater than Homer's compound realized return. (*c*) Homer's compound realized return (CRR) equals the IRR or YTM at purchase, *if all cash flows are reinvested* at the rate of the original IRR. In the case of the discount bond, the terminal value with reinvestment at 16.13 percent is $1,689.71 and the CRR is 16.13 percent. For the par bond, the terminal value with reinvestment at 10.0 percent is

Table 12–5
Five Year Bond Study

	Discount Bond	Premium Bond	Par Bond
Purchase price	$ 800	$1,200	$1,000
Number of years to maturity	5	5	5
Coupon rate	100	100	100
Maturity value	$1,000	$1,000	$1,000
Reinvestment percentage	10.00%	10.00%	10.00%

Cash Flow at End of Years	No Reinvestment			Reinvestment		
	Discount	Premium	Par	Discount	Premium	Par
0	−800	−1,200	−1,000	−800	−1,200	−1,000
1	100	100	100	100	100	100
2	100	100	100	110	110	110
3	100	100	100	121	121	121
4	100	100	100	133	133	133
5	1,100	1,100	1,100	1,146	1,146	1,146
Totals (including amortization of premium or discount)	700	300	500	811	411	611
Interest plus maturity value	1,500	1,500	1,500	1,611	1,611	1,611
Internal rate of return	16.13%	5.34%	10.00%			
Revised internal rate of return				18.26%	7.15%	11.95%
With dividend reinvestment: Homer's method						
Value of annuity				611	611	611
Maturity value plus annuity value				1,611	1,611	1,611
Homer's compound realized yield	13.40%	4.56%	8.45%	15.02%	6.06%	10.00%
Rosen's revised IRR				18.26%	7.15%	11.95%

$1,611 and the CRR is 10 percent; and for the premium bond, the terminal value with reinvestment at 5.34 percent is $1,556.33, and the CRR is 5.34 percent.

The par bond performance shown in Table 12–5 is similar to that previously described. Let's focus first on the discount bond where a different pattern exists. The comparative results are:

Discount Bond

IRR without reinvestment (Table 12–6)	16.13%
Rosen's revised IRR (with reinvestment at 10 percent)	18.26%
Homer's compound realized return (with reinvestment at 10 percent)	15.02%

The progression of values implicit in Homer's method, as shown in Table 12–7, is:

year 0	$ 800
year 1	920
year 2	1,058
. . . year 5	1,611

At Homer's 15.02 percent compound realized return, the terminal value is $1,611 for the following: An $800 bond, paying a coupon of $120.16 (i.e., 15.02% times $800), with reinvestment at a rate of 15.02 percent, until maturity in five years at $800. This is the same terminal value obtained from an investment of $800, at a 10 percent reinvestment rate, and IRR of 16.13 percent (before reinvestment) and 18.26 percent revised IRR.

Premium Bond

IRR without reinvestment (Table 12–6)	5.34%
Rosen's revised IRR (with reinvestment at 10 percent)	7.15%
Homer's compound realized return (with reinvestment at 10 percent)	6.06%
Homer's CRR (with reinvestment at 16.13%)	16.13%

Homer's 6.06 percent "CRR" produces a terminal value of $1.611—for a $1,200 bond with $72.72 coupon ($1,200 × 6.06%) and reinvestment at a rate of 6.06%.

Perhaps the easiest way to distinguish between the Homer and Rosen methods is to view bonds with interest reinvested at ZERO percentage rate; in other words, without reinvestment. The results are:

	Discount	Premium	Par
Homer's compound realized return* (Table 12–7)	13.40%	4.56%	8.45%
Rosen's revised IRR (Table 12–6)	16.13	5.34	10.00
IRR (Table 12–5)	16.13	5.34	10.00
Homer's CRR (with reinvestment at 5.34%)		5.34%	

*In this case, without reinvestment, the terminal value with Homer's method, is $1,500, determined as follows:

$$\text{Future Value} = \text{Annuity} + \text{Maturity Value}$$
$$= \quad 500 \quad + \quad 1,000 \quad = 1,500$$

The value of the bond at the end of each year is shown in Table 12–6.

Table 12–6
Rosen's Method: Year End Values, Including Interest *(Coupon $100)*

	Without Reinvestment			With 10 Percent Reinvestment		
	Discount	Premium	Par	Discount	Premium	Par
Bond Purchase Price	$ 800	$1,200	$1,000	$ 800	$1,200	$1,000
Value after 1st year, including interest	929	1,264	1,100	929	1,264	1,100
Value after 2nd year, including interest	1,063	1,326	1,200	1,073	1,336	1,210
Value after 3rd year, including interest	1,202	1,386	1,300	1,233	1,417	1,331
Value after 4th year, including interest	1,347	1,444	1,400	1,411	1,508	1,464
Value after 5th year, including interest	1,500	1,500	1,500	1,611	1,611	1,611
IRR	16.13%	5.34%	10.0%	18.26%	7.15%	11.95%

The value at any year is the sum of:

1. The present value of the future maturity amount, discounted to such year at the IRR (yield to maturity) at purchase.

2. The present value of future interest payments discounted to such year at the IRR.

3. Interest received with (or without, as applicable) reinvestment of such interest receipts.

The annual year-end value by Homer's method (shown in Table 12–7) is determined by increasing each preceding year's value by the rate of the compound realized return.

Inspect and compare the year-end bond values for several years as shown in Tables 12–6 and 12–7. *The "shortcut" method of equating purchase price to terminal value employed by Mr. Homer generally*

Table 12–7
Homer's Method: Year End Values, Including Interest *(Coupon $100)*

	Without Reinvestment			With 10 Percent Reinvestment		
	Discount	Premium	Par	Discount	Premium	Par
Bond Purchase Price	$ 800	$1,200	$1,000	$ 800	$1,200	$1,000
Value after 1st year, including interest	907	1,255	1,084	920	1,273	1,100
Value after 2nd year, including interest	1,028	1,312	1,176	1,058	1,350	1,210
Value after 3rd year, including interest	1,166	1,372	1,275	1,217	1,432	1,331
Value after 4th year, including interest	1,323	1,435	1,383	1,400	1,518	1,464
Value after 5th year, including interest	1,500	1,500	1,500	1,611	1,611	1,611
Homer's compound realized return	13.40%	4.56%	8.45%	15.02%	6.06%	10.00%

understates the year-end by year-end values of the investment (as compared to the IRR method) until the final year, when the values are equal. The comparison between Homer and Rosen's year-end values is shown in Table 12–8.

Table 12–8
Comparison of Rosen and Homer's Year End Values, Including Interest *(Coupon $100)*

Rosen value exceeds Homer's by:

	Without Reinvestment			With Reinvestment		
	Discount	Premium	Par	Discount	Premium	Par
Year 0	$ 0	$ 0	$ 0	$ 0	$ 0	$0
Year 1	22	9	16	9	−9	0
Year 2	35	14	25	15	−24	0
Year 3	36	14	25	16	−15	0
Year 4	24	9	17	11	−10	0
Year 5	0	0	0	0	0	0

Bond Sale Prior to Maturity

Compare the IRRs in Table 12–9 if the investment is sold at the end of any year, 1 through 5. The sale price is the one that will yield 16.13 percent to a buyer; that is, the original IRR at which the bond was first acquired. The IRR realized for the period of time the investment was held (1 through 5 years) remains constant at about 16.13 percent. But compare the IRR to Homer's compound realized return. Homer's compound realized return is 13.40 percent irrespective of the year of sale.

Summary

The concept of terminal value has merit in some circumstances. Recall that Proposal A and Proposal B both have the same IRR, 10 percent, before reinvestment. If reinvestment is to take place, then the better investment alternative depends on the estimated percentage rate to be earned on such reinvestment. *The revised IRR can then be determined to select the better investment.* In the illustration, Proposal B is equivalent to a "locked-in" reinvestment rate of the initial IRR, 10 percent. At reinvestment rates in excess of 10 percent, Proposal A produces superior results.

The concept of compound realized return is confusing, requires reinvestment of earnings, and makes it difficult to compare alternatives. Its problems are eliminated by the use of the IRR concept, and revised IRRs.

In the next chapter, we shall determine the after tax revised internal rates of return for bonds at various rates of earnings from reinvestment of interest receipts.

Table 12-9
IRR if Bond Sale Occurs Prior to Maturity

Rosen's method:
Reinvestment 0.00%
Purchase price $800.00
IRR 16.13%
Coupon $100.00

Year	Present Value of Maturity Value Discounted at 16.13% A	Present Value of Coupons Discounted at 16.13% B	Total Present Value (A + B) C	Previous Interest Receipts D	Total Value (C + D) E	Annual Interest Received F	Annual Interest Received Plus Amortization of Principal G	Cash Flow if Sold Year 1 H	Cash Flow if Sold Year 2 I	Cash Flow if Sold Year 3 J	Cash Flow if Sold Year 4 K	Cash Flow if Sold Year 5 L
0	473	326	800	0	800	0		-800	-800	-800	-800	-800
1	550	279	829	100	929	100	129	929	100	100	100	100
2	639	224	863	200	1,063	100	134		963	100	100	100
3	741	160	902	300	1,202	100	139			1,002	100	100
4	861	86	947	400	1,347	100	145				1,047	100
5	1,000	0	1,000	500	1,500	100	153					1,100
						500	700					

		H	I	J	K	L
Rosen's internal rate of return		16.11%	16.12%	16.12%	16.13%	16.13%
Homer's compound realized return*		13.40%	13.40%	13.40%	13.40%	13.40%

*The compound rate which equates the purchase price, $800, to Homer's year end values, as follows: Year 1—$907; Year 2—$1,028; Year 3—$1,166; Year 4—$1,323; Year 5—$1,500.

Bond Revised IRRs at Various Reinvestment Rates (After Taxes)

In investing, what counts is what your results are after considering all relevant factors. Certainly taxes are a relevant factor and so is the effect of reinvesting earnings, if that is your intention.

In this chapter, graphs are presented that allow you to determine the **revised IRR** for taxable bond investments taking several variables into account.

1. All purchase prices.

2. A variety of number of years until maturity (5, 10, 15, 20, 25, and 30).

3. A choice of three pre-tax rates (4, 8, and 12 percent) at which all interest income is presumed to be reinvested.

4. Ordinary income taxation at a rate of 50 percent.

5. Capital gains tax (at 20 percent) on the disposition of the bond at maturity.

In the case of **taxable** bonds purchased at a **premium,** the tax benefit is included in the results from the capital **loss** that is recognized when the bond matures at less than the purchase price.

Marshall Denver is an astute investor, in a 50 percent tax bracket, who is considering the possible purchase of two bonds, both of which are priced with an after tax yield to maturity of 6 percent. Alternative A is a premium bond that he can purchase for $1,134. It pays $140 per year in interest and has 25 years until maturity. The stated yield to maturity is 6 percent after taxes and ignoring reinvestment. (The before tax, before reinvestment yield to maturity, or IRR, is 12.3 percent.) Alternative B is a discount bond that is offered to Marshall at $531, has annual interest of $50, and also matures in 25 years. Its yield to maturity is also 6 percent after taxes and ignoring reinvestment. (The discount bond's before tax, before reinvestment IRR is 10.3 percent.)

After consulting with his CPA, Anita Mandlebaum, Marshall decides that it is unwise to ignore either taxes or reinvestment because his intention is to reinvest all the earnings to build up funds for the purchase of a vacation condo in Aspen. He anticipates that he will earn 8 percent (before taxes), at least, on reinvesting the interest receipts as he receives them.

Anita and Marshall turn to Graph 13–14, **Bond Interest Reinvestment,** which covers reinvestment of interest at a pre-tax rate of 8 percent, in a tax bracket of 50 percent, and where the bond has 25 years until maturity.[1]

For the premium bond, they enter the graph along the vertical axis at the $1,134 purchase price, proceed horizontally to the $140 coupon rate curve, then down to the bottom axis where it is intersected at the **8.6** percent point. For alternative A, the premium bond, 8.6 percent is the revised IRR *after taxes and after reinvesting all interest receipts.*

Next, for the discount bond, they enter the same Graph 13–14, along the left axis at the $531 purchase price, proceed horizontally to the $50 coupon curve, then down to the point intersection at the bottom axis, **7.8** percent.

So the premium bond produces a revised IRR of **8.6** percent versus only **7.8** percent for the discount bond, even though both bonds were priced to yield 6 percent after taxes but before considering reinvestment returns. Clearly then, for Marshall Denver's purposes, the premium bond is the more attractive purchase in the foregoing example where the IRR after tax (6 percent) is greater than the interest reinvestment rate after tax (4 percent).

But what if the 6 percent interest reinvestment rate after tax (12 percent before tax) is equal to the IRR after tax (6 percent)? Graph 13–15 has the ready answers! The revised IRR for the premium bond after reinvestment of earnings at 12 percent (before tax) is **10.1** percent, and for the discount bond, it is only **8.9** percent.

If the interest reinvestment rate after tax is 6 percent (12 percent before tax) and the bond is priced at an after tax IRR of only 3.6 percent (before reinvestment—use Graph 6–25), which is then the better investment **after** considering reinvestment of earnings? In this case, the premium bond is priced at $1,600 with a coupon of $140, to provide

---

[1]The 8 percent interest reinvestment rate is a before tax amount. However, the revised IRRs determined from the graphs are after taxes.

an after tax IRR of 3.6 percent, and the discount bond provides the same 3.6 percent after tax IRR with an $800 purchase price and a coupon of $50. Under these circumstances, the revised IRRs (after reinvestment at a before tax 12 percent rate) are **6.9** percent for the premium bond versus **6.1** percent for the discount bond.

So in the three situations presented, where the IRR after tax was greater than, equal to, or less than the after tax rate on reinvestment, the *premium bond produced results superior to the discount bond.* The results are summarized below:

	Premium	Discount
Case 1:		
IRR after tax at purchase	6.0%	6.0%
Reinvestment percentage rate after tax	4.0	4.0
Revised IRR (with reinvestment)	8.6	7.8
Case 2:		
IRR after tax at purchase	6.0%	6.0%
Reinvestment percentage rate after tax	6.0	6.0
Revised IRR (with reinvestment)	10.1	8.9
Case 3:		
IRR after tax at purchase	3.6%	3.6%
Reinvestment percentage rate after tax	6.0	6.0
Revised IRR (with reinvestment)	6.9	6.1

Please refer to Table 13–1 for a complete year-by-year presentation of the effects of reinvesting interest. The $60 entries in the first column represent each year's interest receipts of $120 less 50 percent income tax, leaving a $60 remainder. The column entitled **Before Reinvestment Balance** is the cumulative sum of all cash flow receipts, excluding interest earned from reinvesting. The three columns under the heading **Interest Reinvestment** are comparable to a bank account, to which is credited the coupon interest and interest earned on such coupon interest (after taxes at 50 percent). The last column, **Cash Flow per Year,** is the after tax cash flow for each year including initial investment, receipt of bond maturity value, annual interest coupons, and interest earned on interest—all after applicable income or long-term capital gains taxation. The earnings from reinvestment after taxes are $12.24 in the example, and the IRR after tax without reinvestment is 13.78 percent, and increases to 14.06 percent with reinvestment.

The final step in determining the revised IRR, after taxes with reinvestment of earnings is to determine the IRR for the cash flows that result in each year. The IRR is of course the interest rate that equates such cash flows to the original investment. The detailed process is displayed in Table 13–1 for a bond with five years until maturity, purchased for $700, and paying $120 per year in interest that

Table 13–1
Bonds: After Tax with Reinvestment

Rosen's Method:

Number years until maturity	5
Maturity value	$1,000
Tax bracket	50%
Percentage interest on reinvestment	4%
Purchase price	$ 700
Coupon	$ 120

Before Reinvestment Cash Flows	Year	Before Reinvestment Balance	Interest Reinvestment			Cash Flow per Year
			Old Balance	Interest on Interest	New Balance	
−700	0	0	0	0	0	−700
60	1	60	0	0.00	60	60
60	2	120	60	1.20	121	61
60	3	180	121	2.42	184	62
60	4	240	184	3.67	247	64
1,000	5	1,240	247	4.95	1,252	1,005
1,240				12.24		1,252

IRR	13.78%

Revised IRR	14.06%

is reinvested at 4 percent per year. The tax bracket is 50 percent. The cash flows displayed are after taxes, as such cash flows have already been reduced, before printing, by 50 percent.

In the fifth year, the first column shows a cash flow of $1,000. It is the sum of the maturity value after capital gains tax plus the interest coupon for the fifth year after tax.

a.	Maturity value	$1,000	
b.	Less: Cost	700	
c.	Long-term capital gain	300	
d.	Capital gains tax, 20% × c	60	
e.	Proceeds, after tax a less d		$ 940
f.	Interest coupon before reinvestment	120	
g.	Tax at 50% on interest	60	
h.	Interest, after tax $f - g$		60
i.	Cash flow in years before income from reinvestment		$1,000

Municipals or Tax-Exempt IRRs

Graphs 13–19 through 13–36 in this chapter may also be used to calculate the revised IRR or yield to maturity after tax with interest reinvestment from investments in municipals or tax-exempts purchased at **par** or a **premium**. Graphs 13–1 through 13–18, with slight adaptation, may be used to find revised IRRs of municipals purchased at a **discount.**. Although the interest receipts from a municipal are not normally subject to federal income tax, the *capital gain or loss upon sale or redemption at maturity is taxable.*[2] The procedure to follow for obtaining the after tax yield to maturity (IRR) from an investment in a tax-exempt bond by a 50 percent tax bracket investor is as follows:

1. Choose the graph closest to the bond's number of years until maturity (5, 10, . . . 30 years). (For *par* or *premium* bonds, use in the normal manner, Graphs *13–19* through *13–36.* For **discount** bonds, use Graphs *13–1* through *13–18 and* adjust the coupon rate, as follows.)

2. Calculate an adjusted coupon rate for discount bonds as follows:

$$\frac{\text{Adjusted}}{\text{coupon}} = \frac{\text{Tax-exempt bond's coupon rate}}{0.5}$$

Example: Sally Abelson, who is in a 50 percent tax bracket, is considering the purchase of a tax-exempt sewer bond for $600, with 25 years until maturity. It pays $70 per year in interest per bond. The adjusted coupon rate (for using the graphs) for Sally's bond is:

$$\frac{\text{Adjusted}}{\text{coupon}} = \frac{\$70 \text{ (Tax exempt's coupon rate)}}{0.5 \text{ (1} - \text{ Sally's tax bracket)}}$$

$$= \frac{70}{0.5} = \$140.00$$

Sally estimates that she can reinvest the interest receipts at 12 percent (before tax) in taxable CDs. To find the after-capital-gains-tax yield to maturity with reinvestment at 12 percent, refer to Graph 13–15. Enter the graph on the vertical axis at the bond's purchase price, $600. Proceed horizontally to the adjusted coupon rate, 14 percent ($140); then descend to the horizontal axis. The intersection at the horizontal axis is the after tax yield to maturity with reinvestment of interest, 17 percent.

The revised IRR, 17 percent, for Sally's purchase, takes into consideration reinvestment of interest, the tax-free nature of the $70 annual interest, as well as the ultimate capital gains tax of $80; 20 percent of the $400 gain ($1,000 redemption less $600 cost).[3] A 50 percent tax

---

[2]When tax-exempt bonds are purchased as a premium (i.e., over $1,000), the premium **must** be amortized over the life of the bonds. Such amortization each year reduces the "tax basis." At the maturity date, the "taxable basis" will have been reduced to an amount equal to the maturity value. Thus, there is **no taxable loss** at the maturity of a tax-exempt bond purchased at a premium.

[3]The revised IRR at an 8 percent reinvestment rate (before tax) is 15.27 percent (use Graph 13–14); at a 4 percent reinvestment rate it is 13.6 percent (Graph 13–13). The IRR without reinvestment is 12.06 percent (Graph 6–25 using an adjusted coupon).

bracket investor in a tax-exempt discount bond *must* use an adjusted coupon rate, as described and determined above, and use Graphs 13–1 through 13–18.

Par Bond—Revised IRR for Tax-Exempts

Judy Blank, a successful proprietor of a business brokerage firm, is in a 50 percent tax bracket. Judy is considering the purchase of a tax-exempt San Jose Sewer and Water Bond, at its par value of $1,000. The tax-exempt bond matures in 25 years and has a $110 coupon. Judy has no immediate need for the income from the investment and estimates that she can conservatively reinvest the coupon income at 8 percent before taxes in taxable CDs or the like (i.e. a rate of earnings on reinvestment of 4 percent after tax in a 50 percent tax bracket). But Judy wants to know what her revised IRR will be after reinvesting all the income.

To find the revised IRR for a par bond use Graphs 13–19 through 13–36. These graphs are based on a zero tax-bracket investor. Since a tax-exempt investor in either a par or premium tax-exempt bond is subject to neither tax on the coupon income nor is the investor able to deduct a capital loss at maturity. These graphs may be used in the normal fashion without any adjustments. The reinvestment percentage rate, e.g. 8 percent, should be the rate the investor anticipates earning after paying applicable taxes on the reinvested earnings. Judy enters Graph 13–31 (the graph for 25 years to maturity, 4 percent after tax reinvestment rate) along the vertical axis at the $1,000 purchase price; crosses to the $110 coupon curve; then descends to the bottom axis where the revised IRR is found, 14.3 percent.

Judy wonders what the results will be if she is able to reinvest the income at higher rates. The revised IRR jumps to 17.94 percent at an 8 percent (after tax) reinvestment rate (Graph 13–32); and if she can reinvest at 12 percent (after tax) reinvestment rate, the revised IRR soars to 21.69 percent (Graph 13–33).

Premium Bond—Revised IRR for Tax-Exempts

Janice Platte is also in a 50 percent bracket; and is considering the purchase of a premium bond at a purchase price of $1,450. The bond's annual coupon is $140 and it matures in 25 years. Janice can determine the revised IRR in the same manner as Judy choosing the appropriate Graphs from the 13–19 through 13–36 series. At a reinvestment rate of 4 percent after tax, the revised IRR is 12.65 percent (Graph 13–31); at 8 percent reinvestment after tax, the revised IRR is 16.26 percent (Graph 13–32); and at 12 percent after tax reinvestment, Janice reaps the rewards of a 20.0 percent revised IRR (Graph 13–33).

Tax-Exempt Investors; e.g., Pensions, Keoghs, IRAs

The tax-exempt investor bears a status even more favorable than the investor in tax-exempt securities. That may sound a bit peculiar at first reading. The tax-exempt investor is normally free from any taxation. Examples include pension plans, Keogh (HR-10) plans, and IRAs. On the other hand, a tax-exempt security such as a municipal bond is normally free of federal income tax and state tax of the issuer, but it is subject to the federal capital gains tax. Investments in tax-exempt bonds were described earlier in this chapter.

Now let's look at the tax-exempt *investor*. **Graphs 13–19** through **13–36** show revised IRRs, after reinvesting cash receipts at various percentage rates, *for the tax-exempt investor*. Nothing has been deducted for taxation—either from the regular coupon, the interest-on-interest receipts from reinvestment, or as the result of the capital gain or loss at maturity. These graphs are established for the following number of years until maturity: 5, 10, 15, 20, 25, and 30. A choice of three rates of interest reinvestment is available: 4, 8 or 12 percent.

So if you are interested in knowing the revised IRR of a 10-year bond, with reinvestment at 12 percent, you would use Graph 13–24. The graphs follow the typical pattern found throughout the book. Enter along the left axis at the bond purchase price, proceed horizontally to the curve representing the appropriate interest coupon rate, then descend to the bottom axis to find the revised IRR without taxation.

Zero Coupon Bonds

Zero coupon bonds have been actively promoted by brokers in recent years. Typically the investor is offered a bond at an extraordinarily low purchase price. The bond matures in x years for $1,000. No interest is received during the intervening years. Such a bond is precisely equivalent to buying a conventional bond for the same purchase price, with coupon interest equal to the purchase price times the IRR or YTM of the zero bond, reinvesting all income at that same rate, and maturing at a value equal to the purchase price. The rate earned on reinvestment is fixed and irrevocable at the rate of IRR or YTM at purchase.

Normally, ordinary taxpaying citizens should not buy these bonds because taxpayers must pay tax on income *each year* even though they have not received any cash flow and won't receive any until the bond's maturity. But for the tax-exempt *investor*, such bonds may have appeal depending on quality and pricing.

Dr. Markman has a pension plan, and he is the trustee. He is phoned by one of his brokers (as I was a couple of days ago) and offered the following "deal" for his pension plan. Buy Hagendagen Milk Shake zero coupon bonds that mature for $1,000 in 10 years and are rated AA by Moody's. The *price is only $463.19 per $1,000 bond*. That provides an 8 percent fully compounded yield to maturity (IRR). That's *more* *than double your money in 10 years.* How many bonds would you like to buy?

Dr. Markman says, "Wait just a minute. The zero coupon bond you are offering me is the same as buying a bond with a maturity value of $463.19, an 8 percent coupon, and a $463.19 purchase price. In other words, it's the same return as an 8 percent IRR with compulsory reinvestment at an irrevocable 8 percent rate. That's the same as a revised IRR of 10.86 percent (Graph 13–23). How much do I have to pay to buy a normal high-grade Treasury or corporate bond maturing in 10 years with a coupon rate of, let's say, $80?"

"Well," said the broker, "Hagendagen has some regular bonds maturing in 10 years with an $80 coupon that are selling at about $774."

Dr. Markman quickly thumbs through the book to Graph 5–10, where he finds the before tax IRR for this regular bond to be about 12 percent. He says, "So that's about 12 percent IRR, isn't it?"

"I'll have to check," says the surprised broker. Several minutes later he returns, and says, "That's right, it's 12 percent. How did you know?"

"So," says Dr. Markman, "I can buy the 8 percent fully compounded bonds you offered me that, reinvesting all income (since I don't receive anything until maturity with a zero coupon issue), provide the equivalent of an 8 percent IRR. Or, to look at it with all income reinvested until maturity, the zero coupon bond has a revised IRR of 10.86 percent. But the regular Hagendagen bond—at the same 8 percent earned on reinvestment—has a revised IRR of how much? That is, if I buy the normal bond for $774 with an $80 coupon, and I reinvest the income at 8 percent (after tax of zero) until maturity in 10 years, what will my revised IRR be in that case?"

"Our tables don't show that," says the broker. "I can contact our office in New York and maybe they can tell us."

Meanwhile the Doctor has turned to Graph 13–23 where he enters along the left axis at $774, proceeds to the 8 percent ($80) coupon curve, and then descends to the bottom axis, at 15.1 percent revised IRR. He says, "Oh, don't bother, I've already figured it out; it's about 15.1 percent. So, Mr. Broker, I think I'll pass on the Hagendagen zero coupon bonds. Why should my pension plan buy at an 8 percent IRR (revised IRR of 10.86 percent)when it can make 12 percent (revised IRR of 15.1 percent) from the same issuer?"

Beware of *zero coupon price volatility.* Some zero coupon bonds (those with longer time periods with maturity) are extremely volatile in price. That is, *small* changes in market interest rates cause much larger percentage changes in the market value of the zero coupon bond. For example, Roger Shafer buys zero coupon bonds for $3,338 at 12 percent fully compounded (12 percent IRR with compulsory reinvestment at a 12 percent rate). But, if the market interest rate, 12 percent fully compounded, increases by **25** percent (to 15 percent), then the market value of the bonds **will fall by 55 percent** from $3,338 to $1,510.

Graph 13–1
Bond Interest Reinvestment Rate of 4%

Bond purchase price

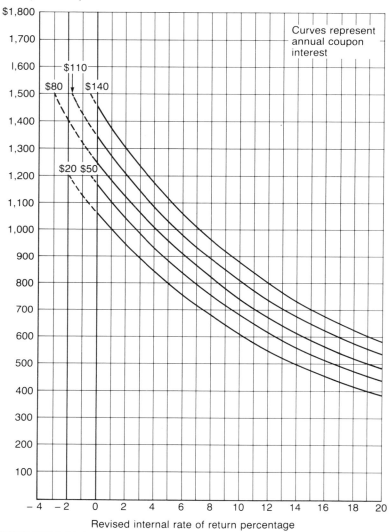

Revised internal rate of return percentage

Note: Tax bracket   50%
         Years until maturity   5 years
         Revised internal rate of return is after applicable taxes, if any.

Graph 13–2
Bond Interest Reinvestment Rate of 8%

Bond purchase price

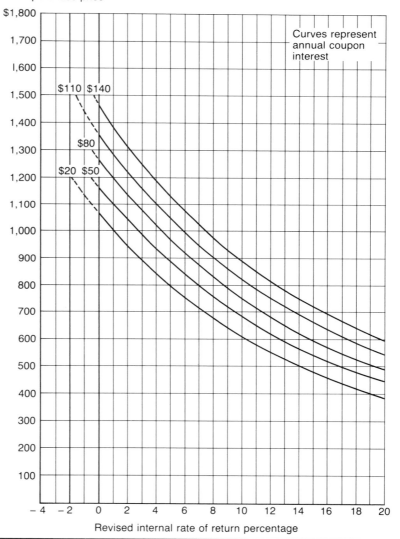

Revised internal rate of return percentage

Note: Tax bracket   50%
         Years until maturity   5 years
         Revised internal rate of return is after applicable taxes, if any.

Graph 13–3
Bond Interest Reinvestment Rate of 12%

Bond purchase price

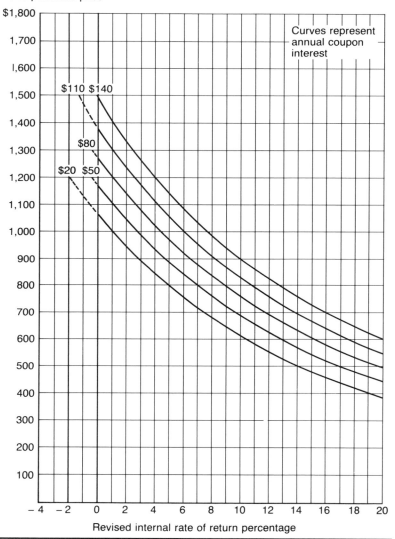

Revised internal rate of return percentage

Note: Tax bracket   50%
       Years until maturity   5 years
       Revised internal rate of return is after applicable taxes, if any.

Graph 13–4
Bond Interest Reinvestment Rate of 4%

Bond purchase price

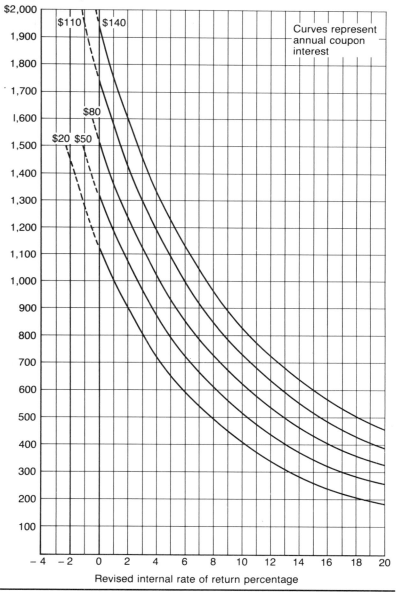

Revised internal rate of return percentage

Note: Tax bracket   50%
       Years until maturity   10 years
       Revised internal rate of return is after applicable taxes, if any.

Graph 13–5
Bond Interest Reinvestment Rate of 8%

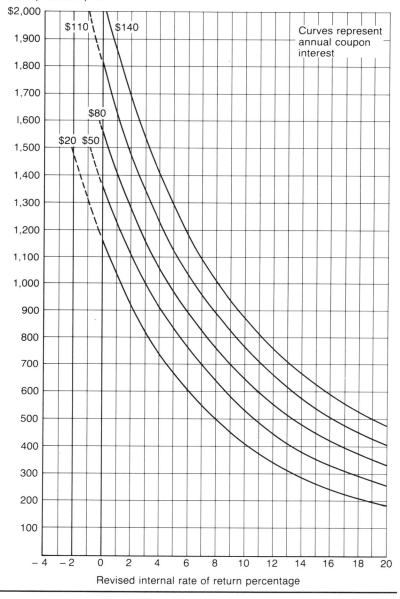

Bond purchase price

Curves represent annual coupon interest

$110 $140

$80

$20 $50

Revised internal rate of return percentage

Note: Tax bracket   50%
         Years until maturity   10 years
         Revised internal rate of return is after applicable taxes, if any.

Graph 13–6
Bond Interest Reinvestment Rate of 12%

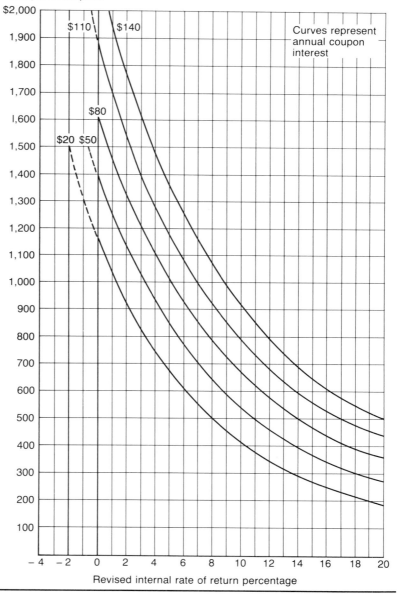

Bond purchase price

Revised internal rate of return percentage

Note: Tax bracket 50%
Years until maturity 10 years
Revised internal rate of return is after applicable taxes, if any.

Graph 13–7
Bond Interest Reinvestment Rate of 4%

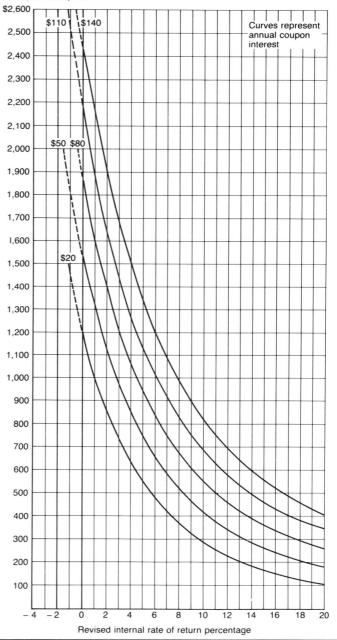

Bond purchase price

Curves represent
annual coupon
interest

$110 $140

$50 $80

$20

Revised internal rate of return percentage

Note: Tax bracket   50%
        Years until maturity   15 years
        Revised internal rate of return is after applicable taxes, if any.

Graph 13–8
Bond Interest Reinvestment Rate of 8%

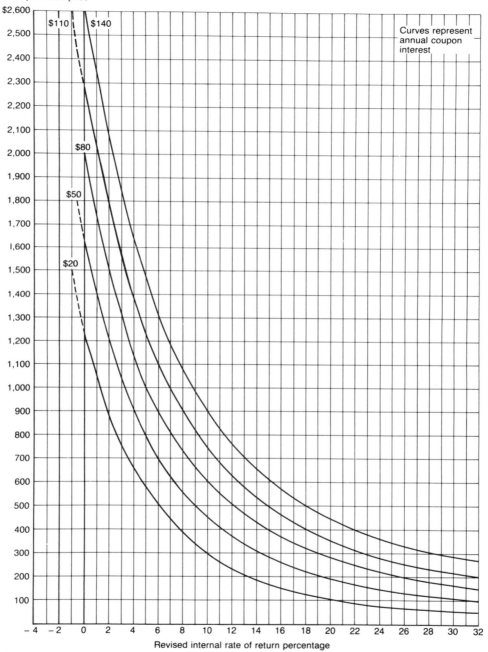

Bond purchase price

Curves represent
annual coupon
interest

Revised internal rate of return percentage

Note: Tax bracket   50%
       Years until maturity   15 years
       Revised internal rate of return is after applicable taxes, if any.

Graph 13–9
Bond Interest Reinvestment Rate of 12%

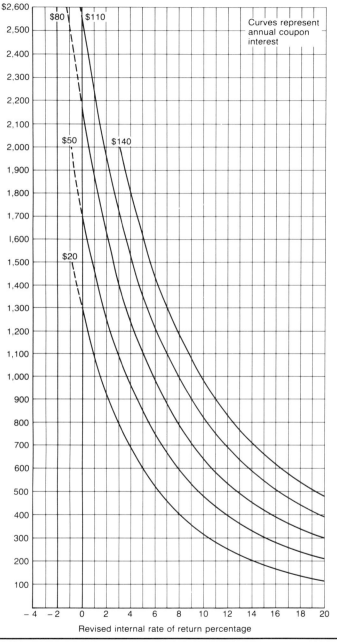

Bond purchase price

Curves represent annual coupon interest

Revised internal rate of return percentage

Note: Tax bracket   50%
      Years until maturity   15 years
      Revised internal rate of return is after applicable taxes, if any.

Graph 13–10
Bond Interest Reinvestment Rate of 4%

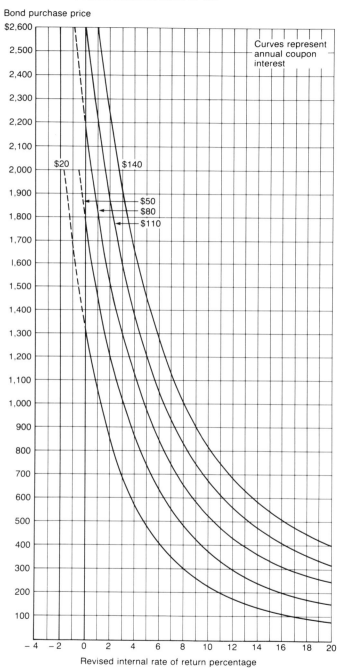

Bond purchase price

Curves represent annual coupon interest

$20

$140

$50
$80
$110

Revised internal rate of return percentage

Note: Tax bracket   50%
       Years until maturity   20 years
       Revised internal rate of return is after applicable taxes, if any.

Graph 13–11
Bond Interest Reinvestment Rate of 8%

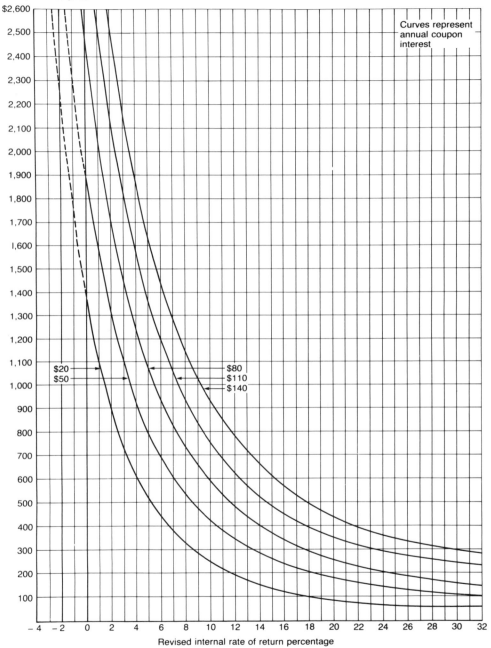

Bond purchase price

Curves represent annual coupon interest

$20
$50
$80
$110
$140

Revised internal rate of return percentage

Note: Tax bracket   50%
       Years until maturity   20 years
       Revised internal rate of return is after applicable taxes, if any.

Graph 13–12
Bond Interest Reinvestment Rate of 12%

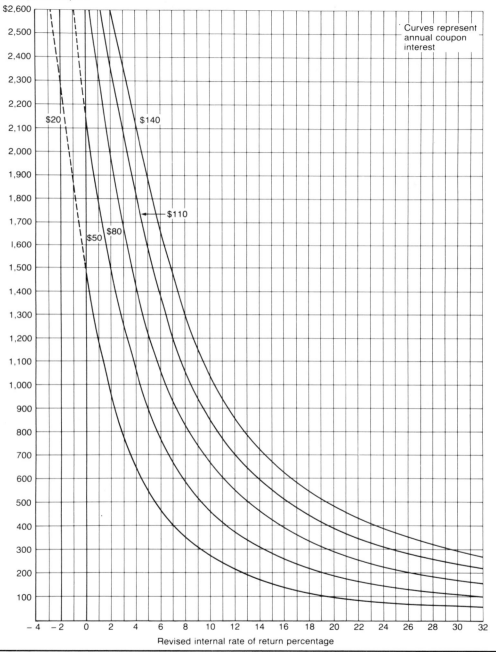

Bond purchase price

Curves represent annual coupon interest

$20 $140

$110

$50 $80

Revised internal rate of return percentage

Note: Tax bracket   50%
        Years until maturity   20 years
        Revised internal rate of return is after applicable taxes, if any.

Graph 13–13
Bond Interest Reinvestment Rate of 4%

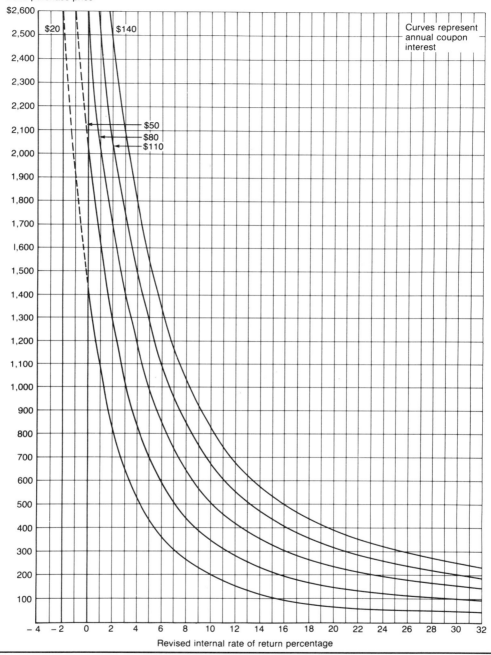

Bond purchase price

Revised internal rate of return percentage

Note: Tax bracket   50%
       Years until maturity   25 years
       Revised internal rate of return is after applicable taxes, if any.

Graph 13–14
Bond Interest Reinvestment Rate of 8%

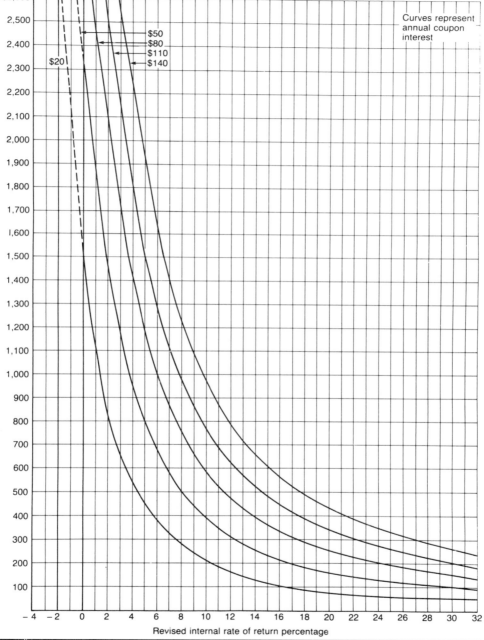

Bond purchase price

Curves represent
annual coupon
interest

$50
$80
$110
$140

$20

Revised internal rate of return percentage

Note: Tax bracket   50%
       Years until maturity   25 years
       Revised internal rate of return is after applicable taxes, if any.

Graph 13-15
Bond Interest Reinvestment Rate of 12%

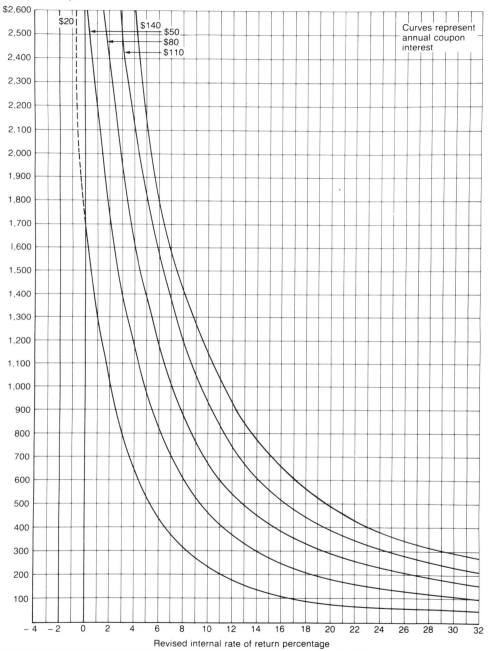

Bond purchase price

Curves represent annual coupon interest

$20 $140 $50 $80 $110

Revised internal rate of return percentage

Note: Tax bracket   50%
      Years until maturity   25 years
      Revised internal rate of return is after applicable taxes, if any.

Graph 13–16
Bond Interest Reinvestment Rate of 4%

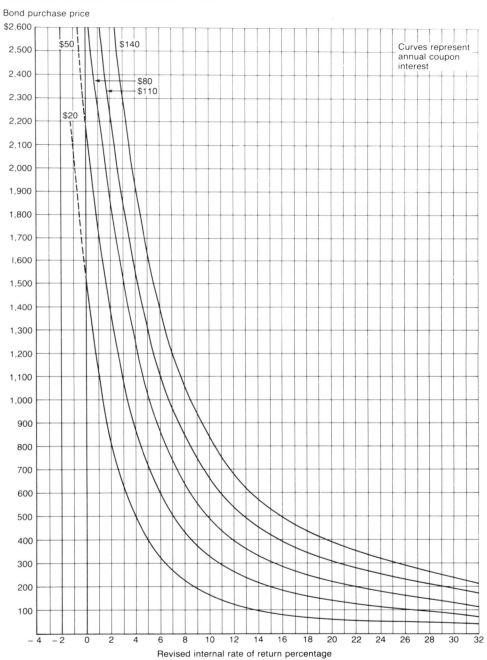

Bond purchase price

Curves represent annual coupon interest

$50 $140 $80 $110 $20

Revised internal rate of return percentage

Note: Tax bracket   50%
         Years until maturity   30 years
         Revised internal rate of return is after applicable taxes, if any.

Graph 13–17
Bond Interest Reinvestment Rate of 8%

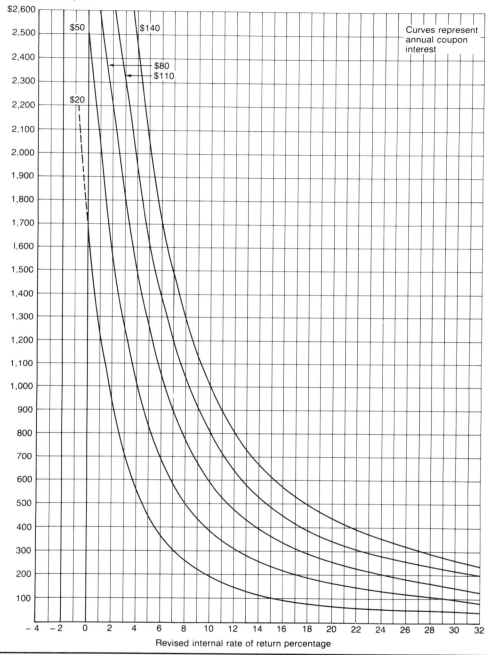

Bond purchase price

Revised internal rate of return percentage

Note: Tax bracket   50%
       Years until maturity   30 years
       Revised internal rate of return is after applicable taxes, if any.

Graph 13–18
Bond Interest Reinvestment Rate of 12%

Bond purchase price

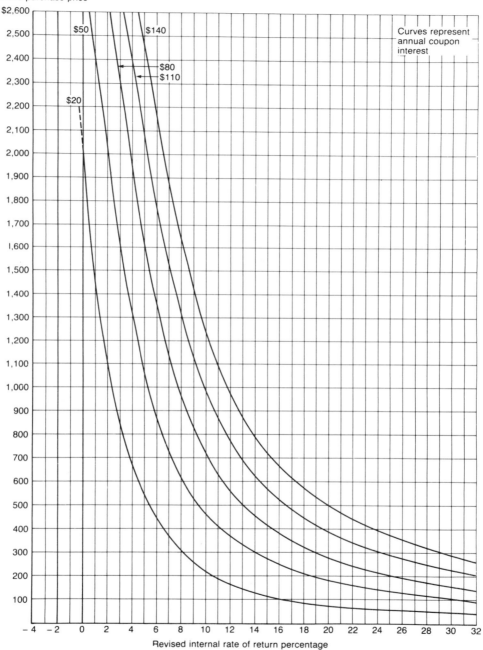

Note: Tax bracket   50%
       Years until maturity   30 years
       Revised internal rate of return is after applicable taxes, if any.

Graph 13–19
Bond Interest Reinvestment Rate of 4%

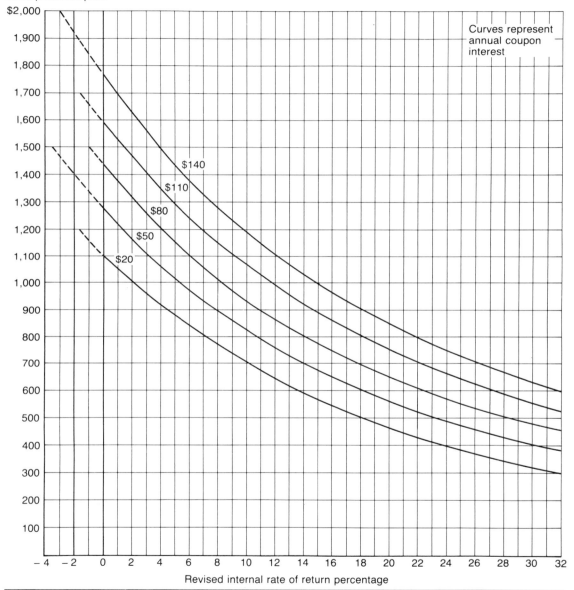

Bond purchase price

Curves represent annual coupon interest

$140
$110
$80
$50
$20

Revised internal rate of return percentage

Note: Tax bracket   0%
        Years until maturity   5 years
        Revised internal rate of return is after applicable taxes, if any.

Graph 13–20
Bond Interest Reinvestment Rate of 8%

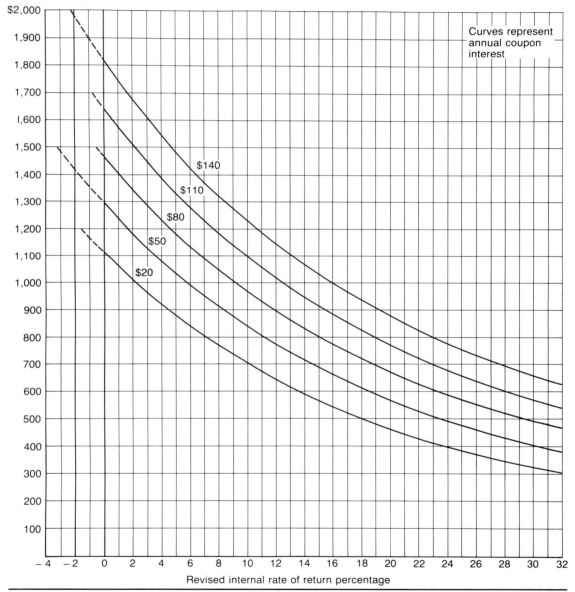

Bond purchase price

Curves represent annual coupon interest

$140
$110
$80
$50
$20

Revised internal rate of return percentage

Note: Tax bracket   0%
        Years until maturity   5 years
        Revised internal rate of return is after applicable taxes, if any.

Graph 13–21
Bond Interest Reinvestment Rate of 12%

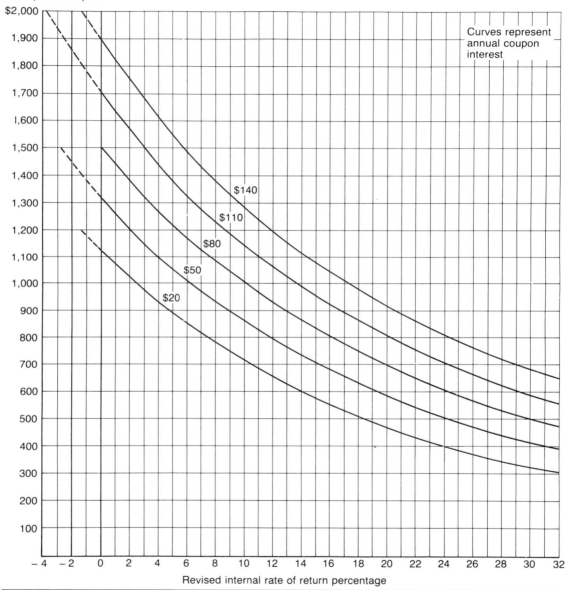

Bond purchase price

Curves represent
annual coupon
interest

$140
$110
$80
$50
$20

Revised internal rate of return percentage

Note: Tax bracket   0%
        Years until maturity   5 years
        Revised internal rate of return is after applicable taxes, if any.

Graph 13–22
Bond Interest Reinvestment Rate of 4%

Bond purchase price

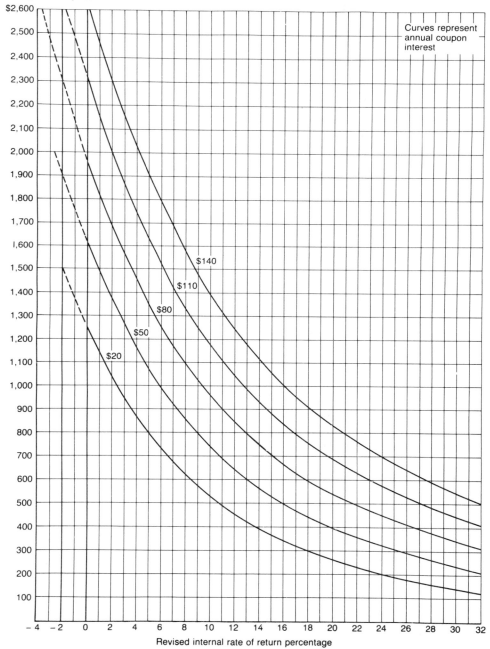

Curves represent annual coupon interest

$140

$110

$80

$50

$20

Revised internal rate of return percentage

Note: Tax bracket   0%
       Years until maturity   10 years
       Revised internal rate of return is after applicable taxes, if any.

Graph 13–23
Bond Interest Reinvestment Rate of 8%

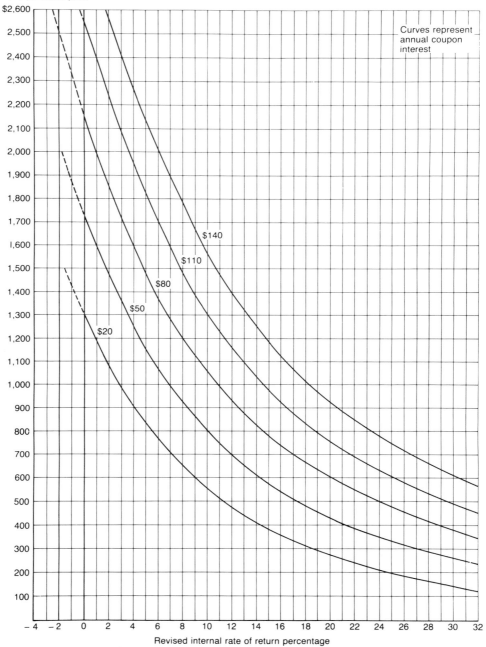

Bond purchase price

Curves represent
annual coupon
interest

$140

$110

$80

$50

$20

Revised internal rate of return percentage

Note: Tax bracket   0%
       Years until maturity   10 years
       Revised internal rate of return is after applicable taxes, if any.

Graph 13–24
Bond Interest Reinvestment Rate of 12%

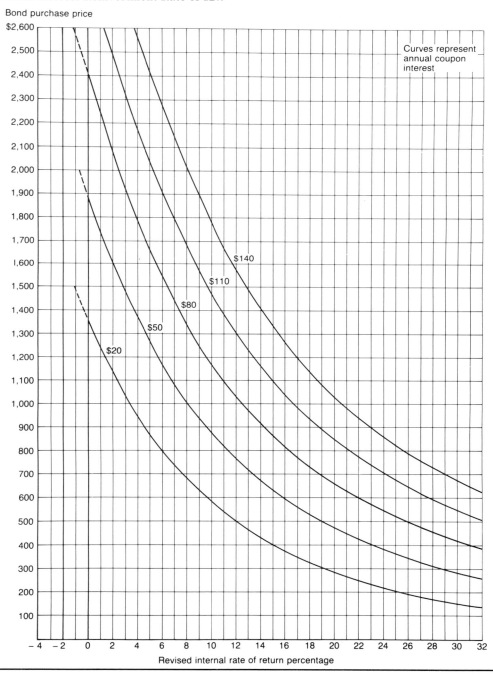

Bond purchase price

Curves represent annual coupon interest

$140

$110

$80

$50

$20

Revised internal rate of return percentage

Note: Tax bracket   0%
Years until maturity   10 years
Revised internal rate of return is after applicable taxes, if any.

Graph 13–25
Bond Interest Reinvestment Rate of 4%

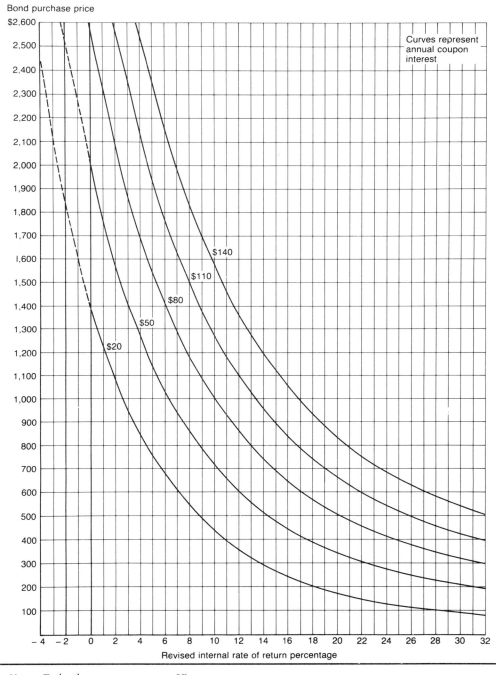

Bond purchase price

Curves represent
annual coupon
interest

$140

$110

$80

$50

$20

Revised internal rate of return percentage

Note: Tax bracket   0%
        Years until maturity   15 years
        Revised internal rate of return is after applicable taxes, if any.

Graph 13–26
Bond Interest Reinvestment Rate of 8%

Bond purchase price

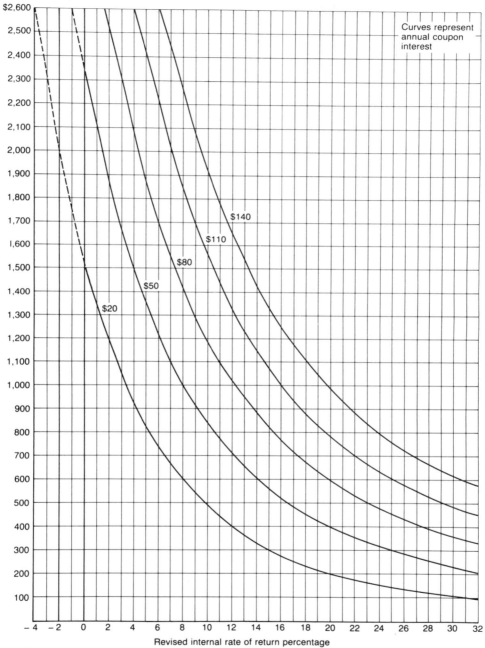

Curves represent annual coupon interest

$140

$110

$80

$50

$20

Revised internal rate of return percentage

Note: Tax bracket   0%
       Years until maturity   15 years
       Revised internal rate of return is after applicable taxes, if any.

Graph 13–27
Bond Interest Reinvestment Rate of 12%

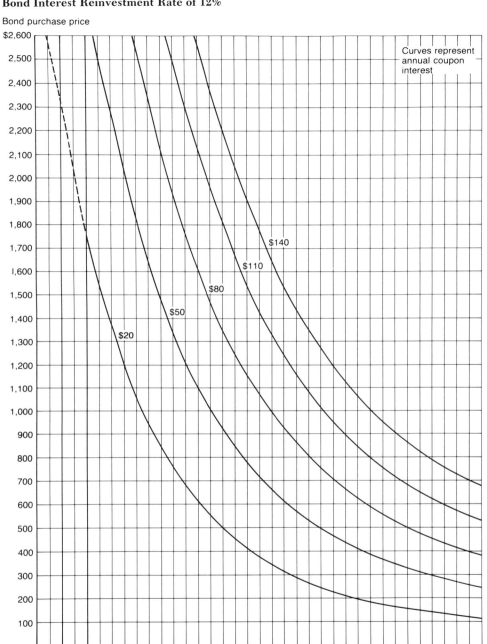

Bond purchase price

Curves represent annual coupon interest

$140

$110

$80

$50

$20

Revised internal rate of return percentage

Note: Tax bracket   0%
       Years until maturity   15 years
       Revised internal rate of return is after applicable taxes, if any.

Graph 13–28
Bond Interest Reinvestment Rate of 4%

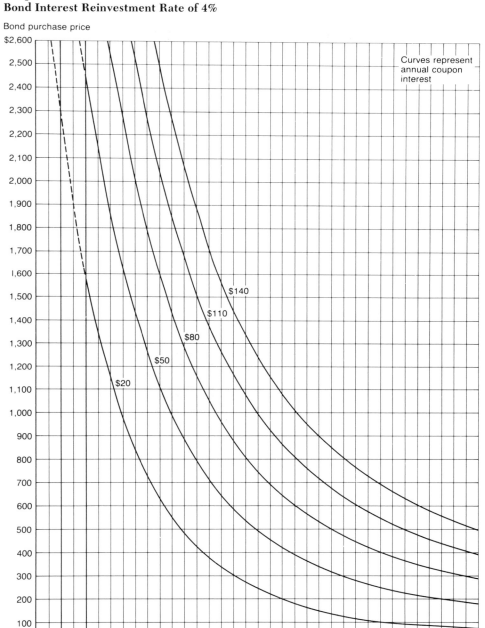

Bond purchase price

Curves represent annual coupon interest

$140

$110

$80

$50

$20

Revised internal rate of return percentage

Note: Tax bracket   0%
Years until maturity   20 years
Revised internal rate of return is after applicable taxes, if any.

Graph 13–29
Bond Interest Reinvestment Rate of 8%

Bond purchase price

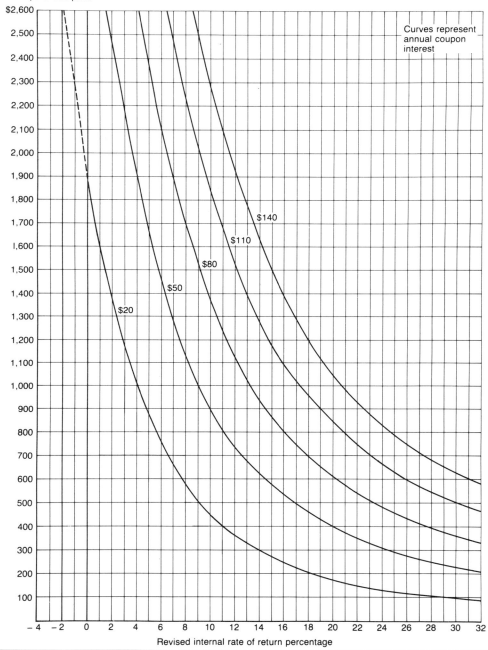

Curves represent
annual coupon
interest

$140

$110

$80

$50

$20

Revised internal rate of return percentage

Note: Tax bracket   0%
       Years until maturity   20 years
       Revised internal rate of return is after applicable taxes, if any.

Graph 13–30
Bond Interest Reinvestment Rate of 12%

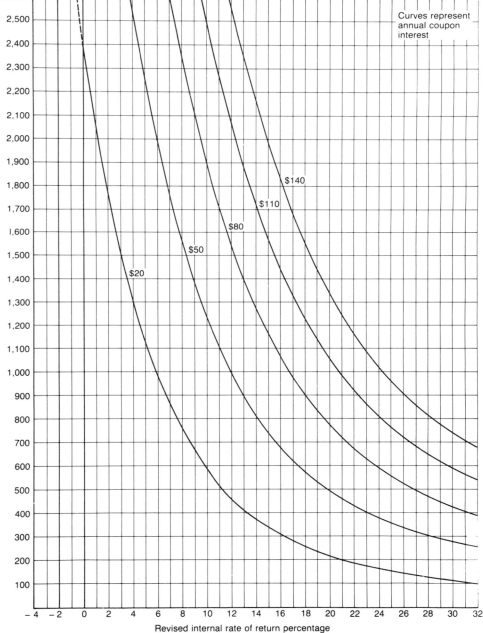

Bond purchase price

Revised internal rate of return percentage

Curves represent annual coupon interest

$140
$110
$80
$50
$20

Note: Tax bracket   0%
        Years until maturity   20 years
        Revised internal rate of return is after applicable taxes, if any.

Graph 13–31
Bond Interest Reinvestment Rate of 4%

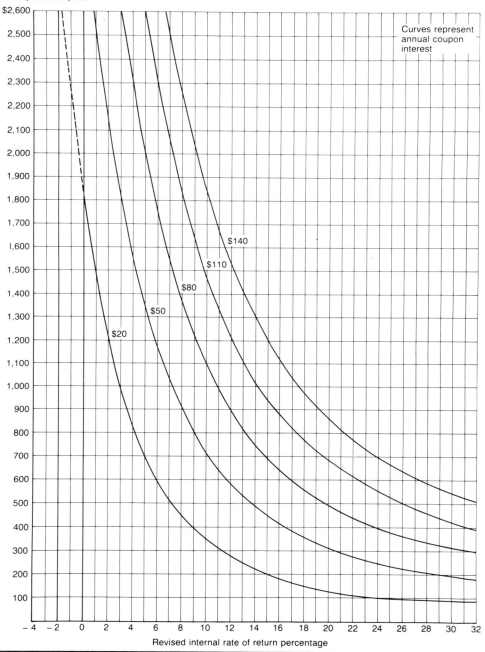

Bond purchase price

Curves represent annual coupon interest

$140

$110

$80

$50

$20

Revised internal rate of return percentage

Note: Tax bracket   0%
      Years until maturity   25 years
      Revised internal rate of return is after applicable taxes, if any.

Graph 13–32
Bond Interest Reinvestment Rate of 8%

Bond purchase price

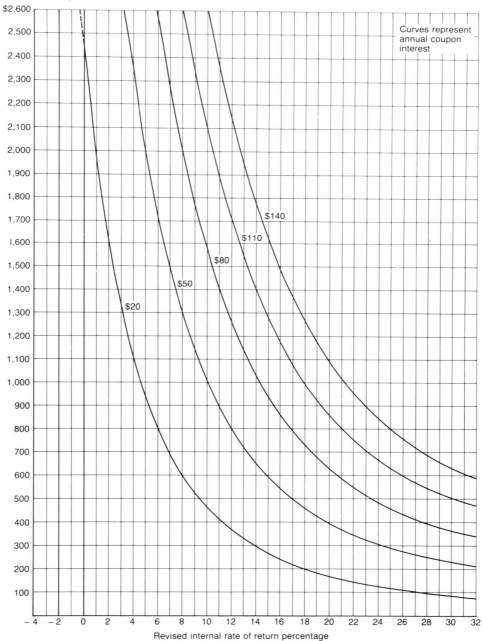

Curves represent
annual coupon
interest

$140

$110

$80

$50

$20

Revised internal rate of return percentage

Note: Tax bracket   0%
        Years until maturity   25 years
        Revised internal rate of return is after applicable taxes, if any.

Graph 13–33
Bond Interest Reinvestment Rate of 12%

Bond purchase price

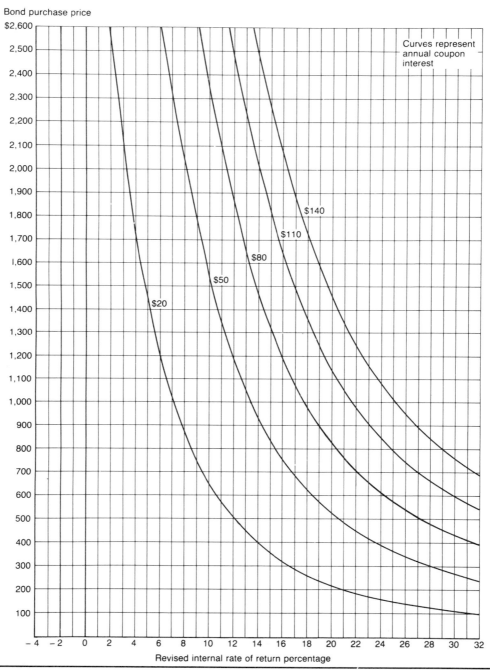

Curves represent annual coupon interest

$140
$110
$80
$50
$20

Revised internal rate of return percentage

Note: Tax bracket   0%
         Years until maturity   25 years
         Revised internal rate of return is after applicable taxes, if any.

Graph 13–34
Bond Interest Reinvestment Rate of 4%

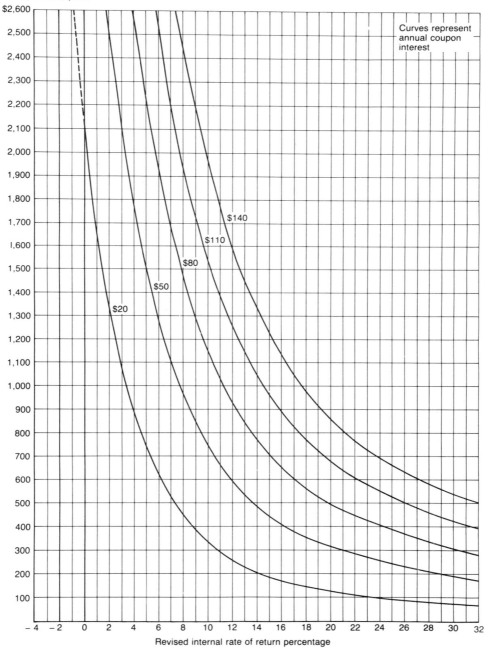

Bond purchase price

Curves represent annual coupon interest

$140
$110
$80
$50
$20

Revised internal rate of return percentage

Note: Tax bracket   0%
       Years until maturity   30 years
       Revised internal rate of return is after applicable taxes, if any.

Graph 13–35
Bond Interest Reinvestment Rate of 8%

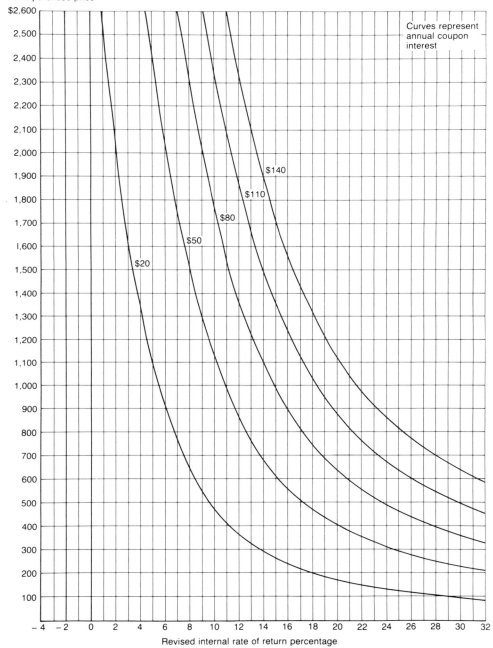

Bond purchase price

Curves represent annual coupon interest

$140
$110
$80
$50
$20

Revised internal rate of return percentage

Note: Tax bracket   0%
       Years until maturity   30 years
       Revised internal rate of return is after applicable taxes, if any.

Graph 13–36
Bond Interest Reinvestment Rate of 12%

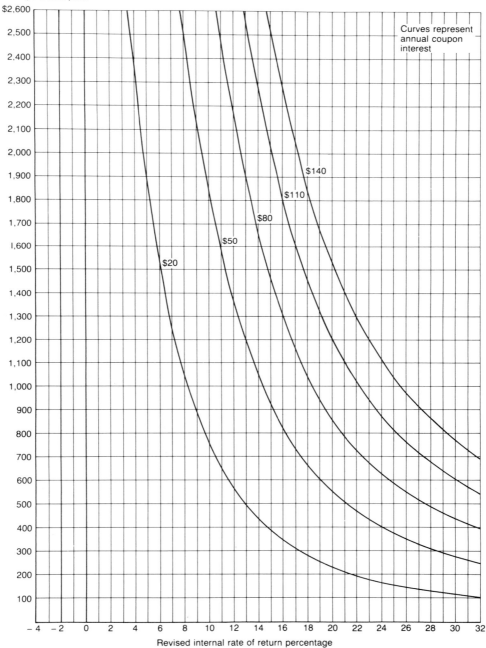

Bond purchase price

Curves represent
annual coupon
interest

$140

$110

$80

$50

$20

Revised internal rate of return percentage

Note: Tax bracket   0%
       Years until maturity   30 years
       Revised internal rate of return is after applicable taxes, if any.

Reinvestment of Dividends (Before and After Tax)

Reinvestment of Dividends—Before Tax

We know that reinvestment of dividends at any positive percentage rate will cause the revised IRR to exceed the original IRR prior to any reinvestment. Also, we have determined that no reinvestment is required to achieve a return equal to the original IRR. But how much difference does reinvestment make? For example, suppose Judy Blank invests $10,000 today to buy a stock with a 6 percent initial yield, and a 10 percent growth is anticipated in earnings and dividends. What IRR will Judy earn with no reinvestment of dividends as compared to the revised IRR that will result if she reinvests all dividends at 10 percent?

Refer to Graph 14–3, **Reinvestment of Cash Flows at Various Rates: 10 Percent Earnings and Dividend Annual Growth Rate.** Enter the graph on the left axis at the 6 percent initial yield; proceed horizontally to the curve representing the 10 percent rate to be earned on reinvestments; at that intersection, descend to the bottom axis. The point of intersection with the bottom axis, 19.7 percent, is the revised IRR. The same graph also shows that with 0 percent earned on reinvestment, the original IRR is 16 percent. Details of the year-by-year calculations are shown in Table 14–1 (at the end of this chapter).

The graphs may also be used in reverse. Judy Blank wants to invest to earn 20 percent after reinvestment of dividends. What are her choices? There are a number, as can be discerned from Graphs 14–1 through 14–4. To illustrate just one option from each graph, that will allow Judy to achieve her objective, she could follow any of the following patterns:

Growth Rate of Dividends and Earnings	Percent Earned on Reinvestment	Initial Yield	Graph
0%	10%	12.0%	14–1
6%	0%	14.0	14–2
10%	8%	7.0	14–3
14%	10%	3.8	14–4

These combinations illustrate but a few of a myriad of options available to Judy as can be deduced from the graphs.

The foregoing options were based on a static P-E ratio and zero tax bracket—at time of purchase and time of sale. Now let's consider the situation when the P-E ratio is expected to materially fluctuate.

Shrinking P-E Multiples

Sally Abelson buys a "glamour" stock at a P-E ratio of 20:1. That simply means that she pays $20 of market price for each $1 per share that the company is presently earning. Glamour, or high growth stocks, tend to sell at higher P-E multiples than other stocks. When the company disappoints the market (analysts and institutional investors in particular), there is frequently a substantial sell-off in the stock, its market price declines, and, concurrently, its P-E multiple is reduced.

In projecting the economic results, IRR, or revised IRR, it is necessary to predict the price at which the stock will ultimately be sold. The sales price is the product of the number of shares purchased, the P-E ratio, and the earnings per share at the time of sale. For example, if 10 shares are owned, the earnings per share are $2, and the P-E multiple is 20:1; the market value of the holdings is $400, which is $10 \times 2 \times 20$. But if the P-E multiple is only 10:1, then the market value drops to $200.

In some instances, it is warranted to project a shrinking multiple, that is the P-E multiple declines from the time of purchase to the time of sale. At other times, it may be more reasonable to predict a static multiple (no change from time of purchase until sale), or a mounting multiple, where the P-E multiple increases from time of purchase until time of sale. *Graphs 14–5 through 14–8* allow computation of *revised IRR* at various rates of earnings on *reinvestment* of dividends, a *shrinking multiple*, and a decline in the P-E from 20:1 at purchase to 10:1 at sale. *Graphs 14–9* through *14–12* allow similar computations with *mounting multiples* where the P-E increases from 10:1 at purchase to

20:1 at sale. *Graphs 14–1 through 14–4* present revised IRR calculations with a *static multiple*.

Let's return to Sally's purchase of a stock selling at a 20:1 P-E multiple. Sally figures that over a 20-year holding period, the stock ought to increase dividends and earnings per share at 10 percent per year. The initial yield (current dividend divided by market price) is 4 percent. If the multiple drops to 10:1 at sale, and Sally reinvests all dividends over the 20 years at a reinvestment rate of 10 percent, what is the revised internal rate of return (the IRR after considering reinvestment)?

Finding the answer with the graphs will take you less time than it is taking to write this description. Turn to the shrinking multiple graph for stocks with earnings and dividend growth of 10 percent per year, which is Graph 14–7. Enter the graph at the yield rate of 4 percent on the left axis; proceed horizontally to the curve representing 10 percent earnings on reinvested dividends; from the point of intersection, descend to the bottom axis. The intersection at the bottom axis is at 15.2 percent, and that is the revised IRR for Sally's investment. (Without reinvestment the original IRR is 11.6 percent.) Further detail of this example is shown in Table 14–2, where it is evident that if Sally invests $100 initially under the described conditions, with reinvested earnings she will receive $825.65.

By using the graphs, exactly comparable procedures may be followed to find the revised IRR for mounting multiple situations or other combinations of expected growth, initial yield, and earnings reinvestment rates.

Graphs 14–1 through 14–12 are all before tax (or for zero tax bracket investors). To find after tax results, the annual cash flows must be reduced by the income tax applicable to the dividends or interest, and the proceeds of sale must be adjusted for the capital gain (or loss) at sale. We shall assume a capital gains tax rate of 40 percent of the tax rate on ordinary income.

Next we shall look at the *after tax results*, as measured by the revised IRR, in a *50 percent tax bracket* for stock investments with dividend reinvestment.

Reinvestment of Dividends—After Tax

The first element that is implicit in Graphs 14–13 through 14–25 is that annual dividends as well as the interest earned from reinvesting such dividends are both *reduced by taxes* at the *rate of 50 percent*. The sales proceeds less cost (the capital gain) is taxed at a 20 percent rate (40 percent of 50 percent = 20 percent). Three distinct types of situations are dealt with: *static P-E multiples, mounting multiples*, and *shrinking multiples*. Graphs 14–13 through 14–16 are for static multiples, Graphs 14–17 through 14–20 cover shrinking multiples, and Graphs 14–21 through 14–24 are based on mounting multiples. Finally, *four* different *choices* are available as to the *projected growth rate of dividends and earnings per share:* 0, 6, 10, and 14 percent.

David Wolfson and Celia Melin have a partnership and are considering a stock investment. They narrow their choice to the following two stocks, Attorney's Library Services, a young rapidly growing firm just starting to spread nationwide, and Teacher's Publishing Company, an old-line, staid and stable publisher of educational materials. Here are the facts about the two alternatives:

	Attorney's Library Services, Inc.	Teacher's Publishing Company
Anticipated growth rate of dividends and earnings	14%	6%
Present dividend yield	0%	10%
Tax bracket of Celia and David	50%	50%
P-E multiple at purchase	20:1	10:1
P-E multiple at sale	10:1	10:1
Percent return on reinvestment of dividends	10%	10%

Attorney's Library Services was started a few years ago by a lawyer who saw the benefits of providing centralized legal libraries in major office buildings to provide lawyers with more complete facilities than they would normally maintain on their own, at a much lower cost than they incur for less material.

Teacher's Publishing Company is a company that began operation in 1881 and is presently headed by a former teacher. The company publishes and distributes textbooks in elementary schools throughout the United States.

Which investment appears to have the better prospects?

The growth company, Attorney's Library Services, can be analyzed by referring to Graph 14–20 (14 percent growth, shrinking multiples, 50 percent tax bracket). Enter the graph on the left axis at the present yield of 0 percent. Proceed horizontally until the 10 percent curve for reinvestment of dividends is reached. Then descend to the bottom axis, where the point of intersection is at 9.1 percent. This is the revised internal rate of return for a 20-year investment in Attorney's Library Services.

Graph 14–14 (6 percent growth of earnings and dividends, static multiple, 50 percent tax bracket) does the trick for Teacher's Publishing. Enter the graph on the left axis at the 10 percent initial yield point; proceed horizontally to the 10 percent rate earned on reinvestment of dividends. Then descend to the point of intersection with the bottom axis, which is about 12.6 percent. Thus 12.6 percent is the revised IRR for the staid, mature investment.

To summarize:

Revised IRR for Attorney's Library Services	9.1%
Revised IRR for Teacher's Publishing	12.6%

So not only is Teacher's Publishing less risky, it also offers the greater after tax return. *With facts like these, the decision is easy.*

Remember that a small percentage difference in after tax revised IRR results means a substantial amount of money over time. To illustrate, consider the following summary of the results shown in Tables 14–4 through 14–15.

Initial investment	$100
Holding period	20 yrs.
Tax bracket	50%
Initial dividend yield	4%
Earnings on reinvestment of cash flows	10%

	Dividend and Earnings Growth	End Value	Revised IRR
Static multiples:			
	0%	$ 169	3.25%
	6%	392	8.26%
	10%	728	11.89%
	14%	1,377	15.64%
Shrinking multiples:			
	0%	129	1.65%
	6%	264	6.10%
	10%	459	9.45%
	14%	827	12.97%
Mounting multiples:			
	0%	249	5.44%
	6%	649	10.96%
	10%	1,267	14.85%
	14%	2,476	18.81%

A bit of analysis of the above results shows that a *1 percent increase in the revised IRR usually results in between 20 and 25 percent more money after tax at the conclusion of the investment.* You, too, can join Mr. Wolfson and Miss Melin and find quick answers to the tough question of where to invest. Just use the graphs and find your answers in seconds.

Graph 14–1

Reinvestment of Cash Flow at Various Rates: 0 Percent Earnings and Dividend Annual Growth Rate

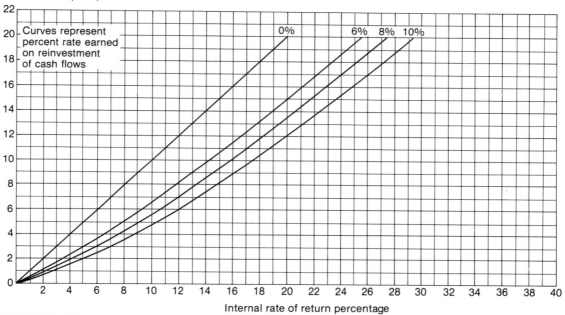

Percent yield
(annual initial
dividend divided by
initial market price)

Internal rate of return percentage

Curves represent percent rate earned on reinvestment of cash flows

0% 6% 8% 10%

Notes: Static multiple
        Holding period   20 yrs.
        P-E ratio at purchase   10:1
        P-E ratio at sale   10:1
        Tax bracket   0%

Graph 14–2
Reinvestment of Cash Flow at Various Rates: 6 Percent Earnings and Dividend Annual Growth Rate

Percent yield
(annual initial
dividend divided by
initial market price)

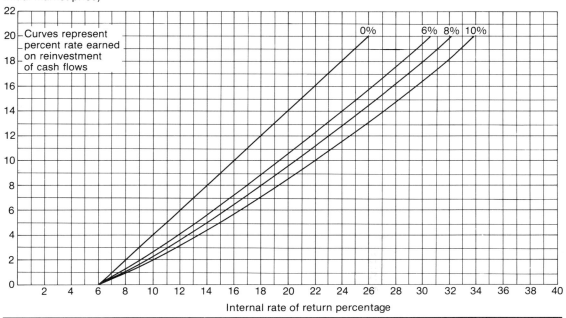

Internal rate of return percentage

Notes: Static multiple
          Holding period   20 yrs.
          P-E ratio at purchase   10:1
          P-E ratio at sale   10:1
          Tax bracket   0%

Graph 14–3
Reinvestment of Cash Flow at Various Rates: 10 Percent Earnings and Dividend Annual Growth Rate

Percent yield
(annual initial
dividend divided by
initial market price)

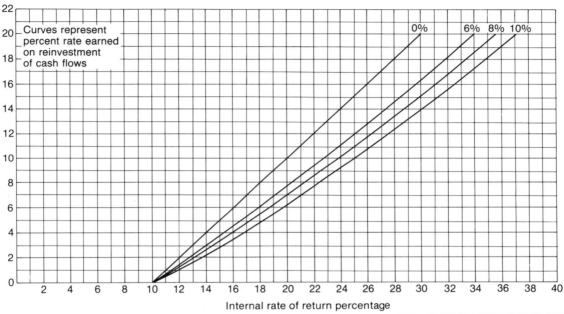

Internal rate of return percentage

Notes: Static multiple
Holding period   20 yrs.
P-E ratio at purchase   10:1
P-E ratio at sale   10:1
Tax bracket   0%
Example: Table 14–1

Graph 14–4
Reinvestment of Cash Flow at Various Rates: 14 Percent Earnings and Dividend Annual Growth Rate

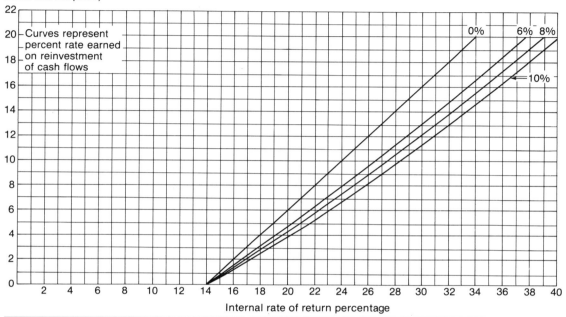

Percent yield
(annual initial
dividend divided by
initial market price)

Internal rate of return percentage

Notes: Static multiple
       Holding period   20 yrs.
       P-E ratio at purchase 10:1
       P-E ratio at sale   10:1
       Tax bracket   0%

Graph 14–5
Reinvestment of Cash Flow at Various Rates: 0 Percent Earnings and Dividend Annual Growth Rate

Percent yield
(annual initial
dividend divided by
initial market price)

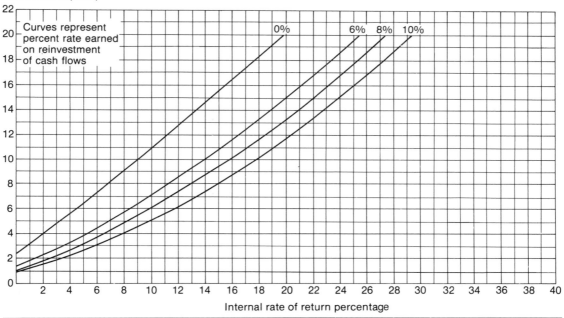

Internal rate of return percentage

Notes: Shrinking multiple
Holding period   20 yrs.
P-E ratio at purchase   20:1
P-E ratio at sale   10:1
Tax bracket   0%

Graph 14–6
Reinvestment of Cash Flow at Various Rates: 6 Percent Earnings and Dividend Annual Growth Rate

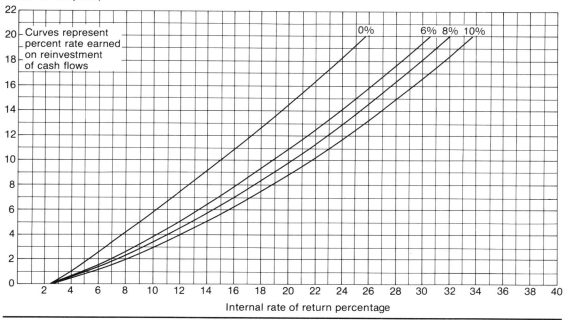

Percent yield
(annual initial
dividend divided by
initial market price)

Internal rate of return percentage

Notes: Shrinking multiple
          Holding period   20 yrs.
          P-E ratio at purchase   20:1
          P-E ratio at sale   10:1
          Tax bracket   0%

Graph 14–7
Reinvestment of Cash Flow at Various Rates: 10 Percent Earnings and Dividend Annual Growth Rate

Percent yield
(annual initial
dividend divided by
initial market price)

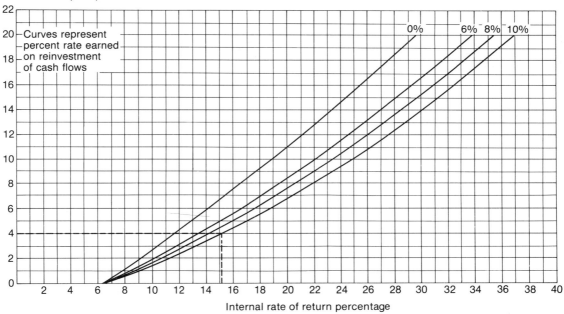

Internal rate of return percentage

Notes: Shrinking multiple
Holding period   20 yrs.
P-E ratio at purchase   20:1
P-E ratio at sale   10:1
Tax bracket   0%
Example: Table 14–2

Graph 14–8
Reinvestment of Cash Flow at Various Rates: 14 Percent Earnings and Dividend Annual Growth Rate

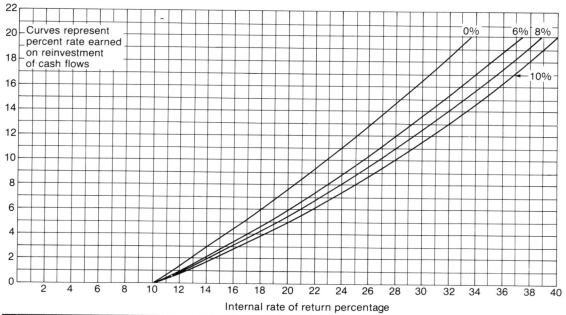

Notes: Shrinking multiple
Holding period   20 yrs.
P-E ratio at purchase   20:1
P-E ratio at sale   10:1
Tax bracket   0%

Graph 14–9
Reinvestment of Cash Flow at Various Rates: 0 Percent Earnings and Dividend Annual Growth Rate

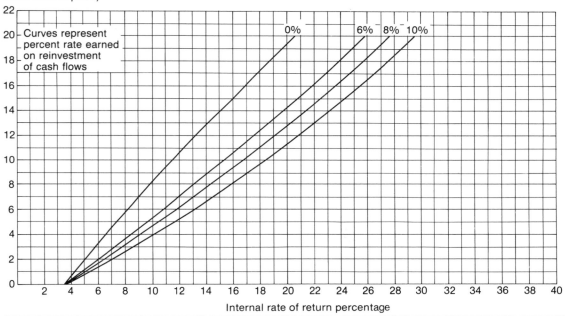

Percent yield
(annual initial
dividend divided by
initial market price)

Curves represent
percent rate earned
on reinvestment
of cash flows

0%   6% 8% 10%

Internal rate of return percentage

Notes: Mounting multiple
          Holding period   20 yrs.
          P-E ratio at purchase   10:1
          P-E ratio at sale   20:1
          Tax bracket   0%

Graph 14–10
Reinvestment of Cash Flow at Various Rates: 6 Percent Earnings and Dividend Annual Growth Rate

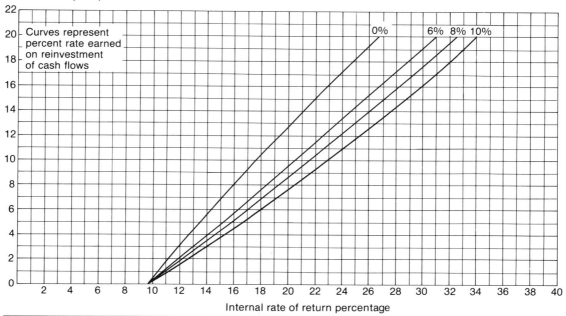

Percent yield
(annual initial
dividend divided by
initial market price)

Internal rate of return percentage

Notes: Mounting multiple
Holding period   20 yrs.
P-E ratio at purchase   10:1
P-E ratio at sale   20:1
Tax bracket   0%

Graph 14–11
Reinvestment of Cash Flow at Various Rates: 10 Percent Earnings and Dividend Annual Growth Rate

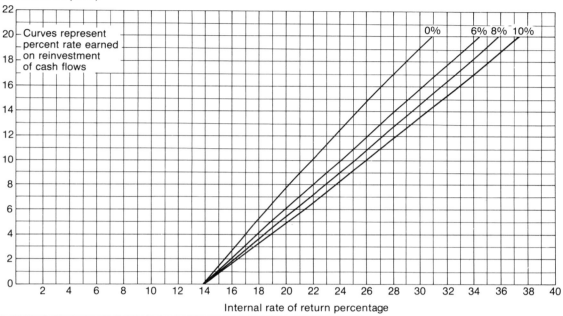

Percent yield
(annual initial
dividend divided by
initial market price)

Internal rate of return percentage

Notes:	Mounting multiple	
	Holding period	20 yrs.
	P-E ratio at purchase	10:1
	P-E ratio at sale	20:1
	Tax bracket	0%
	Example:	Table 14–3

Graph 14–12
Reinvestment of Cash Flow at Various Rates: 14 Percent Earnings and Dividend Annual Growth Rate

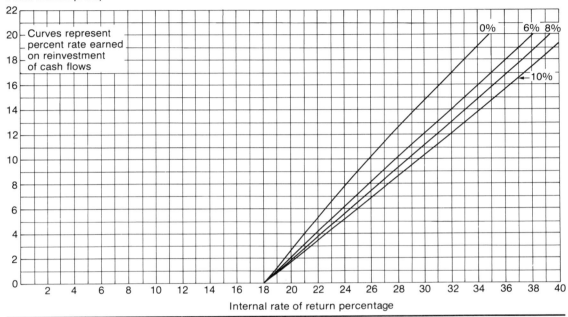

Percent yield
(annual initial
dividend divided by
initial market price)

Internal rate of return percentage

Notes:	Mounting multiple	
	Holding period	20 yrs.
	P-E ratio at purchase	10:1
	P-E ratio at sale	20:1
	Tax bracket	0%

Graph 14–13
Reinvestment of Cash Flow at Various Rates: 0 Percent Earnings and Dividend Annual Growth Rate

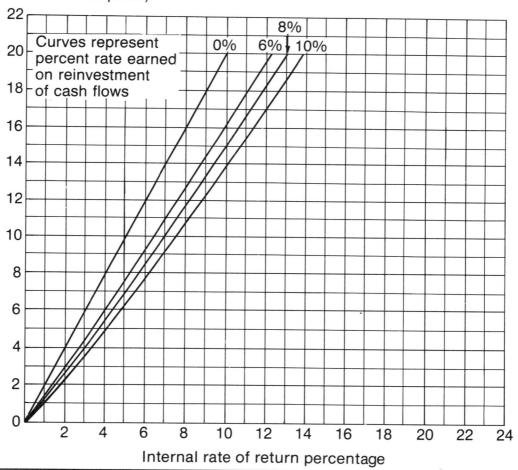

Percent yield
(annual initial
dividend divided by
initial market price)

Curves represent percent rate earned on reinvestment of cash flows

Internal rate of return percentage

Notes: Static multiple
Holding period   20 yrs.
P-E ratio at purchase   10:1
P-E ratio at sale   10:1
Tax bracket   50%
Example: Table 14–4

Graph 14–14
Reinvestment of Cash Flow at Various Rates: 6 Percent Earnings and Dividend Annual Growth Rate

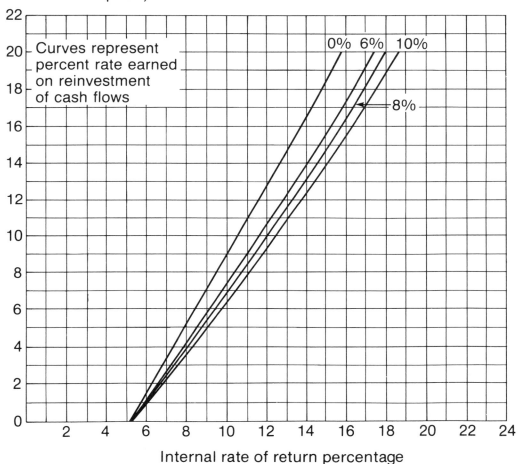

Percent yield
(annual initial
dividend divided by
initial market price)

Internal rate of return percentage

Notes: Static multiple
          Holding period   20 yrs.
          P-E ratio at purchase   10:1
          P-E ratio at sale   10:1
          Tax bracket   50%
          Example: Table 14–5

Graph 14–15
Reinvestment of Cash Flow at Various Rates: 10 Percent Earnings and Dividend Annual Growth Rate

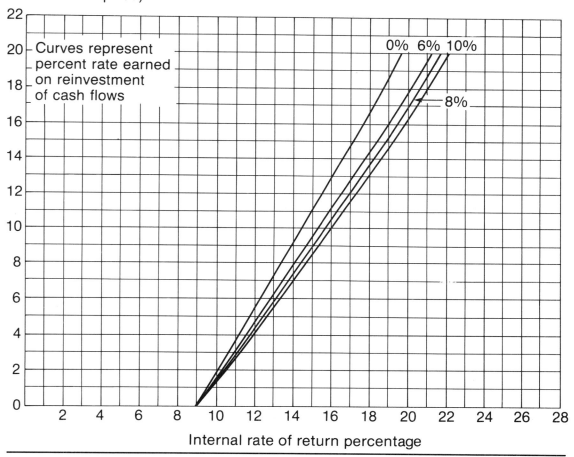

Percent yield
(annual initial
dividend divided by
initial market price)

Internal rate of return percentage

Notes: Static multiple
Holding period 20 yrs.
P-E ratio at purchase 10:1
P-E ratio at sale 10:1
Tax bracket 50%
Example: Table 14–6

Graph 14–16
Reinvestment of Cash Flow at Various Rates: 14 Percent Earnings and Dividend Annual Growth Rate

Percent yield
(annual initial
dividend divided by
initial market price)

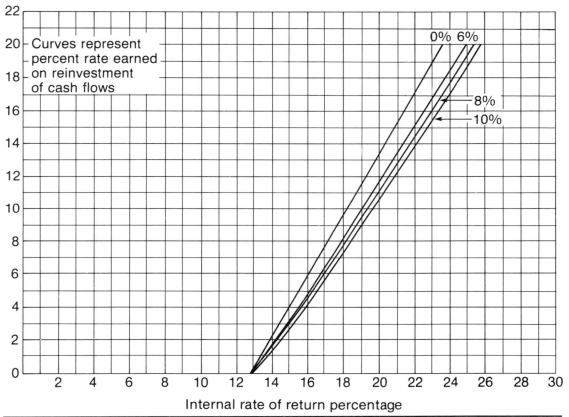

Internal rate of return percentage

Notes: Static multiple
          Holding period   20 yrs.
          P-E ratio at purchase   10:1
          P-E ratio at sale   10:1
          Tax bracket   50%
          Example: Table 14–7

Graph 14–17
Reinvestment of Cash Flow at Various Rates: 0 Percent Earnings and Dividend Annual Growth Rate

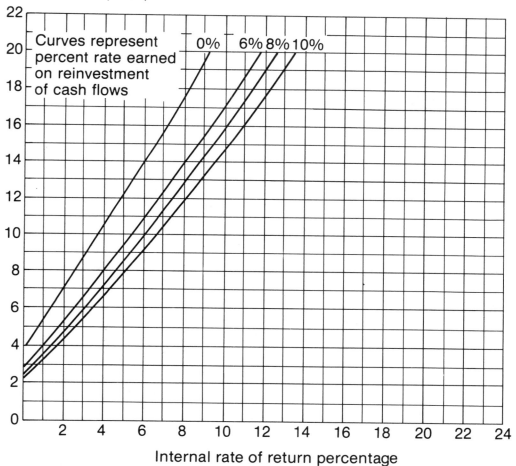

Notes: Shrinking multiple
      Holding period   20 yrs.
      P-E ratio at purchase 20:1
      P-E ratio at sale   10:1
      Tax bracket   50%
      Example: Table 14–8

Graph 14–18
Reinvestment of Cash Flow at Various Rates: 6 Percent Earnings and Dividend Annual Growth Rate

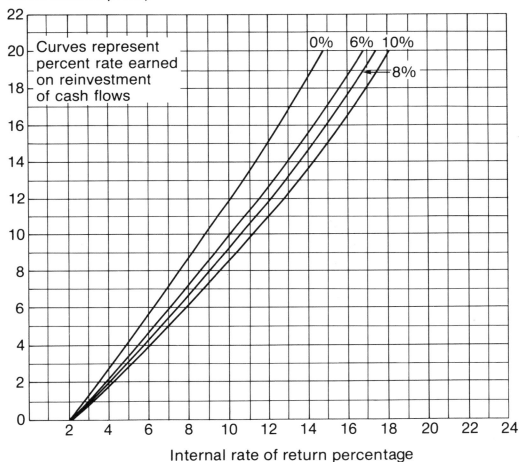

Percent yield
(annual initial
dividend divided by
initial market price)

Internal rate of return percentage

Notes: Shrinking multiple
          Holding period   20 yrs.
          P-E ratio at purchase   20:1
          P-E ratio at sale   10:1
          Tax bracket   50%
          Example: Table 14–9

Graph 14–19
Reinvestment of Cash Flow at Various Rates: 10 Percent Earnings and Dividend Annual Growth Rate

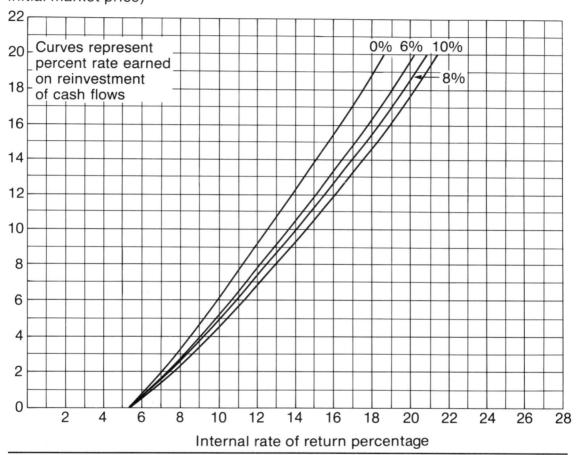

Percent yield
(annual initial
dividend divided by
initial market price)

Curves represent
percent rate earned
on reinvestment
of cash flows

0% 6% 10%

8%

Internal rate of return percentage

Notes: Shrinking multiple
       Holding period   20 yrs.
       P-E ratio at purchase 20:1
       P-E ratio at sale   10:1
       Tax bracket   50%
       Example: Table 14–10

Graph 14–20
Reinvestment of Cash Flow at Various Rates: 14 Percent Earnings and Dividend Annual Growth Rate

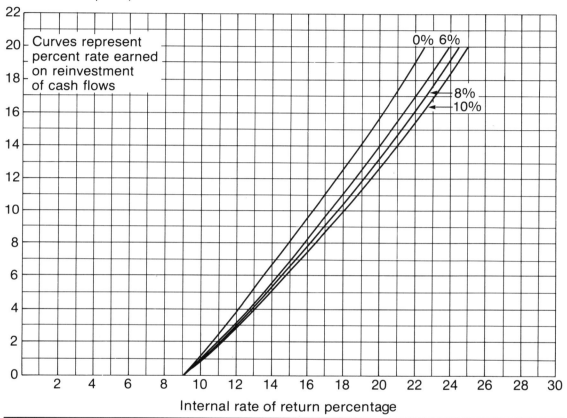

Percent yield
(annual initial
dividend divided by
initial market price)

Internal rate of return percentage

Notes: Shrinking multiple
         Holding period   20 yrs.
         P-E ratio at purchase   20:1
         P-E ratio at sale   10:1
         Tax bracket   50%
         Example: Table 14–11

Graph 14–21
Reinvestment of Cash Flow at Various Rates: 0 Percent Earnings and Dividend Annual Growth Rate

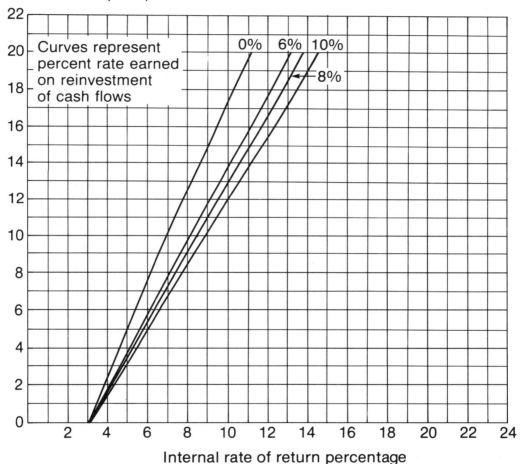

Percent yield
(annual initial
dividend divided by
initial market price)

Internal rate of return percentage

Notes: Mounting multiple
Holding period   20 yrs.
P-E ratio at purchase   10:1
P-E ratio at sale   20:1
Tax bracket   50%
Example: Table 14–12

Graph 14–22
Reinvestment of Cash Flow at Various Rates: 6 Percent Earnings and Dividend Annual Growth Rate

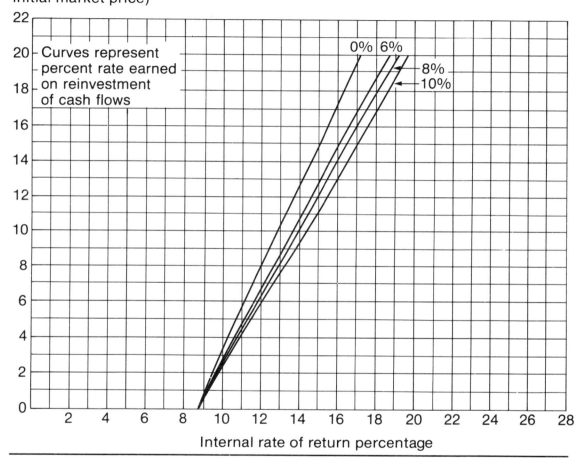

Notes: Mounting multiple
          Holding period   20 yrs.
          P-E ratio at purchase   10:1
          P-E ratio at sale   20:1
          Tax bracket   50%
          Example: Table 14–13

Graph 14–23
Reinvestment of Cash Flow at Various Rates: 10 Percent Earnings and Dividend Annual Growth Rate

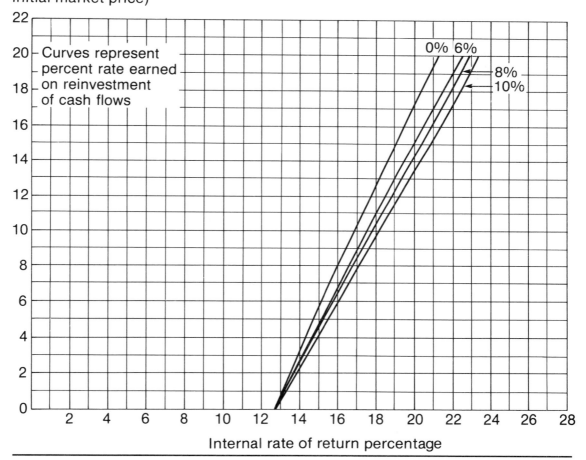

Percent yield
(annual initial
dividend divided by
initial market price)

Curves represent
percent rate earned
on reinvestment
of cash flows

0% 6%
8%
10%

Internal rate of return percentage

Notes: Mounting multiple
          Holding period   20 yrs.
          P-E ratio at purchase   10:1
          P-E ratio at sale   20:1
          Tax bracket   50%
          Example: Table 14–14

Graph 14–24
Reinvestment of Cash Flow at Various Rates: 14 Percent Earnings and Dividend Annual Growth Rate

Percent yield
(annual initial
dividend divided by
initial market price)

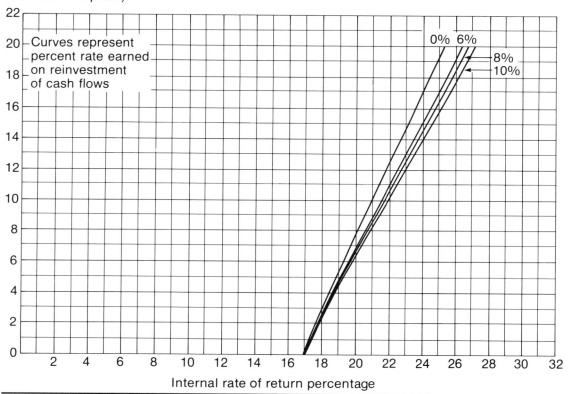

Internal rate of return percentage

Notes: Mounting multiple
          Holding period   20 yrs.
          P-E ratio at purchase   10:1
          P-E ratio at sale   20:1
          Tax bracket   50%
          Example: Table 14–15

Table 14–1
Calculation of IRR and Revised IRR

		Year	Cash Dividend	Old Balance	Interest	New Balance	New Flows
Dividend growth	10.00%						
Initial investment		0	−100.00	0.00	0	0	−100.00
Initial dividend	6.00%	1	6.00	0.00	0.00	6.00	6.00
P-E ratio at purchase	10.00	2	6.60	6.00	0.60	13.20	7.20
P-E ratio at sale	10.00	3	7.26	13.20	1.32	21.78	8.58
Earnings growth	10.00%	4	7.99	21.78	2.18	31.94	10.16
Earnings per share at purchase	$1.00	5	8.78	31.94	3.19	43.92	11.98
Number of years investment is held	20.00	6	9.66	43.92	4.39	57.98	14.06
Reinvestment of cash flows percent rate	10.00%	7	10.63	57.98	5.80	74.41	16.43
Tax bracket	0.00%	8	11.69	74.41	7.44	93.54	19.13
		9	12.86	93.54	9.35	115.75	22.22
		10	14.15	115.75	11.58	141.48	25.72
		11	15.56	141.48	14.15	171.19	29.71
		12	17.12	171.19	17.12	205.42	34.24
		13	18.83	205.42	20.54	244.80	39.37
		14	20.71	244.80	24.48	289.99	45.19
		15	22.78	289.99	29.00	341.77	51.78
		16	25.06	341.77	34.18	401.02	59.24
		17	27.57	401.02	40.10	468.69	67.67
		18	30.33	468.69	46.87	545.88	77.20
		19	33.36	545.88	54.59	633.83	87.95
Includes sales proceeds		20	709.45	633.83	63.38	1406.66	772.83

Internal rate of return
  Original   16.00%

  Revised   19.72%

Note: Earnings on reinvestment   10%
        Dividend and earnings growth   10%
        Yield at purchase   6%

Table 14–2
Calculation of IRR and Revised IRR

		Year	Cash Dividend	Old Balance	Interest	New Balance	New Flows
Dividend growth	10.00%						
Initial investment		0	−100.00	0.00	0	0	−100.00
Initial dividend	4.00%	1	4.00	0.00	0.00	4.00	4.00
P-E ratio at purchase	20.00	2	4.40	4.00	0.40	8.80	4.80
P-E ratio at sale	10.00	3	4.84	8.80	0.88	14.52	5.72
Earnings growth	10.00%	4	5.32	14.52	1.45	21.30	6.78
Earnings per share at purchase	$1.00	5	5.86	21.30	2.13	29.28	7.99
Number of years investment is held	20.00	6	6.44	29.28	2.93	38.65	9.37
Reinvestment of cash flows percent rate	10.00%	7	7.09	38.65	3.87	49.60	10.95
Tax bracket	0.00%	8	7.79	49.60	4.96	62.36	12.76
		9	8.57	62.36	6.24	77.17	14.81
		10	9.43	77.17	7.72	94.32	17.15
		11	10.37	94.32	9.43	114.12	19.81
		12	11.41	114.12	11.41	136.95	22.82
		13	12.55	136.95	13.69	163.20	26.25
		14	13.81	163.20	16.32	193.33	30.13
		15	15.19	193.33	19.33	227.85	34.52
		16	16.71	227.85	22.78	267.34	39.49
		17	18.38	267.34	26.73	312.46	45.11
		18	20.22	312.46	31.25	363.92	51.46
		19	22.24	363.92	36.39	422.55	58.63
Includes sales proceeds		20	360.84	422.55	42.26	825.65	403.09
Internal rate of return							
Original					11.61%		
Revised					15.19%		

Table 14–3
Calculation of IRR and Revised IRR

		Year	Cash Dividend	Old Balance	Interest	New Balance	New Flows
Dividend growth	10.00%						
Initial investment		0	−100.00	0.00	0	0	−100.00
Initial dividend	4.00%	1	4.00	0.00	0.00	4.00	4.00
P-E ratio at purchase	10.00	2	4.40	4.00	0.40	8.80	4.80
P-E ratio at sale	20.00	3	4.84	8.80	0.88	14.52	5.72
Earnings growth	10.00%	4	5.32	14.52	1.45	21.30	6.78
Earnings per share at purchase	$1.00	5	5.86	21.30	2.13	29.28	7.99
Number of years investment is held	20.00	6	6.44	29.28	2.93	38.65	9.37
Reinvestment of cash flows percent rate	10.00%	7	7.09	38.65	3.87	49.60	10.95
Tax bracket	0.00%	8	7.79	49.60	4.96	62.36	12.76
		9	8.57	62.36	6.24	77.17	14.81
		10	9.43	77.17	7.72	94.32	17.15
		11	10.37	94.32	9.43	114.12	19.81
		12	11.41	114.12	11.41	136.95	22.82
		13	12.55	136.95	13.69	163.20	26.25
		14	13.81	163.20	16.32	193.33	30.13
		15	15.19	193.33	19.33	227.85	34.52
		16	16.71	227.85	22.78	267.34	39.49
		17	18.38	267.34	26.73	312.46	45.11
		18	20.22	312.46	31.25	363.92	51.46
		19	22.24	363.92	36.39	422.55	58.63
Includes sales proceeds		20	1369.96	422.55	42.26	1834.77	1412.22
Internal rate of return							
Original				16.90%			
Revised				18.92%			

Table 14-4
Calculation of IRR and Revised IRR

		Year	Cash Dividend	Old Balance	Interest	New Balance	New Flows
Dividend growth	0.00%						
Initial investment	100.00	0	−100.00	0.00	0	0	−100.00
Initial dividend	4.00%	1	2.00	0.00	0.00	2.00	2.00
P-E ratio at purchase	10.00	2	2.00	2.00	0.10	4.10	2.10
P-E ratio at sale	10.00	3	2.00	4.10	0.20	6.30	2.20
Earnings growth	0.00%	4	2.00	6.30	0.32	8.62	2.32
Earnings per share at purchase	$1.00	5	2.00	8.62	0.43	11.05	2.43
Number of years investment is held	20.00	6	2.00	11.05	0.55	13.60	2.55
Reinvestment of cash flows percent rate	10.00%	7	2.00	13.60	0.68	16.28	2.68
Tax bracket	50.00%	8	2.00	16.28	0.81	19.10	2.81
		9	2.00	19.10	0.95	22.05	2.95
		10	2.00	22.05	1.10	25.16	3.10
		11	2.00	25.16	1.26	28.41	3.26
		12	2.00	28.41	1.42	31.83	3.42
		13	2.00	31.83	1.59	35.43	3.59
		14	2.00	35.43	1.77	39.20	3.77
		15	2.00	39.20	1.96	43.16	3.96
		16	2.00	43.16	2.16	47.31	4.16
		17	2.00	47.31	2.37	51.68	4.37
		18	2.00	51.68	2.58	56.26	4.58
Sale before tax	100.00	19	2.00	56.26	2.81	61.08	4.81
Includes sales proceeds after tax		20	102.00	61.08	6.11	169.19	108.11
Internal rate of return							
Original					2.00%		
Revised					3.25%		

Table 14–5
Calculation of IRR and Revised IRR

		Year	Cash Dividend	Old Balance	Interest	New Balance	New Flows
Dividend growth	6.00%						
Initial investment	100.00	0	−100.00	0.00	0	0	−100.00
Initial dividend	4.00%	1	2.00	0.00	0.00	2.00	2.00
P-E ratio at purchase	10.00	2	2.12	2.00	0.10	4.22	2.22
P-E ratio at sale	10.00	3	2.25	4.22	0.21	6.68	2.46
Earnings growth	6.00%	4	2.38	6.68	0.33	9.39	2.72
Earnings per share at purchase	$1.00	5	2.52	9.39	0.47	12.39	2.99
Number of years investment is held	20.00	6	2.68	12.39	0.62	15.68	3.30
Reinvestment of cash flows percent rate	10.00%	7	2.84	15.68	0.78	19.31	3.62
Tax bracket	50.00%	8	3.01	19.31	0.97	23.28	3.97
		9	3.19	23.28	1.16	27.63	4.35
		10	3.38	27.63	1.38	32.39	4.76
		11	3.58	32.39	1.62	37.59	5.20
		12	3.80	37.59	1.88	43.27	5.68
		13	4.02	43.27	2.16	49.46	6.19
		14	4.27	49.46	2.47	56.19	6.74
		15	4.52	56.19	2.81	63.53	7.33
		16	4.79	63.53	3.18	71.50	7.97
		17	5.08	71.50	3.57	80.15	8.66
		18	5.39	80.15	4.01	89.54	9.39
Sale before tax	320.71	19	5.71	89.54	4.48	99.73	10.19
Includes sales proceeds after tax		20	282.62	99.73	9.97	392.32	292.60
Internal rate of return							
Original					7.63%		
Revised					8.26%		

Table 14–6
Calculation of IRR and Revised IRR

		Year	Cash Dividend	Old Balance	Interest	New Balance	New Flows
Dividend growth	10.00%						
Initial investment	100.00	0	−100.00	0.00	0	0	−100.00
Initial dividend	4.00%	1	2.00	0.00	0.00	2.00	2.00
P-E ratio at purchase	10.00	2	2.20	2.00	0.10	4.30	2.30
P-E ratio at sale	10.00	3	2.42	4.30	0.21	6.93	2.63
Earnings growth	10.00%	4	2.66	6.93	0.35	9.94	3.01
Earnings per share at purchase	$1.00	5	2.93	9.94	0.50	13.37	3.43
Number of years investment is held	20.00	6	3.22	13.37	0.67	17.26	3.89
Reinvestment of cash flows percent rate	10.00%	7	3.54	17.26	0.86	21.66	4.41
Tax bracket	50.00%	8	3.90	21.66	1.08	26.65	4.98
		9	4.29	26.65	1.33	32.26	5.62
		10	4.72	32.26	1.61	38.59	6.33
		11	5.19	38.59	1.93	45.71	7.12
		12	5.71	45.71	2.29	53.70	7.99
		13	6.28	53.70	2.69	62.66	8.96
		14	6.90	62.66	3.13	72.70	10.04
		15	7.59	72.70	3.64	83.93	11.23
		16	8.35	83.93	4.20	96.48	12.55
		17	9.19	96.48	4.82	110.50	14.01
		18	10.11	110.50	5.52	126.13	15.63
Sale before tax	672.75	19	11.12	126.13	6.31	143.56	17.43
Includes sales proceeds after tax		20	570.43	143.56	14.36	728.35	584.79
Internal rate of return							
Original					11.15%		
Revised					11.89%		

Table 14–7
Calculation of IRR and Revised IRR

		Year	Cash Dividend	Old Balance	Interest	New Balance	New Flows
Dividend growth	14.00%						
Initial investment	100.00	0	−100.00	0.00	0	0	−100.00
Initial dividend	4.00%	1	2.00	0.00	0.00	2.00	2.00
P-E ratio at purchase	10.00	2	2.28	2.00	0.10	4.38	2.38
P-E ratio at sale	10.00	3	2.60	4.38	0.22	7.20	2.82
Earnings growth	14.00%	4	2.96	7.20	0.36	10.52	3.32
Earnings per share at purchase	$1.00	5	3.38	10.52	0.53	14.43	3.90
Number of years investment is held	20.00	6	3.85	14.43	0.72	19.00	4.57
Reinvestment of cash flows percent rate	10.00%	7	4.39	19.00	0.95	24.34	5.34
Tax bracket	50.00%	8	5.00	24.34	1.22	30.56	6.22
		9	5.71	30.56	1.53	37.79	7.23
		10	6.50	37.79	1.89	46.19	8.39
		11	7.41	46.19	2.31	55.91	9.72
		12	8.45	55.91	2.80	67.16	11.25
		13	9.64	67.16	3.36	80.15	12.99
		14	10.98	80.15	4.01	95.14	14.99
		15	12.52	95.14	4.76	112.42	17.28
		16	14.28	112.42	5.62	132.32	19.90
		17	16.27	132.32	6.62	155.21	22.89
		18	18.55	155.21	7.76	181.52	26.31
Sale before tax	1374.35	19	21.15	181.52	9.08	211.75	30.23
Includes sales proceeds after tax		20	1143.59	211.75	21.17	1376.52	1164.77
Internal rate of return							
Original					15.03%		
Revised					15.64%		

Table 14–8
Calculation of IRR and Revised IRR

		Year	Cash Dividend	Old Balance	Interest	New Balance	New Flows
Dividend growth	0.00%						
Initial investment	100.00	0	−100.00	0.00	0	0	−100.00
Initial dividend	4.00%	1	2.00	0.00	0.00	2.00	2.00
P-E ratio at purchase	20.00	2	2.00	2.00	0.10	4.10	2.10
P-E ratio at sale	10.00	3	2.00	4.10	0.20	6.30	2.20
Earnings growth	0.00%	4	2.00	6.30	0.32	8.62	2.32
Earnings per share at purchase	$1.00	5	2.00	8.62	0.43	11.05	2.43
Number of years investment is held	20.00	6	2.00	11.05	0.55	13.60	2.55
Reinvestment of cash flows percent rate	10.00%	7	2.00	13.60	0.68	16.28	2.68
Tax bracket	50.00%	8	2.00	16.28	0.81	19.10	2.81
		9	2.00	19.10	0.95	22.05	2.95
		10	2.00	22.05	1.10	25.16	3.10
		11	2.00	25.16	1.26	28.41	3.26
		12	2.00	28.41	1.42	31.83	3.42
		13	2.00	31.83	1.59	35.43	3.59
		14	2.00	35.43	1.77	39.20	3.77
		15	2.00	39.20	1.96	43.16	3.96
		16	2.00	43.16	2.16	47.31	4.16
		17	2.00	47.31	2.37	51.68	4.37
		18	2.00	51.68	2.58	56.26	4.58
Sale before tax	50.00	19	2.00	56.26	2.81	61.08	4.81
Includes sales proceeds after tax		20	62.00	61.08	6.11	129.19	68.11
Internal rate of return							
Original					0.00%		
Revised					1.65%		

Table 14–9
Calculation of IRR and Revised IRR

		Year	Cash Dividend	Old Balance	Interest	New Balance	New Flows
Dividend growth	6.00%						
Initial investment	100.00	0	−100.00	0.00	0	0	−100.00
Initial dividend	4.00%	1	2.00	0.00	0.00	2.00	2.00
P-E ratio at purchase	20.00	2	2.12	2.00	0.10	4.22	2.22
P-E ratio at sale	10.00	3	2.25	4.22	0.21	6.68	2.46
Earnings growth	6.00%	4	2.38	6.68	0.33	9.39	2.72
Earnings per share at purchase	$1.00	5	2.52	9.39	0.47	12.39	2.99
Number of years investment is held	20.00	6	2.68	12.39	0.62	15.68	3.30
Reinvestment of cash flows percent rate	10.00%	7	2.84	15.68	0.78	19.31	3.62
Tax bracket	50.00%	8	3.01	19.31	0.97	23.28	3.97
		9	3.19	23.28	1.16	27.63	4.35
		10	3.38	27.63	1.38	32.39	4.76
		11	3.58	32.39	1.62	37.59	5.20
		12	3.80	37.59	1.88	43.27	5.68
		13	4.02	43.27	2.16	49.46	6.19
		14	4.27	49.46	2.47	56.19	6.74
		15	4.52	56.19	2.81	63.53	7.33
		16	4.79	63.53	3.18	71.50	7.97
		17	5.08	71.50	3.57	80.15	8.66
		18	5.39	80.15	4.01	89.54	9.39
Sales before tax	160.36	19	5.71	89.54	4.48	99.73	10.19
Includes sales proceeds after tax		20	154.34	99.73	9.97	264.04	164.31

Internal rate of return
  Original   4.84%

  Revised   6.10%

Table 14–10
Calculation of IRR and Revised IRR

		Year	Cash Dividend	Old Balance	Interest	New Balance	New Flows
Dividend growth	10.00%						
Initial investment	100.00	0	−100.00	0.00	0	0	−100.00
Initial dividend	4.00%	1	2.00	0.00	0.00	2.00	2.00
P-E ratio at purchase	20.00	2	2.20	2.00	0.10	4.30	2.30
P-E ratio at sale	10.00	3	2.42	4.30	0.21	6.93	2.63
Earnings growth	10.00%	4	2.66	6.93	0.35	9.94	3.01
Earnings per share at purchase	$1.00	5	2.93	9.94	0.50	13.37	3.43
Number of years investment is held	20.00	6	3.22	13.37	0.67	17.26	3.89
Reinvestment of cash flows percent rate	10.00%	7	3.54	17.26	0.86	21.66	4.41
Tax bracket	50.00%	8	3.90	21.66	1.08	26.65	4.98
		9	4.29	26.65	1.33	32.26	5.62
		10	4.72	32.26	1.61	38.59	6.33
		11	5.19	38.59	1.93	45.71	7.12
		12	5.71	45.71	2.29	53.70	7.99
		13	6.28	53.70	2.69	62.66	8.96
		14	6.90	62.66	3.13	72.70	10.04
		15	7.59	72.70	3.64	83.93	11.23
		16	8.35	83.93	4.20	96.48	12.55
		17	9.19	96.48	4.82	110.50	14.01
		18	10.11	110.50	5.52	126.13	15.63
Sale before tax	336.37	19	11.12	126.13	6.31	143.56	17.43
Includes sales proceeds after tax		20	301.33	143.56	14.36	459.25	315.69
Internal rate of return							
Original					8.41%		
Revised					9.45%		

Table 14–11
Calculation of IRR and Revised IRR

		Year	Cash Dividend	Old Balance	Interest	New Balance	New Flows
Dividend growth	14.00%						
Initial investment	100.00	0	−100.00	0.00	0	0	−100.00
Initial dividend	4.00%	1	2.00	0.00	0.00	2.00	2.00
P-E ratio at purchase	20.00	2	2.28	2.00	0.10	4.38	2.38
P-E ratio at sale	10.00	3	2.60	4.38	0.22	7.20	2.82
Earnings growth	14.00%	4	2.96	7.20	0.36	10.52	3.32
Earnings per share at purchase	$1.00	5	3.38	10.52	0.53	14.43	3.90
Number of years investment is held	20.00	6	3.85	14.43	0.72	19.00	4.57
Reinvestment of cash flows percent rate	10.00	7	4.39	19.00	0.95	24.34	5.34
Tax bracket	50.00%	8	5.00	24.34	1.22	30.56	6.22
		9	5.71	30.56	1.53	37.79	7.23
		10	6.50	37.79	1.89	46.19	8.39
		11	7.41	46.19	2.31	55.91	9.72
		12	8.45	55.91	2.80	67.16	11.25
		13	9.64	67.16	3.36	80.15	12.99
		14	10.98	80.15	4.01	95.14	14.99
		15	12.52	95.14	4.76	112.42	17.28
		16	14.28	112.42	5.62	132.32	19.90
		17	16.27	132.32	6.62	155.21	22.89
		18	18.55	155.21	7.76	181.52	26.31
Sale before tax	687.17	19	21.15	181.52	9.08	211.75	30.23
Includes sales proceeds after tax		20	593.85	211.75	21.17	826.78	615.03
Internal rate of return							
Original				12.11%			
Revised				12.97%			

Table 14–12
Calculation of IRR and Revised IRR

		Year	Cash Dividend	Old Balance	Interest	New Balance	New Flows
Dividend growth	0.00%						
Initial investment	100.00	0	−100.00	0.00	0	0	−100.00
Initial dividend	4.00%	1	2.00	0.00	0.00	2.00	2.00
P-E ratio at purchase	10.00	2	2.00	2.00	0.10	4.10	2.10
P-E ratio at sale	20.00	3	2.00	4.10	0.20	6.30	2.20
Earnings growth	0.00%	4	2.00	6.30	0.32	8.62	2.32
Earnings per share at purchase	$1.00	5	2.00	8.62	0.43	11.05	2.43
Number of years investment is held	20.00	6	2.00	11.05	0.55	13.60	2.55
Reinvestment of cash flows percent rate	10.00%	7	2.00	13.60	0.68	16.28	2.68
Tax bracket	50.00%	8	2.00	16.28	0.81	19.10	2.81
		9	2.00	19.10	0.95	22.05	2.95
		10	2.00	22.05	1.10	25.16	3.10
		11	2.00	25.16	1.26	28.41	3.26
		12	2.00	28.41	1.42	31.83	3.42
		13	2.00	31.83	1.59	35.43	3.59
		14	2.00	35.43	1.77	39.20	3.77
		15	2.00	39.20	1.96	43.16	3.96
		16	2.00	43.16	2.16	47.31	4.16
		17	2.00	47.31	2.37	51.68	4.37
		18	2.00	51.68	2.58	56.26	4.58
Sale before tax	200.00	19	2.00	56.26	2.81	61.08	4.81
Includes sales proceeds after tax		20	182.00	61.08	6.11	249.19	188.11
Internal rate of return							
Original					4.54%		
Revised					5.44%		

Table 14–13
Calculation of IRR and Revised IRR

		Year	Cash Dividend	Old Balance	Interest	New Balance	New Flows
Dividend growth	6.00%						
Initial investment	100.00	0	−100.00	0.00	0	0	−100.00
Initial dividend	4.00%	1	2.00	0.00	0.00	2.00	2.00
P-E ratio at purchase	10.00	2	2.12	2.00	0.10	4.22	2.22
P-E ratio at sale	20.00	3	2.25	4.22	0.21	6.68	2.46
Earnings growth	6.00%	4	2.38	6.68	0.33	9.39	2.72
Earnings per share at purchase	$1.00	5	2.52	9.39	0.47	12.39	2.99
Number of years investment is held	20.00	6	2.68	12.39	0.62	15.68	3.30
Reinvestment of cash flows percent rate	10.00%	7	2.84	15.68	0.78	19.31	3.62
Tax bracket	50.00%	8	3.01	19.31	0.97	23.28	3.97
		9	3.19	23.28	1.16	27.63	4.35
		10	3.38	27.63	1.38	32.39	4.76
		11	3.58	32.39	1.62	37.59	5.20
		12	3.80	37.59	1.88	43.27	5.68
		13	4.02	43.27	2.16	49.46	6.19
		14	4.27	49.46	2.47	56.19	6.74
		15	4.52	56.19	2.81	63.53	7.33
		16	4.79	63.53	3.18	71.50	7.97
		17	5.08	71.50	3.57	80.15	8.66
		18	5.39	80.15	4.01	89.54	9.39
Sale before tax	641.43	19	5.71	89.54	4.48	99.73	10.19
Includes sales proceeds after tax		20	539.19	99.73	9.97	648.90	549.17
Internal rate of return							
Original					10.34%		
Revised					10.96%		

Table 14–14
Calculation of IRR and Revised IRR

		Year	Cash Dividend	Old Balance	Interest	New Balance	New Flows
Dividend growth	10.00%						
Initial investment	100.00	0	−100.00	0.00	0	0	−100.00
Initial dividend	4.00%	1	2.00	0.00	0.00	2.00	2.00
P-E ratio at purchase	10.00	2	2.20	2.00	0.10	4.30	2.30
P-E ratio at sale	20.00	3	2.42	4.30	0.21	6.93	2.63
Earnings growth	10.00%	4	2.66	6.93	0.35	9.94	3.01
Earnings per share at purchase	$1.00	5	2.93	9.94	0.50	13.37	3.43
Number of years investment is held	20.00	6	3.22	13.37	0.67	17.26	3.89
Reinvestment of cash flows percent rate	10.00%	7	3.54	17.26	0.86	21.66	4.41
Tax bracket	50.00%	8	3.90	21.66	1.08	26.65	4.98
		9	4.29	26.65	1.33	32.26	5.62
		10	4.72	32.26	1.61	38.59	6.33
		11	5.19	38.59	1.93	45.71	7.12
		12	5.71	45.71	2.29	53.70	7.99
		13	6.28	53.70	2.69	62.66	8.96
		14	6.90	62.66	3.13	72.70	10.04
		15	7.59	72.70	3.64	83.93	11.23
		16	8.35	83.93	4.20	96.48	12.55
		17	9.19	96.48	4.82	110.50	14.01
		18	10.11	110.50	5.52	126.13	15.63
Sale before tax	1345.50	19	11.12	126.13	6.31	143.56	17.43
Includes sales proceeds after tax		20	1108.63	143.56	14.36	1266.55	1122.99
Internal rate of return							
Original					14.34%		
Revised					14.85%		

Table 14–15
Calculation of IRR and Revised IRR

		Year	Cash Dividend	Old Balance	Interest	New Balance	New Flows
Dividend growth	14.00%						
Initial investment	100.00	0	−100.00	0.00	0	0	−100.00
Initial dividend	4.00%	1	2.00	0.00	0.00	2.00	2.00
P-E ratio at purchase	10.00	2	2.28	2.00	0.10	4.38	2.38
P-E ratio at sale	20.00	3	2.60	4.38	0.22	7.20	2.82
Earnings growth	14.00%	4	2.96	7.20	0.36	10.52	3.32
Earnings per share at purchase	$1.00	5	3.38	10.52	0.53	14.43	3.90
Number of years investment is held	20.00	6	3.85	14.43	0.72	19.00	4.57
Reinvestment of cash flows percent rate	10.00%	7	4.39	19.00	0.95	24.34	5.34
Tax bracket	50.00%	8	5.00	24.34	1.22	30.56	6.22
		9	5.71	30.56	1.53	37.79	7.23
		10	6.50	37.79	1.89	46.19	8.39
		11	7.41	46.19	2.31	55.91	9.72
		12	8.45	55.91	2.80	67.16	11.25
		13	9.64	67.16	3.36	80.15	12.99
		14	10.98	80.15	4.01	95.14	14.99
		15	12.52	95.14	4.76	112.42	17.28
		16	14.28	112.42	5.62	132.32	19.90
		17	16.27	132.32	6.62	155.21	22.89
		18	18.55	155.21	7.76	181.52	26.31
Sale before tax	2748.70	19	21.15	181.52	9.08	211.75	30.23
Includes sales proceeds after tax		20	2243.07	211.75	21.17	2475.99	2264.24
Internal rate of return							
Original				18.39%			
Revised				18.81%			

Real Estate IRRs with Reinvestment of Cash Flow

After reading the last couple of chapters, the effect of reinvesting cash flow from an investment has probably become clear. The original IRR is increased to a new revised IRR as the result of the reinvestment. This is generally true with real estate investments, but *not invariably true*. There are instances where the reinvestment of real estate cash flows results in lower revised IRRs than the original IRR. We'll discuss that in more detail later.

Max Melin is an affluent, elderly gentleman in a 50 percent tax bracket. He is offered an investment in an office building, with the following characteristics:

IRR	10%
Loan as percent of total investment	75%
Loan interest rate	12%
Years, loan amortization	25
Building as percent of total investment	90%

Mr. Melin makes the following assumptions:

Period of time he will hold the investment	15 years
Depreciation method	Straight line
Number of years of depreciation	15
Capitalization rate when he sells the property	12%

Mr. Melin has no immediate need for the cash flow that he will receive from the investment and plans to reinvest the cash flow until he sells the property after 15 years. What will his revised internal rate of return be then at reinvestment rates of 4, 8, and 12 percent?

He first checks in Table 15–1 to find the graph closest to the circumstances of his situation. Graph 15–2 has the same characteristics as his proposed investment. He uses this graph by entering it on the vertical axis at the IRR rate of 10 percent. He proceeds horizontally to the curves for 4, 8, and 12 percent earnings on reinvestment. At the point of intersection with each curve, he proceeds downward to the intersection with the horizontal axis, where he finds:

Interest on Reinvestment	Revised IRR
4%	10.6%
8	11.3
12	12.2

That's all there is to it. First, find the appropriate graph in Table 15–1. Enter the graph with the IRR you expect from the investment, and find the revised IRRs.

Graphs 15–1 to 15–8 are all based on an inflation rate of 6 percent. If the inflation rate were more or less than 6 percent, the cash flow pattern before reinvestment would change and so would the revised IRRs after reinvestment. The change would *not* be significant, in most cases. Refer to Table 15–3. This table shows various combinations of inflation rate and net operating income divided by total investment. The various combinations all result in the *same IRR*, 12.01 percent. But since each combination produces a unique set of cash flows, the *revised IRRs are different.* For example, at a reinvestment rate of 12 percent, the lowest revised IRR is 13.14 percent (at the lowest NOI/Total investment rate of 4.78 percent and the highest inflation rate, 10 percent. The highest revised IRR is 16.53 percent (produced at the highest NOI/Total investment of 10.9 percent and the lowest inflation rate, 0 percent). The indication is that with equal IRRs, higher revised IRRs will result from higher initial NOI/Total investment percentages. The early, larger cash flow in such cases has more impact on reinvestment results than cash flow that comes later from inflation.

The normal pattern of cash flow evolution, interplay between the starting levels of net operating income and inflation, and calculation of IRR and revised IRRs is shown in Table 15–2. The revised IRRs determined by *the analysis in Table 15–2 represent one point on each of the three curves* in Graph 15–4—at the IRR level of 21.19 percent.

The exception to the general pattern of revised IRRs being in excess of the original IRR occurs when the cash flows in early years are negative. In such event, the negative balance compounds upon reinvestment, and the higher the reinvestment percentage rate, the higher the negative balance becomes. Later, when cash flows become positive, the negative balance is whittled away until it becomes positive, and a normal pattern is established.

The exception is evident in Graph 15–4 at IRRs below 8.6 percent, where the higher the reinvestment percentage rate, the lower the revised IRR. Similar results may be observed in Graph 15–8 at IRRs below 12.6 percent.

Table 15–1
Key to Reinvestment Graphs

Situation:	Graph 15–1	Graph 15–2	Graph 15–3	Graph 15–4	Graph 15–5	Graph 15–6	Graph 15–7	Graph 15–8	Graph 15–9
Tax bracket	40%	50%	50%	30%	30%	50%	40%	0%	0%
Loan/Total investment	75%	75%	0%	75%	75%	75%	75%	75%	0%
Loan interest rate	10%	12%	n/a	12%	12%	12%	12%	12%	n/a
Years, loan amortization	25	25	n/a	25	int. only	int. only	25	25	n/a
Rates of inflation	various	various	various	various	various	various	various	various	various
Initial yield (NOI)	various	various	various	various	various	various	various	various	various
Capitalization rate at sale	10%	12%	12%	10%	12%	12%	16%	12%	12%
Year of sale	15	15	15	15	15	15	15	15	15
Years, straight line depreciation	15	15	15	15	15	15	15	15	15
Building/Total investment	90%	90%	90%	90%	90%	90%	90%	90%	90%
Prior reference, Graph	8–1	8–2	8–3	8–4	8–5	8–6	8–7	8–8	8–13

Table 15–2
Real Estate Revised IRR, with Reinvestment of Cash Flow, 30% Tax Bracket

	Year															
	1	2	3	4	5	6	7	8	9	10	11	12	13	14	15	Totals
Loan (beginning)	750	744	738	731	723	714	704	693	681	667	651	634	614	592	568	
Interest, annual	90	89	89	88	87	86	85	83	82	80	78	76	74	71	68	1,225
Principal reduction	6	6	7	8	9	10	11	12	14	16	17	20	22	25	27	210
Loan (end)	744	738	731	723	714	704	693	681	667	651	634	614	592	568	540	
NOI/Investment*	10%															
NOI (net operating income)	100	106	112	119	126	134	142	150	159	169	179	190	201	213	226	2,328
NOI/Total investment	0.10	0.11	0.11	0.12	0.13	0.13	0.14	0.15	0.16	0.17	0.18	0.19	0.20	0.21	0.23	
Less: loan principal and interest	96	96	96	96	96	96	96	96	96	96	96	96	96	96	96	1,434
Cash flow before tax	4	10	17	23	31	38	46	55	64	73	83	94	106	118	130	893
Cash flow/Cash investment	0.02	0.04	0.07	0.09	0.12	0.15	0.18	0.22	0.26	0.29	0.33	0.38	0.42	0.47	0.52	
− Depreciation	60	60	60	60	60	60	60	60	60	60	60	60	60	60	60	900
+ Loan Principal	6	6	7	8	9	10	11	12	14	16	17	20	22	25	27	210
Taxable Income	−50	−43	−36	−29	−21	−12	−3	7	18	29	41	54	68	82	98	203
Income tax (− = Savings)	−15	−13	−11	−9	−6	−4	−1	2	5	9	12	16	20	25	29	61
Cash flow after tax, before sale	19	23	28	32	37	42	47	53	58	65	71	78	85	93	101	832
Sales proceeds in year 15															2,261	2,261
Capital gains tax on sale															259	259
Cash from sale after tax and loan repayment															1,461	1,461
Cash flow after tax	19	23	28	32	37	42	47	53	58	65	71	78	85	93	1,562	2,294
Internal rate of return							21.19%									
Beginning balance, 4% reinvestment	0	19	43	72	106	146	192	244	304	371	446	529	622	725	838	
4% on beginning balance	0	1	1	2	3	4	5	7	9	10	12	15	17	20	23	
Cash flow	19	24	29	34	40	46	52	59	67	75	84	93	103	113		1,586
Ending balance	19	43	72	106	146	192	244	304	371	446	529	622	725	838		2,424
Revised IRR at 4% reinvestment							22.07%									
Beginning balance, 8% reinvested	0	19	44	74	110	153	203	262	329	406	493	592	703	828	967	
8% on beginning balance	0	1	2	4	6	9	11	15	18	23	28	33	39	46	54	
Cash flow	19	24	30	36	43	50	58	67	77	87	99	111	125	139		1,617
Ending balance	19	44	74	110	153	203	262	329	406	493	592	703	828	967		2,584

Table 15–2 *(concluded)*

	\multicolumn{15}{c}{Year}														
	1	2	3	4	5	6	7	8	9	10	11	12	13	14	15	Totals
Revised IRR at																
8% reinvestment								23.06%								
Beginning balance, 12% reinvested	0	19	44	76	114	160	216	281	357	446	548	665	799		951	1,124
12% on beginning balance	0	2	4	6	10	13	18	24	30	37	46	56	67		80	94
Cash flow	19	25	31	38	46	55	65	76	88	102	117	134	152		173	1,657
Ending balance	19	44	76	114	160	216	281	357	446	548	665	799	951	1,124	2,781	
Revised IRR at																
12% reinvestment								24.17%								

*NOI is net operating income; that is, rental income less operating expenses excluding debt service and depreciation. NOI/investment is the NOI divided by the total investment in the property, which includes loan proceeds, if any.

Initial yield	10.0%
Tax bracket	30.0%
Cash investment	250
Loan	750
Total investment	1000
Years loan amortization	25
Loan interest	12.0%
Loan principal and interest	96
Building/Total investment	90.0%
Initial depreciable assets	900
Years straight line depreciation	15
Year of sale	15
Capitalization rate	10.0%
Inflation	6.0%
Mortgage constant	12.75%

Table 15–3
Variations in Revised IRRs with Equal Starting IRR

IRR (0% Reinvestment)	NOI/Total Investment	Inflation	\multicolumn{3}{c}{Revised Internal Rates of Return with Interest Reinvestment Rate of}		
			4%	8%	12%
12.01%	4.78%	10.00%	12.35%	12.73%	13.14%
12.01	6.70	12.64	12.64	13.33	14.09
12.01	5.71	8.00	12.48	12.99	13.56
12.01	8.00	4.00	12.84	13.75	14.73*
12.01	9.38	2.00	13.10	14.28	15.53
12.01	10.91	0.00	13.45	14.95	16.53

*See Table 15–4 for complete details.

Table 15–4
Real Estate Revised IRR, with Reinvestment of Cash Flow, 40% Tax Bracket

	Year															Totals
	1	2	3	4	5	6	7	8	9	10	11	12	13	14	15	
Loan (beginning)	750	744	738	731	723	714	704	693	681	667	651	634	614	592	568	
Interest, annual	90	89	89	88	87	86	85	83	82	80	78	76	74	71	68	1,225
Principal reduction	6	6	7	8	9	10	11	12	14	16	17	20	22	25	27	210
Loan (end)	744	738	731	723	714	704	693	681	667	651	634	614	592	568	540	
NOI/Investment*	8.00%															
NOI (net operating income)	80	83	87	90	94	97	101	105	109	114	118	123	128	133	139	1,602
NOI/Total investment	0.08	0.08	0.09	0.09	0.09	0.10	0.10	0.11	0.11	0.11	0.12	0.12	0.13	0.13	0.14	
Less: loan principal and interest	96	96	96	96	96	96	96	96	96	96	96	96	96	96	96	1,434
Cash flow before tax	−16	−12	−9	−6	−2	2	6	10	14	18	23	28	32	38	43	168
Cash flow/Cash investment	−0.06	−0.05	−0.04	−0.02	−0.01	0.01	0.02	0.04	0.06	0.07	0.09	0.11	0.13	0.15	0.17	
− Depreciation	60	60	60	60	60	60	60	60	60	60	60	60	60	60	60	900
+ Loan Principal	6	6	7	8	9	10	11	12	14	16	17	20	22	25	27	210
Taxable Income	−70	−66	−62	−58	−53	−48	−43	−38	−32	−26	−20	−13	−6	2	10	−523
Income tax (− = Savings)	−35	−33	−31	−29	−27	−24	−22	−19	−16	−13	−10	−6	−3	1	5	−261
Cash flow after tax, before sale	19	21	22	23	25	26	27	29	30	31	33	34	35	37	38	429
Sales proceeds in year 15															1,154	1,154
Capital gains tax on sale															211	211
Cash from sale after tax and loan repayment															403	403
Cash flow after tax	19	21	22	23	25	26	27	29	30	31	33	34	35	37	441	832
Internal rate of return																12.01%

							Year									Totals
	1	2	3	4	5	6	7	8	9	10	11	12	13	14	15	
Beginning balance, 4% reinvestment	0	19	40	63	88	114	142	172	204	238	274	313	353	395	440	
4% on balance, after tax per year	0	0	1	1	2	2	3	3	4	5	5	6	7	8	9	
Cash flow	19	21	23	24	26	28	30	32	34	36	38	40	42	44	450	
Ending balance	19	40	63	88	114	142	172	204	238	274	313	353	395	440	889	
Revised IRR							12.84%									
Beginning balance, 8% reinvested	0	19	41	64	90	118	149	182	218	257	298	343	391	442	496	
8% on balance	0	1	2	3	4	5	6	7	9	10	12	14	16	18	20	
Cash flow	19	21	24	26	28	31	33	36	39	42	45	48	51	54	461	
Ending balance	19	41	64	90	118	149	182	218	257	298	343	391	442	496	956	
Revised IRR							13.75%									
Beginning balance, 12% reinvested	0	19	41	66	93	123	156	193	233	277	325	377	434	495	561	
12% on balance	0	1	2	4	6	7	9	12	14	17	19	23	26	30	34	
Cash flow	19	22	24	27	30	33	37	40	44	48	52	57	61	66	475	
Ending balance	19	41	66	93	123	156	193	233	277	325	377	434	495	561	1,036	
Revised IRR							14.73%									

Initial yield	8.0%
Tax bracket	40.0%
Cash investment	250
Loan	750
Total investment	1000
Years loan amortization	25
Loan interest	10.0%
Loan principal and interest	96
Building/Total investment	90.0%
Initial depreciable assets	900
Years straight line depreciation	15
Year of sale	15
Capitalization rate at sale	10.0%
Inflation	4.0%
Mortgage constant	12.75%

*NOI is net operating income; that is, rental income less operating expenses excluding debt service and depreciation. NOI/investment is the NOI divided by the total investment in the property, which includes loan proceeds, if any.

Graph 15–1
Real Estate Investment: Revised IRR with Reinvestment *(Using Assumptions Contained in Table 15–1 with 6 Percent Inflation)*; **40 Percent Tax Bracket; with Loan**

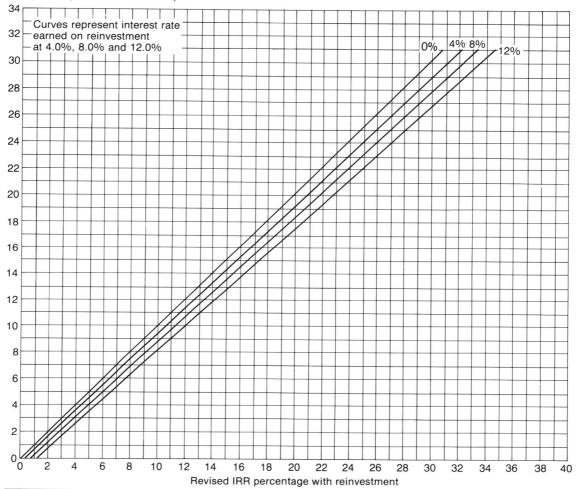

IRR (at zero percent reinvestment)

Curves represent interest rate earned on reinvestment at 4.0%, 8.0% and 12.0%

0%   4% 8%   12%

Revised IRR percentage with reinvestment

Assumptions:		
Tax bracket	40%	
Loan/Total investment	75%	
Loan interest rate	10%	
Years, loan amortization	25	
Rates of inflation	6%	
Capitalization rate at sale	10%	
Year of sale	15	
Year, straight line depreciation	15	
Building/Total investment	90%	
Prior reference Graph	8–1	

Graph 15–2
Real Estate Investment: Revised IRR with Reinvestment *(Using Assumptions Contained in Table 15–1 with 6 Percent Inflation);* **50 Percent Tax Bracket; with Loan**

IRR (at zero percent reinvestment)

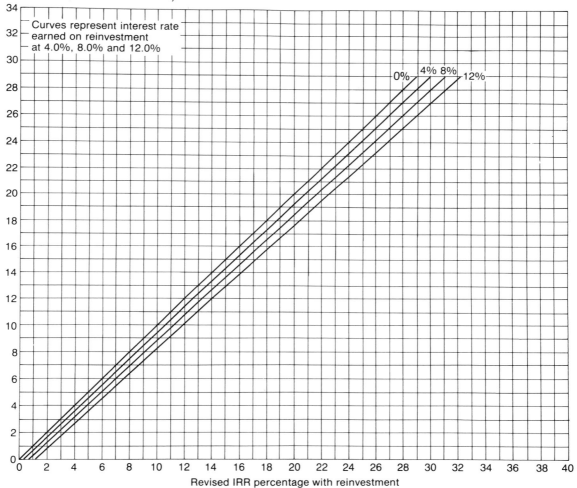

Revised IRR percentage with reinvestment

Assumptions:		
	Tax bracket	50%
	Loan/Total investment	75%
	Loan interest rate	12%
	Years, loan amortization	25
	Rates of inflation	6%
	Capitalization rate at sale	12%
	Year of sale	15
	Year, straight line depreciation	15
	Building/Total investment	90%
	Prior reference Graph	8–2

Graph 15–3
Real Estate Investment: Revised IRR with Reinvestment *(Using Assumptions Contained in Table 15–1 with 6 Percent Inflation)*; **50 Percent Tax Bracket; No Loan**

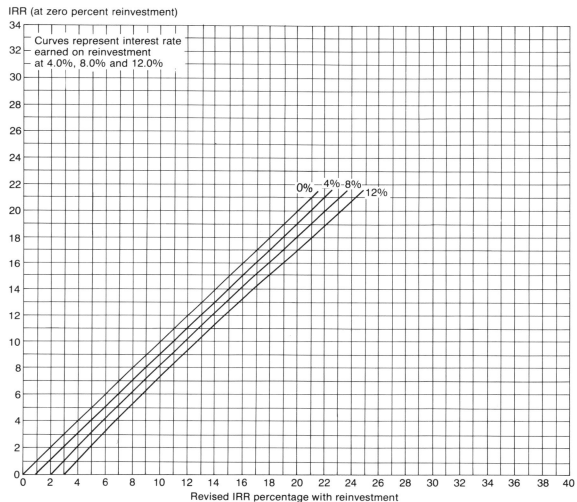

IRR (at zero percent reinvestment)

Curves represent interest rate earned on reinvestment at 4.0%, 8.0% and 12.0%

0% 4% 8% 12%

Revised IRR percentage with reinvestment

Assumptions:		
Tax bracket	50%	
Loan/Total investment	0%	
Loan interest rate	n/a	
Years, loan amortization	n/a	
Rates of inflation	6%	
Capitalization rate at sale	12%	
Year of sale	15	
Year, straight line depreciation	15	
Building/Total investment	90%	
Prior reference Graph	8–3	

Graph 15–4
Real Estate Investment: Revised IRR with Reinvestment *(Using Assumptions Contained in Table 15–1 with 6 Percent Inflation);* **30 Percent Tax Bracket; with Loan**

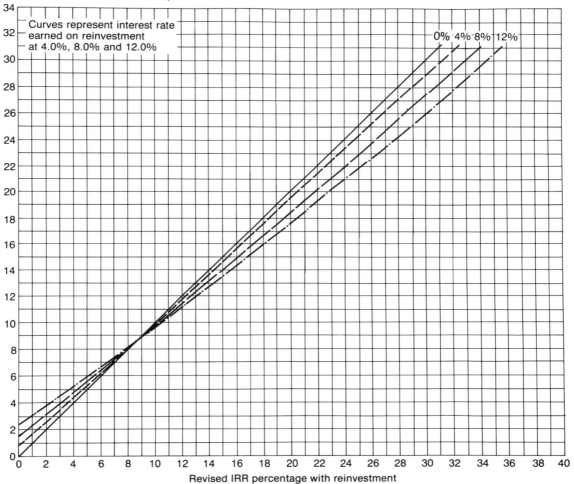

IRR (at zero percent reinvestment)

Curves represent interest rate earned on reinvestment at 4.0%, 8.0% and 12.0%

0% 4% 8% 12%

Revised IRR percentage with reinvestment

Assumptions:		
Tax bracket	30%	
Loan/Total investment	75%	
Loan interest rate	12%	
Years, loan amortization	25	
Rates of inflation	6%	
Capitalization rate at sale	10%	
Year of sale	15	
Year, straight line depreciation	15	
Building/Total investment	90%	
Prior reference Graph	8–4	

Graph 15–5
Real Estate Investment: Revised IRR with Reinvestment *(Using Assumptions Contained in Table 15–1 with 6 Percent Inflation);* **30 Percent Tax Bracket; with "Interest Only" Loan**

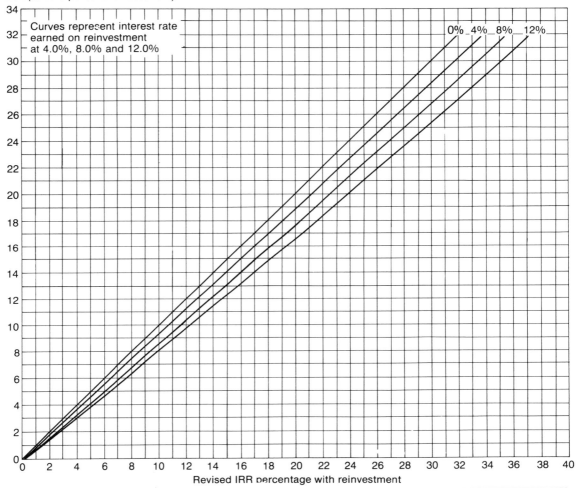

IRR (at zero percent reinvestment)

Curves represent interest rate earned on reinvestment at 4.0%, 8.0% and 12.0%

0%   4%   8%   12%

Revised IRR percentage with reinvestment

Assumptions:		
	Tax bracket	30%
	Loan/Total investment	75%
	Loan interest rate	12%
	Years, loan amortization	int. only
	Rates of inflation	6%
	Capitalization rate at sale	12%
	Year of sale	15
	Year, straight line depreciation	15
	Building/Total investment	90%
	Prior reference Graph	8–5

Graph 15–6
Real Estate Investment: Revised IRR with Reinvestment *(Using Assumptions Contained in Table 15–1 with 6 Percent Inflation);* **50 Percent Tax Bracket; with "Interest Only" Loan**

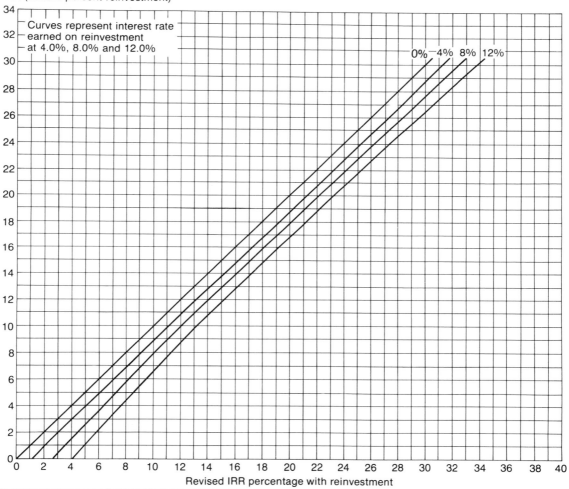

IRR (at zero percent reinvestment)

Curves represent interest rate earned on reinvestment at 4.0%, 8.0% and 12.0%

0% 4% 8% 12%

Revised IRR percentage with reinvestment

Assumptions:	Tax bracket	50%
	Loan/Total investment	75%
	Loan interest rate	12%
	Years, loan amortization	int. only
	Rates of inflation	6%
	Capitalization rate at sale	12%
	Year of sale	15
	Year, straight line depreciation	15
	Building/Total investment	90%
	Prior reference Graph	8–6

Graph 15–7
Real Estate Investment: Revised IRR with Reinvestment *(Using Assumptions Contained in Table 15–1 with 6 Percent Inflation)*; **40 Percent Tax Bracket; with Loan**

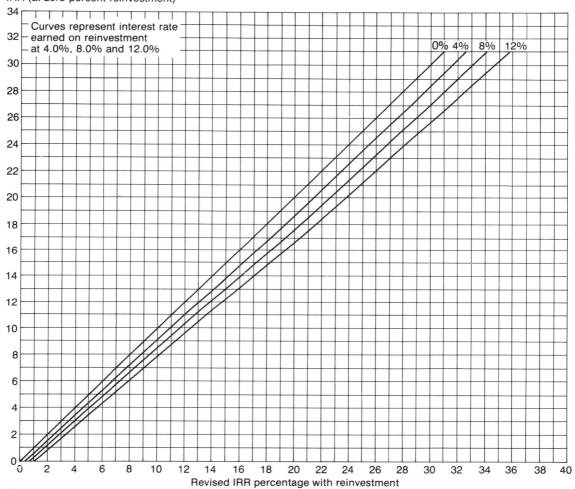

IRR (at zero percent reinvestment)

Curves represent interest rate earned on reinvestment at 4.0%, 8.0% and 12.0%

0% 4% 8% 12%

Revised IRR percentage with reinvestment

Assumptions:	Tax bracket	40%
	Loan/Total investment	75%
	Loan interest rate	12%
	Years, loan amortization	25
	Rates of inflation	6%
	Capitalization rate at sale	16%
	Year of sale	15
	Year, straight line depreciation	15
	Building/Total investment	90%
	Prior reference Graph	8–7

Graph 15–8
Real Estate Investment: Revised IRR with Reinvestment *(Using Assumptions Contained in Table 15–1 with 6 Percent Inflation);* **0 Percent Tax Bracket; with Loan**

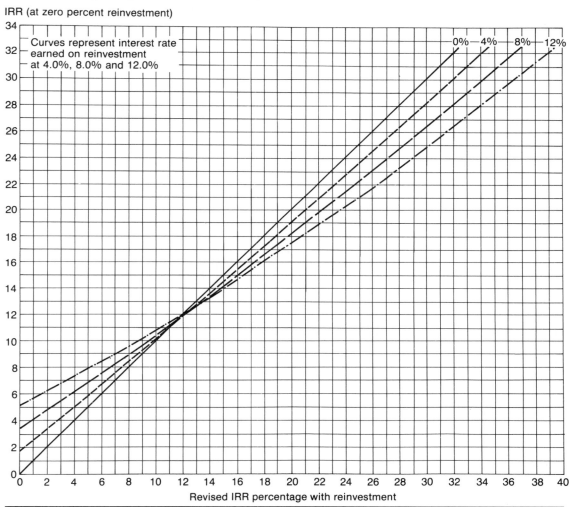

IRR (at zero percent reinvestment)

Curves represent interest rate earned on reinvestment at 4.0%, 8.0% and 12.0%

0%—4%—8%—12%

Revised IRR percentage with reinvestment

Assumptions:	Tax bracket	0%
	Loan/Total investment	75%
	Loan interest rate	12%
	Years, loan amortization	25
	Rates of inflation	6%
	Capitalization rate at sale	12%
	Year of sale	15
	Year, straight line depreciation	15
	Building/Total investment	90%
	Prior reference Graph	8–8

Graph 15–9
Real Estate Investment: Revised IRR with Reinvestment *(Using Assumptions Contained in Table 15–1 with 6 Percent Inflation)*; **0 Percent Tax Bracket; No Loan**

IRR (at zero percent reinvestment)

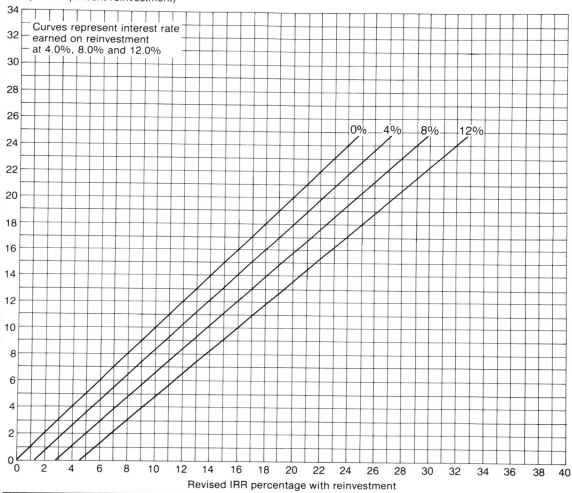

Revised IRR percentage with reinvestment

Assumptions:	Tax bracket	0%
	Loan/Total investment	0%
	Loan interest rate	n/a
	Years, loan amortization	n/a
	Rates of inflation	6%
	Capitalization rate at sale	12%
	Year of sale	15
	Year, straight line depreciation	15
	Building/Total investment	90%
	Prior reference Graph	8–13

C H A P T E R 16

Lump Sum Investments

Simple Annual Interest

If you invest $1,000 today at 4 percent simple annual interest, after one year the account is worth $1,040; after two years, $1,080, and so on. The formula is:

$$I = P \times i \times T$$

where:

I = interest earned
P = principal (e.g., $1,000)
i = rate of annual interest (e.g., 4 percent, or 0.04)
T = time in years (e.g., 1 year).

Thus in the example given, after one year the interest earned (I) is $1,000 × 0.04 × 1, or $40.

The value of the account (S) is the original principal ($1,000) plus the interest earned ($40).
Thus,

$$S = P + I$$

and since

$$I = P \times i \times T,$$
$$S = P + P \times i \times T, \text{ or}$$
$$S = P(1 + iT).$$

After two years, the value of the account, with 4 percent simple annual interest, is:

$$S = P(1 + iT)$$
$$= 1,000(1 + 0.04 \times 2)$$
$$= 1,000(1.08)$$
$$= 1,080.$$

However, this calculation fails to take into consideration the interest earned in the second year on the $40 interest from the first year. Interest paid only on the original principal is called "simple interest."

Compound Interest

Compound interest would be calculated as shown in the 10-year table.

Year	P Principal at Beginning	I Annual Interest Earned During Year at 4% (P × i × T)	S Value at End of Year (P + I)
1	1,000.	40.	1,040.
2	1,040.	41.6000	1,081.6000
3	1,081.6000	43.2640	1,124.8640
4	1,124.8640	44.9946	1,169.8586
5	1,169.8586	46.7943	1,216.6529
6	1,216.6529	48.6661	1,265.3190
7	1,265.3190	50.6128	1,315.9318
8	1,315.9318	52.6373	1,368.5691
9	1,368.5691	54.7428	1,423.3118
10	1,423.3118	56.9326	1,480.2444

The formula for determining S, the value of an account after a period of years, n (e.g., 10), started with an original investment, P (e.g., 1,000), at i annual compound interest (e.g., .04) is:

$$S = P(1 + i)^n$$
$$= 1,000(1.04)^{10}$$
$$= 1,000(1.480244)$$
$$= \$1.480.244$$

Using the Graphs: Examples

Example 1: Refer to Graph 16–1. After 8 years, how much is $1,000 worth if it earns 6 percent compound annual interest? The value would be $1,593.85. The formula is:

$$S = P(1 + i)^n$$
$$= 1,000(1.06)^8$$
$$= 1,000(1,59385)$$
$$= \underline{\$1,593.85}$$

Example 2: Similarly, a $100 investment at 6 percent after 8 years would be worth $159 and an original $10,000 investment about $15,939.

Example 3: A person has $10,000 today and estimates that he can earn 5 percent per year compounded. How many years will it take for his investment to reach $30,000 if no withdrawals are made?

To find the solution in Graph 16–2, the problem may be restated as follows: At 10 percent compound interest, how long does it take an investment of $1,000 ($10,000) to increase to $3,000 ($30,000)?

As the dotted line shows, it would take about 11.5 years.

Example 4: How long would it take $4,000 to increase to $40,000 at 10 percent compound interest? Rephrased, the question is: How long would it take $4,000 to multiply itself 10 times? The solution to the problem is equivalent to the time required for $1,000 to grow to $10,000. This would require 24.1 years, as shown by the dotted line in Graph 16–3.

Refer to Graph 16–3. Your goal is to have $50,000 at the end of 19 years. Assuming money can earn 17 percent compounded, how much must be invested today? Start on the bottom axis of the graph at 19 years, proceed—as the dotted line shows—up to the 17 percent curve, then horizontally to the left axis. This shows that $1,000 will grow to $20,000 after 19 years at the 17 percent rate.

The problem then is as follows. Where x is the sum that must be invested today to reach $50,000 after 19 years at 17 percent compounded:

$$\frac{\$1,000}{\$20,000} = \frac{x}{\$50,000}$$
$$\$20,000x = \$50,000 \times \$1,000$$
$$x = \underline{\$2,500}$$

Hence, $2,500 invested today will be worth $50,000 at 17 percent compounded after 19 years.

Single Investments at Simple Interest, and IRR

A single investment of, say $1,000 paying 10 percent per year simple interest ($100) is equivalent to an IRR of 10 percent. **Simple interest** by definition means that interest is calculated on the original investment (principal) only (i.e., cash flows are not reinvested). If cash flows were reinvested, and if interest were calculated on the combined principal and previously reinvested interest, then the interest would be **compound** rather than simple. Thus the cash flows for a single investment at simple interest would be as follows:

> Initial negative cash flow is the initial investment.
>
> Annual cash flows equal the initial investment times the interest rate.
>
> Cash flow in the final year is the annual interest plus the return of the original investment.
>
> *And the IRR is equal to the simple interest rate.*

For example, a $1,000 investment at 10 percent simple interest has cash flows of a negative $1,000 at the beginning, $100 per year thereafter, plus, in the final year, an additional $1,000 return of principal. The IRR is 10 percent. (Note: Homer's compound realized return, in this case, is 8.45 percent.) No reinvestment is required to achieve the IRR, but at the lower compound realized return rate, reinvestment at that rate is implicit.

Single Investments with Compounded Interest, and IRR

Single Sum at Maturity

The first possibility is when an investment is made today and only a maturity value is received. In this case, you invest today and at some future date receive another sum of money. There are no intervening cash flows. The only cash flow is the initial investment, which is negative, and the amount received at maturity, which is, of course, positive. For example, a $1,000 initial investment compounded at 10 percent annually will be worth, after 30 years, the sum of $17,449. The cash flows are a negative $1,000 at the beginning and a positive $17,449 at the end of 30 years. There is zero cash flow in the intervening years between the beginning and the end. The IRR is 10 percent.

For a $1,000 investment at 10 percent *simple* interest, the initial investment is $1,000, and the sum received at maturity is $4,000 (which is the $1,000 maturity value plus $3,000 in interest). In this case, the IRR is 4.73 percent.

To achieve the same $17,449 result, one could buy a $1,000 bond at par, paying $100 per year interest, and reinvest all the interest at a reinvestment rate of 10 percent, for a revised IRR of 19.13 percent. In this situation, the terminal value of $17,449 is comprised of:

Maturity value	$ 1,000
Interest on interest	13,449
Regular interest	3,000
Revised IRR	19.13%

A single investment (e.g., $1,000) compounded to maturity (e.g., $17,449) at an interest rate of x percent (e.g., 10%) *is the same as* investing the amount of the single investment (e.g., $1,000) in a conventional par bond, purchased at an IRR or yield to maturity of x percent (e.g., 10%), reinvesting all interest income at a rate of x percent (e.g., 10%), to obtain a resulting *revised IRR* of "greater than" x percent (e.g., 19.13%).

Cash Flows Reinvested Periodically

The second possibility is when a single investment occurs, annual (periodic) distributions are received, and those distributions are reinvested at a reinvestment percentage rate. For example, $10,000 is invested for three years in Project A, which returns 10 percent simple interest, $1,000 per year with no reinvestment. In a second project, B, interest is reinvested at a reinvestment rate of 10 percent. In a third project, C, $10,000 is invested at the beginning, no intervening cash flows are received, and $13,310 is recouped at the end of three years. The cash flows and IRRs are:

	Project A	Project B	Project C
Initial investment	$10,000	$10,000	$10,000
IRR	10%	10%	10%
Reinvestment rate	0%	10%	Compulsory 10%
Terminal value	$13,000	$13,310	$13,310

	Project A			Project B			
Year	Interest	Principal	Beginning Balance	Interest	Additional Deposits	Ending Balance	Cash Flow
0	0	− 10,000	0	0	0	0	− 10,000
1	1,000		0	0	1,000	1,000	1,000
2	1,000		1,000	100	1,000	2,100	1,100
3	1,000	+ 10,000	2,100	210	1,000	3,310	11,210

Cash Flows Summary and IRR

Year	Project A		Project B		Project C
	10 Percent Simple	Cumulative	Cash Flows Reinvested at 10 Percent	Cumulative	Single Sum at Maturity
0	− 10,000		− 10,000		− 10,000
1	1,000	1,000	1,000	1,000	
2	1,000	2,000	1,100	2,100	
3	11,000	13,000	11,210	13,310	13,310
Revised IRR	10%*		10.96%†		10.96%‡

*$11,000 (1.1)^{-3} + 1,000 (1.1)^{-2} + 1,000 (1.1)^{-1} = 10,000$
†$11,210 (1.1096)^{-3} + 1,100 (1.1096)^{-2} + 1,000 (1.1096)^{-1} = 10,000$
‡$13,310 (1.1)^{-3} = 10,000$

Project A's cash flow is not reinvested. If Project A's cash flow were reinvested at a 10 percent rate, then Project A is transformed into Project B. The terminal value of Project B is equal to that of Project C, $13,310. Project A is inferior to Project C at reinvestment rates below 10 percent and superior to Project C at reinvestment rates greater than 10 percent. At a 10 percent reinvestment rate, Project A and Project C are equivalent with a revised IRR of 10.96 percent for both.

Project C's IRR (which is "fully compounded") is 10 percent, and the progression of annual values is:

	Value	Change
Year 1 (beg.)	$10,000	
Year 1 (end)	11,000	+ 1,000
Year 2	12,100	+ 1,100
Year 3	13,310	+ 1,210

The revised IRR for Project C is determinable by the "imputed cash flows" ($1,000, $1,100 and $11,210) that are automatically and irrevocably reinvested at the IRR rate of 10 percent. These imputed cash flows are identical to Project B's, as is the revised IRR of Project C, 10.96 percent.

Graph 16–1 *(How $1,000 Grows at Compound Interest)*
Single Compounded Sum at Maturity *(1–10 Year Holding Period/0 Percent Tax Bracket)*

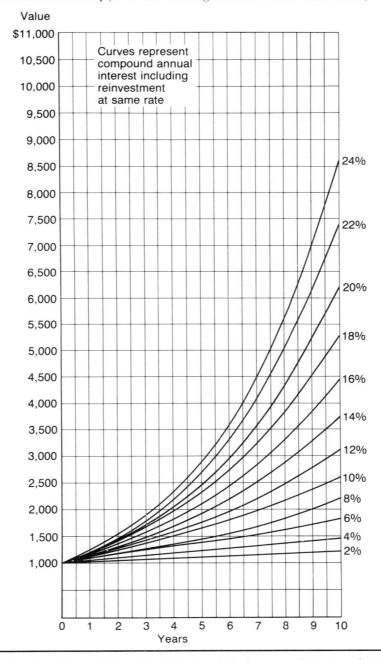

Note: For tax brackets above 0 percent, before using the Graph, multiply the compound interest rate by 1 − tax bracket and use the amount so determined as the curve in the Graph.

Example: Tax bracket   50% $0.20 \times (1 - 0.5) = 0.20 \times 0.5$
              Compound interest   20% $= 10\%$

                                                    Use the 10% curve

Graph 16–2 *(How $1,000 Grows at Compound Interest)*
Single Compounded Sum at Maturity *(1–15 Year Holding Period/0 Percent Tax Bracket)*

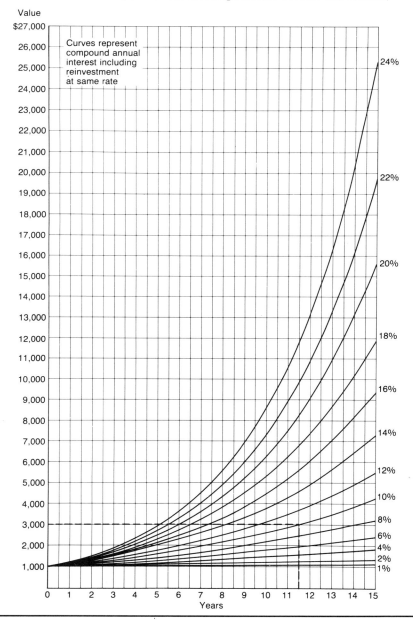

Note: For tax brackets above 0 percent, before using the Graph, multiply the compound interest rate by 1 − tax bracket and use the amount so determined as the curve in the Graph.

Example: Tax bracket   30%
Compound interest   10%

0.10 × (1 − 0.3) = 0.10 × 0.7
                 = 7%

Use the 7% curve

Graph 16–3   *(How $1,000 Grows at Compound Interest)*
Single Compounded Sum at Maturity *(1–30 Year Holding Period/0 Percent Tax Bracket)*

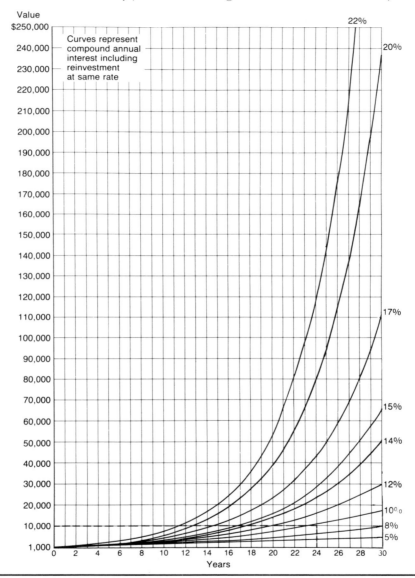

Note: For tax brackets above 0 percent, before using the Graph, multiply the compound interest rate by 1 − tax bracket and use the amount so determined as the curve in the Graph.

Example: Tax bracket   50%
               Compound interest   20%

$$0.20 \times (1 - 0.5) = 0.20 \times 0.5$$
$$= 10\%$$

Use the 10% curve

C H A P T E R   17

The Summing Up

In the twilight of his life, the marvelous novelist and quasi-philosopher, Somerset Maugham, wrote a book bearing the title *The Summing Up.* It is no accident that this chapter bears the same title. Maugham's book summarized the results of his years of study and observations—and succinctly stated his beliefs, many of which he had previously given voice to through the mouths of the characters in his books. This chapter is intended to sum up my observations, in hopes that it will help you invest your assets more efficiently and intelligently—whether they be large or small at present. Even small assets may become large over time if you adopt the methods that have been presented.

Investment results, whether projected into the future or historical, require measurement. If the ruler you use is inaccurate, no matter how painstaking your analysis, your results are sure to be wrong as well. The first point I wish to emphasize is: *Use IRR as your ruler.* Don't be hoodwinked into looking at investments with other measures.

For example, suppose Harold Pidgeon is offered the following "deal" by Sharpy McClintock. Sharpy says, "Invest $10,000 in my hotel project, and I'll give you back $31,000 in 10 years. Triple your money! And you'll have a bank guaranty that I will perform. That means you'll have a $21,000 profit on your investment, Harold. That's a 210 percent gain ($21,000 ÷ $10,000) in 10 years, or 21 percent per year."

But Harold Pidgeon is no pigeon. He knows his ABCs and IRRs. Harold says, "I like the security of your investment, Sharpy, and I don't mind tying up my money for 10 years in an illiquid situation. But let's see what my IRR will be after tax and reinvesting the income (since there is no year-to-year cash flow).

Harold turns to Graph 16–1 in Chapter 16. The increase from $10,000 to $31,000 is equivalent to an investment of $1,000 that reaches $3,100 in 10 years. First, Harold decides to determine the IRR in a zero tax bracket. He enters the graph along the bottom axis at the 10-year point and draws a line vertically up the page. Then he moves to the left axis to the $3,100 point and draws a horizontal line across the page. The zero tax bracket IRR is the curve at or closest to the point where his horizontal and vertical lines meet. This turns out to be on the 12 percent curve. So Harold knows that the *before tax* return from this investment is 12 percent. Thus the IRR is 12 percent.[1]

But what about after taxes in Harold's 50 percent tax bracket? If the annual increase in value of Sharpy's investment is treated as ordinary income by the IRS, as will be the case, then the investment is equivalent to *only a 5.68 percent after tax compound rate of return.* And the IRR is 5.68 percent after taxes. (See Table 17–1.)

Table 17–1

Annual average gain	$ 2,100 (21,000 ÷ 10)
50% bracket	$ 1,050 tax
Initial investment	$10,000
Maturity value	$31,000

Year	Annual Cash Flow*	Present Value at 5.68%
0	− 10,000	
1	− 1,050	− 993.60
2	− 1,050	− 940.23
3	− 1,050	− 889.73
4	− 1,050	− 841.94
5	− 1,050	− 796.72
6	− 1,050	− 753.92
7	− 1,050	− 713.43
8	− 1,050	− 675.11
9	− 1,050	− 638.85
10	− 29,950	17,243.52
IRR after tax	5.68%	TOTAL $10,000.00

*After tax

But *if* the investment is *not* subject to taxes each year as ordinary income, then the $31,000 at maturity might be subject to long-term capital gains tax. If 40 percent of the $21,000 gain is taxed at 50 percent, the tax is $4,200, and the maturity value after tax is $31,000 less $4,200, or $26,800. Thus the $10,000 after tax increases to $26,800; which is equivalent to $1,000 increasing to $2,680. Harold goes back

---

[1]Before considering taxation, this fully compounded 12 percent return is equivalent to investing $10,000 in a par bond, with a $120 coupon, and reinvesting at a rate of 12 percent. Graph 13–24 shows the before tax revised IRR to be about 18 percent (after reinvestment of all income).

to Graph 16–1. He enters the graph along the left axis at $2,680 and draws a horizontal line across the graph. He then moves to the bottom axis to the 10-year point, where he draws a vertical line up the graph. The curve where the horizontal and vertical lines meet is the IRR or compound interest rate. It is about 10 percent, if and only if Harold were only subject to long-term capital gains tax on the investment.

On the other hand, if Harold invests and the presumed annual increase on his investment is taxable as ordinary income, then he will have to pay tax of $1,050 each year on cash that he won't receive until the 10th year. And his IRR after tax will be a meager 5.68 percent. In fact, this is probably the way this would be taxed.

So another point to remember is check out the tax implications of proposed investments before you invest. Harold Pidgeon, after completing his homework, calls Sharpy and says: "Mr. McClintock, I have reviewed your proposed investment, and I find I can do better in a tax-free bond or one of Mr. Rosen's real estate deals. So I'll have to pass."

We have seen that Sharpy's promised 21 percent per year return is nothing but an illusion no matter how convincingly he may have presented it. The IRR is a meagre 5.68 percent after tax. Subject your investments to the hard scrutiny of IRR analysis and avoid traps like the one that Sharpy McCintock baited for Harold Pidgeon.

The Glamour Stock

Steve Blank, a 50 percent tax bracket investor, has purchased, over several years, a large block of Fie-Fie's, a fast-growing Japanese restaurant chain that pays no dividend. His earlier purchases were very profitable. But lately the stock has dropped from its high of about $40 per share to $29. He's beginning to worry, especially since some of the purchases were with borrowed money from his brokerage firm. If much further decline in the stock takes place, his broker will require more equity (in the form of cash or securities), and if Steve fails to supply the additional equity, the broker will sell part (or all) of his considerable Fie-Fie's shares. Steve's projections for Fie-Fie's are:

Year	Earnings per Share	Price	P-E Ratio	Annual Sales ($ Millions)
−3	$ .05	$ 2.50	50.00	$ 5.00
−2	.15	7.50	50.00	20.00
−1	.30	15.00	50.00	40.00
present	.80	28.80	36.00	90.00
+1	1.00	30.00	30.00	140.00
+2	1.50	37.50	25.00	210.00
+3	2.00	40.00	20.00	280.00
+4	2.60	39.00	15.00	364.00
+5	3.10	37.00	12.00	434.00

Steve's projections are based on personal conversations with Fie-Fie's management and a study of financial analysts' opinions and recommendations. Alternative uses of the funds presently invested in Fie-Fie's include the purchase of tax-free bonds or a real estate investment. His problem is to decide whether or not to sell.

Steve surmises that Fie-Fie's will be unlikely, at its present size, to maintain its past earnings per share growth rate of 152 percent per year. He figures that a likely scenario is for earnings per share of 80 cents to increase to $3.10 over the next five years. That is about 31.12 percent per year compounded. As a result of the maturation of the company, and a decrease in the rate of increase of its growth, Steve estimates a possible drop in the P-E multiple from 36 to 1 to about 12 to 1, a 67 percent drop. What should he do?

If he is likely to have a lesser IRR by holding the Fie-Fie's stock than by selling it and investing elsewhere, then he should sell. If he holds, his after tax IRR is easily determinable by reference to Graph 4–31. (If he sells, he'll just about break even, so after tax, he'll have the full proceeds of sale available to reinvest.)

He enters Graph 4–31 along the vertical axis at the 31 percent annual increase in earnings per share; proceeds horizontally to the 0 percent dividend curve then down to the bottom axis. The after tax IRR is seen to be a meager 6 percent. So Steve's conclusion is easily determinable—sell! But, where should he reinvest?

Steve's bond broker, Ralph Ronald, has offered him a state sewer bond for $800 that matures in 20 years and pays $80 per year interest. The interest is tax-exempt from federal income tax, but he'll have to pay tax on the long-term gain of $200 at maturity. The adjusted coupon rate on the tax-free bond is:

$$\frac{\$80}{1 - .5} = \$160$$

To find the IRR on the bond, Steve turns to Graph 6–20. Steve enters the Graph at the $800 purchase price, moves across to the $160 coupon curve, then down to the bottom axis where the after tax IRR is determined to be between 10 and 11 percent. Steve decides that the bond is certainly better than holding on to Fie-Fie's. But, what about real estate?

Steve calls his real estate broker, Marshall McGrewder, who proposes an investment in a multitenant warehouse with the following characteristics:

Inflation	5%
Initial percent return	10%
Tax bracket	50%
Loan as percent of total investment	75%

Interest rate	12%
Amortization period of loan	25 yrs
Depreciation method	straight line
Number of years of depreciation	15
Capitalization rate at resale	12%
Building as a percent of total investment	90%

He then turns to Chart 8–1, the match-up worksheet, and selects Graph 8–2 as the one most closely corresponding to his proposed real estate investment.

He enters the Graph at the 10 percent initial yield point on the vertical axis; moves horizontally across to midway between the 4 percent and 6 percent curves (for 5 percent inflation or increase in yield per year); then down to the bottom axis, where the **after tax IRR** is determined to be between **19 and 20** percent. So Steve elects to sell Fie-Fie's, which is likely to return an IRR of only 6 percent and invest in the real estate project at 19 to 20 percent rather than the tax-free bond at about **10** percent.

The Market Situation

Sally Abelson wants to know where to invest her surplus cash. She doesn't want any highly risky investments, she doesn't expect to need the money for many years, and she wants to know the alternatives.

The only sure thing about markets, as Bernard Baruch once said, is that they will fluctuate. The evaluation of possibilities for Sally that follows is based, more or less, on market conditions at the present moment, and the conclusions reached may not be valid in a month, year, or whenever. But the approach should remain indefinitely valid.

Sally, you have three basic choices, **bonds, stocks, and real estate.**

Let's consider a **corporate or U.S. government long-term bond,** where the yields are the highest. Good quality issues can be bought at par of $1,000 with about $130 in annual interest. For a 30-year bond in your 50 percent tax bracket, turn to Graph 6–30. Enter the Graph on the left axis at $1,000 purchase price, proceed horizontally to the $130 curve, then down to the bottom axis, where the after tax IRR is seen to be about **6.5 percent.**

Next, let's look at a typical municipal or **tax-free bond** (subject to tax on long-term gain or loss but not annual interest). Here you can buy a bond at par of $1,000 with a 30-year maturity and a coupon of about 10 percent. What then is the return? The adjusted coupon rate (in order to use the Graphs as described on page 106) is 10 divided by 1 less Sally's tax bracket of 50 percent. That is 10/.5, or 20 percent. Sally turns to Graph 6–30 and enters along the vertical axis at the $1,000 purchase price and proceeds horizontally to the 20 percent curve, then vertically down to the bottom axis, where the point of intersection is 10 percent. (Or Sally could use Graph 5–30 without having to adjust the coupon rate.) Thus the IRR after tax for the municipal bond is **10 percent.**

Finally **real estate.** We are making acquisitions along the following terms in the present market: initial net operating income divided by total investment of 12 percent; seller financing at 75 percent of investment at 10 percent interest, with 25-year amortization, 12 percent estimated capitalization rate upon future sale, and 6 percent inflation, meaning income and operating expenses are projected to increase at that rate. In other words, the assumptions of Graph 8–2 are operative. Sally turns to Graph 8–2. She enters the Graph along the vertical axis at the initial yield (NOI/total investment percent of 12 percent). She proceeds horizontally until the 6 percent inflation (percent increase in yield per year) curve is reached. Then she descends to the bottom axis, where the point of intersection is the after tax IRR of about **25 percent.**

A stock investment with income and growth potential that is not subject to wide market fluctuations might be a possibility. Many utility companies offer about 11 percent dividends with prospects for about 5 percent growth in earnings per share and dividends. On a 20-year investment after tax, what IRR is that equivalent to? Sally turns to Graph 4–20. She enters the graph along the vertical axis at the 11 percent yield; proceeds horizontally to the 5 percent growth curve (for a 50 percent tax bracket), then vertically to the bottom axis, where the point of intersection is **10.1 percent.** (This is with a static P-E multiple, which is a reasonable assumption in the case of a utility stock; other graphs would be used for expected shrinking or mounting multiples.)

So, Sally says to herself, what does this all mean? From an after tax standpoint, with current market conditions, if I invest, I can expect to receive the following:

Corporate or government bond	about 6.5%
Municipal or tax-free bond	about 10.0%
Income-producing real estate	about 25.0%
Utility common stock	about 10.1%

How can there be such a difference, Sally wonders. Why doesn't everybody buy real estate?

That's what makes up a market Sally. Forces of supply and demand interact, prices change, yields change, and the good investment of today may be the poor choice of tomorrow. In addition, remember that the results above were tailored to Sally Abelson's tax bracket. If the investor were tax-free, then the IRR of the government or corporate bond would just about double, and IRR from the real estate would stay about the same in spite of the lack of value of any tax-shelter benefits to the tax-free investor.

So the only generalizations I care to make are not about what investment you should buy but about how you should make the decision. And that is, with precise measurement, **using IRR, or revised IRR, or marginal IRR, the magic number that puts all investments on a directly comparable basis.**

Good luck in your investing.

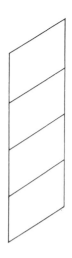

Index